The Beast
Who Once Was

Chris Relitz

The Beast Who Once Was: New Insight into End Times Prophecy
First Printing

© 2014 Chris Relitz. All rights reserved
ISBN 978-1-304-97343-6 90000

Christianity- Prophecy- Conspiracy- Freemason
Daniel11:33 Books
Daniel11.33@hotmail.com

P.O. Box 951
Martensville, Saskatchewan, Canada
S0K2T0

The version of the Bible used herein is the NIV: New International Version, unless
otherwise stated. The NIV is copyright 1973, 1978, 1984 by International Bible
Society, Zondervan Publishing House.

To my daughters

I am sending you out like sheep among wolves.
Therefore be shrewd as snakes and innocent as doves.
Matthew 10: 16

Also by Chris Relitz
Antichrist Osiris: the History of the Luciferian Conspiracy

TABLE OF CONTENTS

FORWARD

When I became a Christian the *Left Behind* series of books was very popular. As I was brought up on a steady diet of superhero comics and Science Fiction, the notion that we may be caught up in the ultimate battle between good and evil really fascinated me. A lot has been written about the end times, a good portion of Bible prophecy deals with it. It is the time when Jesus Christ returns to triumph over evil and set everything right again. It is also a time when the forces of evil will rise up in an attempt to prevent this.

This is a book that will help Christians identify three things.

The first is the end times themselves. The Bible says there was a beginning of things, and that there will be an end. The mythologies and ancient lore of most cultures agree with this. Just look at the frenzy that occurred when the Mayan calendar hit 2012. Throughout history there have been many false alarms, crazed people crying out that "the end is near!" With this book we will be able to identify if we're at all near the end. This may be a darker topic and definitely not one to be fixated on, but it is important to consider what prophecy has to say about the future. After all, Jesus himself told us to always be prepared and keep a watch out for the end times (Matthew 24: 42).

The second thing we will be able to identify is the Antichrist. The Bible says that in the end there would appear a Christ and an Antichrist, a hero and a villain. After reading this book we will be able to spot that son of Satan instantly. Yes, this is a bold claim, but we will, without any doubt whatsoever, be able to spot that individual the moment he appears! The Bible tells us this would otherwise be difficult as he is destined to be a master of deception and many will turn to him believing he is the world's savior. Although appearing glorious and wonderful, in reality he will be leading as many as he can to a spiritual death. God does not want his children following this path. The knowledge that can show this character as evil and thus save many souls has been preserved in the Bible for thousands of years.

And then lastly, we will begin to identify those human followers of

Satan, those who have hid in the shadows, manipulating things and preparing the way for their savior, the Antichrist. These people follow Lucifer as their god, therefore they call themselves Luciferians. They belong to various secret societies, are power hungry, adept at deception and always show their "gang signs," visible symbols of their allegiance to the devil.

Every time Jesus spoke of the end times, the first thing he told his followers was "do not be deceived (Matthew 24: 4, Mark 13: 5, Luke 21: 8)." When the end does come, it will be impossible to deceive those who have been equipped with the knowledge in this book; instead these people will bring many into relationship with God, our loving Father and Creator.

INTRODUCTION

The Bible clearly tells us that someday an *end* will come, but before it does there will be a terrible time of tribulation where the Antichrist, the son of Satan, gets to reign supreme over all the earth. It has been two-thousand years since the prophecies were given about this individual and every generation has tried to guess who he is, watching for signs of his coming. But one prophecy has caused people to stumble in this regard, for it seems to indicate that the Antichrist will not be somebody from our present days, but rather someone who lived long ago, restored to life!

The disciple John wrote about *the Beast,* a prophetic name for the Antichrist, he said:

> The inhabitants of the earth whose names are not written in the book of life from the creation of the world will be astonished when they see the beast, because **he once was, now is not, and yet will come.**
>
> Revelation 17: 8

John said the beast "once was," that is, he lived before the time of John's writing. Then John said that the beast "now is not," indicating that he was no longer alive. John then says "and yet will come" indicating that the beast would somehow be restored to life.

John also tells us that the beast recovers from a fatal wound, not a *nearly*-fatal wound but a fatal wound; he will somehow seem to rise from the dead!

> And I saw a beast coming out of the sea… the beast seemed to have a fatal wound, but the fatal wound had been healed. The whole world was astonished and followed the beast.
>
> Revelation 13: 1, 3

Because of this astonishing recovery the world will follow this individual as a god. Of course Satan has always sought to overthrow God, and has even imitated him at times. His son will seem to rise from the grave just as Jesus did. But his resurrection will not be a miracle, as when Jesus rose from the dead. The Bible tells us that "the coming of the lawless one will be in accordance with the work of Satan displayed in all kinds of counterfeit miracles, signs and wonders… that deceives those who are perishing (2Thessalonians 2: 9, 10)." The Antichrist will rise up from death in a fashion that will bring him a great deal of attention.

Here I will introduce a new concept, interpreting Scripture in a way that just a few years ago would have been unfathomable. We have come to a time when science has developed incredible processes regarding life and death. Genetically modified organisms now sit on our grocery store shelves. Dolly the sheep lived thus proving that a living organism could be cloned. Spielberg's *Jurassic Park* movie introduced the idea of cloning long dead dinosaurs. In real life, scientists have tried to clone extinct Wooly Mammoths from remains found in the icy wastelands of Siberia. But this has been impossible because once cells have been frozen they are far too damaged. There has been success with creatures found preserved not in the ice, but in dry desert conditions. Incredibly, ancient burial customs, such as mummification, has made it far easier!

After examining current advances in science, Bible prophecy and the scriptures held sacred by the ancients, such as the Egyptians, I can show that the Antichrist, the Beast who once lived, now is dead, and will live again, could be resurrected, in part, via the modern science of cloning.

Crazy you say?

What would the ancients possibly know of cloning?

In some legends and myths it appears a very great deal.

In the first book of the Bible there is a very brief mention of a character with a rather memorable name: Nimrod. He was born shortly after Noah's Flood and achieved a great deal of fame. To the Canaanites he was referred as Baal, the Sumerians referred to him as Tammuz: Child of the Abyss, the Ammonites knew him as Moloch and he was Assur to the Assyrians. He has, in fact, been known as the god with a thousand names! But, most importantly, in the Egyptian histories and mythology he is Osiris. It is this individual we will examine most closely because in the legend of Osiris it claims that after he was killed and his corpse cut to pieces his wife, Isis, searched for and reassembled all the pieces but one. The genitals were missing. Legends say a fish ate them. With the help of the god Thoth they mummified Osiris, which the Egyptians, who are known for their mummies, say was the first time this process was ever performed.

Then Isis and Thoth do something very strange. The ancient Egyptian holy book, the Book of the Dead says that:

> Isis sought him untiringly, she wandered round and round about this earth in sorrow… she raised up the inactive members of whose heart was still, she drew **from him his essence, she made an heir,** she reared the child in loneliness, and the place where he was not known, and he grew in strength and stature, and his hand was mighty in the House of Keb. The Company of the Gods rejoiced, rejoiced, at the coming of Horus, the son of Osiris, whose heart was firm, the triumphant, the son of Isis, the heir of Osiris.
>
> Hymn to Osiris, *the Book of the Dead*,
> pg. 61, E.A. Wallis Budge

After Osiris was preserved from deterioration, the Book of the Dead specifically says his "essence" was isolated and Isis "made an heir." Plutarch, the ancient historian, adds that Isis also needed to make a false penis, a phallus, to become pregnant. This might seem rather like our modern in vitro fertilization, but since Osiris' seed producing gentiles were absent we must consider the cloning aspect. Somehow this "essence" contained all that was needed to sire their son Horus. It is most important that we know what this "essence" is. What were the ancient peoples trying to communicate with this concept? Was it the DNA of Osiris? Could Horus have been his genetic duplicate? They both shared the All-Seeing-Eye as their symbol and the legends say Isis was both the wife and mother of Osiris. Osiris is called not only "the soul that liveth again" but "the being who becometh a child again."[1]

Yes, this is a strange story but every ancient Egyptian knew it as it was the key to their religion, in fact the average Egyptian was taught that if it happened once, it may happen again. So they based their funerary practices, preserving the bodies of the dead via mummification, on this notion, everyone hoping to be someday

---

[1] *The Book of the Dead*, E.A. Wallis Budge, pg 58.

resurrected from the dead as their god had.

Since Dolly the sheep, it is commonly known that it is possible to clone organisms. But today we find that the ancient Egyptian's hopes and wishes have been fulfilled. It is possible to clone mummies! The Science Journal *Nature* reported on April 18, 1985, in an article entitled the *Molecular Cloning of Ancient Egyptian Mummy DNA* that Svante Paabo of the Department of Cell Research at the University of Uppsala Sweden, had found that the mummification processes of the ancient Egyptians were sufficient enough to preserve DNA over several millennia so that it "could be molecularly cloned in a plasmid vector."

The astute reader might then say "Phooey! So what if you were able to clone somebody, they wouldn't really be that person because all their collected memories and experiences, what makes a person unique, would be absent!" But I answer this with Bible prophecy that clearly states that in the end times Nimrod, who is known in Greek mythology as Apollo, or Apollyon, is destined to rise from the very pit of hell itself (Revelation 9: 11)! As a demon it would be his duty to possess somebody, his own body should be the easiest, wouldn't you think?

Then what if I told you the tomb of Osiris was discovered by Zahi Hawass in January, 1999, near the Great Pyramid, on the Giza plateau?

Apollyon, Nimrod, Osiris, the Beast, whatever you want to call him, was once considered a god on this earth, the Egyptians claimed he would someday return, rise from the dead and rule the earth again. Today this religion still has its followers who await his return. So, with that in mind, why did the Freemasons have his symbol, the All Seeing Eye, placed on the American dollar bill, the most notorious piece of paper on the planet? It says "In God We trust," but search as you might there is not one iota of Christian symbolism to be found here. The Latin script around this symbol reads "Annuit Coeptis," which is from the ancient Roman poet Virgil's poem the Aeneid, where the god Jupiter is asked for his favor in an undertaking. Remember, quite simply an undertaker is someone who buries and… exhumes dead bodies.

We're about to embark on a journey into mysteries never before examined. We will see that right now there are powerful people who are trying to prepare the way for the Antichrist. We will examine their own writings to see exactly what they believe. By comparing their words to the Word of God we will see the truth. But first we will see that the Antichrist, the Beast-who-once-was, may have first lived during the days of Noah.

CHAPTER ONE
THE DAYS OF NOAH

Just as it was in the Days of Noah, so also will it be in the days
of the Son of Man.

Luke 17: 26

The above verse has been referred to as the Days of Noah Prophecy,
and it was given by Jesus to his disciples when they asked if there
would be any warning signs prior to, and leading up to, the end times.

To break the phrase down, the *Days of Noah* refers to Noah's
lifetime. The term *Son of Man* is used at times to identify Jesus. This is
an important term because he came to earth as a man, not as a spirit or a
demigod, as a man he could live among us as one of us, suffering all
the hardships we do. This makes Jesus a truly merciful savior. Jesus
came once to teach, mark and free the captives, and he will soon come
back to destroy the enemy.

The Days of Noah Prophecy then clearly implies that just prior to
the Second Coming of Christ, something that happened during Noah's
lifetime would happen again just before the end.

I was quite interested in this idea so I set out to learn all I could
about the Great Flood which initially seemed to have been the
predominant event in Noah's life. Everyone knows he was called upon
by God to build a giant boat and house a pile of animals while the
wicked world was washed away. Since the Bible tells us very little of
Noah's days and the pre-Flood world I began to look into the
mythological records of the world's various cultures. I looked for some
trace mention, a record or remnant of a cataclysmic flood story. I was
amazed to find that nearly every culture on the planet has some
memory of this event in their oldest legends!

At first I considered the Greek philosopher Plato's account of
Atlantis. I thought it was likely they were speaking of the same event.
Since then I've collected and documented well over two hundred-fifty
similar stories. It was during this research I heard rumors that the

secretive fraternity of Freemasons had a great deal of knowledge in this area. The information age was just beginning to blossom with the advent of the internet and many stories were circulating about this bunch. They weren't like the Elk's Club or Kinsmen, there were fantastic tales. The Masons apparently counted world leaders among their membership, they claimed to know certain secrets about Jesus and some even say they're in possession of the lost Ark of the Covenant! I didn't really spend much time considering Masonry until one day when I was in my favorite used book shop. On the front counter was a mountain of books they had just bought from someone. I quickly recognized the Masonic symbol, the square and compass, on many of the books. Upon opening one of them I saw stamped within the front cover that the book was "not meant for profane eyes" and was "to be returned to the Masonic Lodge upon death or withdrawal of the member." So what was this enormous pile of volumes doing here? Many were over a hundred years old!

Needless to say, curiosity had the better of me. Besides furthering my research into the days of Noah prophecy I thought I could also be on the verge of discovering the secrets of the Freemasons. So out came the credit card and my library at home grew considerably.

As I read the books certain things struck me, the first was that in the older Masonic writings they did spend a great deal of time studying history, especially that time around Noah's Flood. The next, which was very alarming, is that the Mason's stated goals compare directly to Bible prophecy. What the Bible warns about happening during the end times, the Freemasons seemed to be trying to make happen!

This shocked me; some of my own relatives are members in this group! As I studied more of their own writings I easily concluded that the Freemasons are in fact a religion, a religion imbedded in secrecy and deception, appropriately called by insiders the Mystery religion, or just *the Mysteries.* Some of the membership is unaware of this. Others will deny it because oaths are taken to protect their secrets which have survived for millennia. Slow and agonizing death has been the penalty for those who break Masonic oaths. Ultimately, the Mason's greatest scholars all agree that the heroes of the Mysteries lived during the days of Noah!

In the pages ahead we will examine the history of Freemasonry and many allied secret societies. We will start with the texts of the great Masonic scholars: Albert Pike and Albert G. Mackey. We will then go on to see that many of the most powerful people on earth, whether royalty, big businessmen or politicians, are affiliated with Freemasonry. We will carefully examine their goals and ultimately compare them to what the Bible says about the end times.

The Bible itself is an amazing book. Its importance is recognized around the globe to believers and non-believers alike. It is actually a collection of 66 books by 40 different authors and was written over a fifteen-hundred year period. It is the historical record of the Hebrew people and contains God's teachings for humanity. To verify that these messages are indeed from a higher power, interspersed amongst them are prophecies. This is the main reason I take the Bible seriously. Many of the prophecies in this ancient book have been fulfilled and are therefore empirically verifiable! For example the Hebrew people returned to their homeland, Israel, in 1948, just after suffering the Nazi Holocaust. Their return to Israel and presence there is a fact that cannot be denied. This event alone fulfilled dozens of prophecies. For nearly two millennia the Hebrews had been living scattered in exile. But since the Israelites returned to the Promised Land it seems God's prophetic clock has started ticking again. We're seeing more prophecies fulfilled now than ever before!

Currently, the only prophecies yet to be fulfilled have to do with the end times. Jesus himself gave the most important prophecies regarding this time and these are aimed at helping us identify the son of Satan so we might not be deceived and follow this charismatic being. Satan has often imitated God and desired human worship. His son will be no different. He will trick many into thinking he is the world's savior, he will have his own religion, here called Luciferism, and will teach all humans that they too can be gods and worshipped as well. This alone will lure in many followers. With knowledge of the Luciferian religion, the Bible's sometimes confusing end time's prophecies will be fully decoded here for the first time. Luciferians, those who follow the fallen angel Lucifer and await his son, exist today. We will learn a great deal about the Biblical end times from their own documented teachings!

When it comes to this self worship, what we should take notice of, however, is that when Jesus was on the earth he did not seek worship. He came to serve and save his brothers and sisters.

Your attitude should be the same as that of Christ Jesus: Who being in very nature God, did not consider equality with God

something to be grasped, but made himself nothing, taking the very nature of a servant... he humbled himself.
Philippians 2: 5- 8

It is so important to remember that every time Jesus spoke of the end times, the first thing he always said was "do not be deceived," indicating that deception would be rampant and identifying the heroes and villains in the end time's battles might be difficult. The Luciferians have been hard at work, preparing the way for their coming savior. Their means of preparation included attaining positions of power and influence in order to foment mass deception, to slowly condition and ultimately trick the world to accept their false savior.

There is a war going on right now in the spiritual realms. Extra-dimensional beings are fighting over our souls at this very moment! Some people are aware of this and are taking sides.

It all began back in the Garden of Eden.

IN THE GARDEN: In the Garden of Eden everything was perfect, God walked and talked with Adam and Eve, all their food was abundant and the earth was peaceful. It also seems that work, housing and even clothing itself were not necessary. Something has obviously gone very wrong since that time. The earth is now full of constant strife and turmoil and God seems distant.

What happened to bring us down from this point?

The Bible tells us that something terrible happened when Adam and Eve ate a certain fruit.

God's number one angel, Lucifer, had become jealous of humans. He was a being of light, and he looked down upon us humans who were formed from the dust and mud of the earth. So he approached Eve in the form of a talking serpent, which she did not think surprising or out of place, and got her to first doubt and then question God. He lied and she was deceived and ate the forbidden fruit. She broke the one law God had made. Soon after, Adam chose to eat the fruit as well.

In deceiving the first humans Lucifer offered three specific things: hidden or occult knowledge, immortality and "to be as gods (Genesis 3: 5)." As we move through this book we will repeatedly see that these three tenets form the basis of the Luciferian religion!

WHO WAS LUCIFER? The Biblical story of *the fall* is in the third chapter of Genesis, but we can learn more about Lucifer elsewhere. For instance we can see that he was not always evil. In Genesis 1: 31, it says that when God had finished creating man, "*all* God had made was good," and *all* the sons of God, the angels, shouted for joy (Job 38: 4-7). Lucifer had yet to turn evil at that point. The Book of Revelation tells us it was definitely Lucifer that took the form of a serpent in Eden, but it wasn't a snake as legend has it, it was really something more like a dragon (Revelation 12).

The prophet Ezekiel spoke of Lucifer's rebellion and tells us that Lucifer was initially assigned by God to be mankind's protecting guardian angel. Until then, Lucifer had been the brightest in all creation, but he could not stand being second to creatures made from dust and mud.

This is what the sovereign Lord says:
"You were the model of perfection,
Full of wisdom and perfect in beauty, you were in Eden, the garden of God.
You were anointed as a guardian cherub for so I ordained you...
You were blameless in your ways from the day you were created
Till wickedness was found in you.
You were filled with violence, and you sinned.
So I drove you in disgrace from the mount of God,
And I expelled you, O guardian cherub...
Your heart became proud on account of your beauty,
And you corrupted your wisdom because of your splendor.
So I threw you to the earth.
                              Ezekiel 28: 12- 17

When the angel Lucifer fell his name was changed. Through his actions he became our *Accuser,* or in the Hebrew language, Satan. The prophet Isaiah revealed these bold statements from Satan's heart and mind:

I will ascend to heaven,
I will raise my throne above the stars,
I will sit enthroned on the sacred mountain,
I will ascend above the tops of the clouds,
I will make myself like the most high.
                              Isaiah 14: 12-15

Five times Satan said "I will," basically saying "I will make myself God."

GOD'S PLAN TO SAVE HUMANITY: God came to Adam shortly after he had eaten the fruit. He told our ancestors that they had made a terrible mistake, but he had a plan to set things right. He said to the serpent:

> I will put enmity between you and the woman, and between your offspring and hers: he will crush your head and you will strike his heel.
>
> Genesis 3: 15

In this verse God prophesied that a savior would come, the child of a virgin[2] to crush and put an end to the serpent. But he also prophesied that Lucifer would father a child as well. We know that God's son has come once, fulfilling many ancient prophesies. And since that time many people have wondered and tried to surmise the identity of Satan's son, the dreaded Antichrist. Various kings and popes have been suspected, even Martin Luther, founder of the Protestant denomination was once accused by the Roman Catholic Church.

Furthermore, God said to the serpent "You will crawl on your belly and you will eat *dust* all the days of your life." Interesting, because in creating man "The Lord God formed the man from *dust* (Genesis 3:14 and 2: 7)." God knew full well that Satan would continue to figuratively eat and devour humans.

The part that most people miss is what is said regarding the seed, or offspring, of Satan. Recognize the language used here, most snakes encountering humans have had their heads stomped upon and crushed. On the other side of the situation snakes will strike out and bite people's heels and lower legs. Somehow the Antichrist was to strike out against Jesus. Later we'll, how this may have already occurred when we examine the role Satan had to play in Christ's crucifixion.

We wait for Jesus to crush Satan's head at Armageddon. It has all been planned, it's all arranged. Our God exists in the past, present and future, all times are under his observation. He has already seen the victory, "I saw Satan fall like lightening (Luke 10: 18)."

---

[2] In ancient terminology the offspring, or *seed* in the KJV, is always attributed to the male, or father. In this one Biblical verse the woman is credited with seed, ie: a virgin birth.

CHAPTER TWO
ENOCH AND THE GIANT NEPHILIM

Satan is an angel, one that is destined to have a son.

Can angels have children?

Have angels ever sired children with human women? That is the better question.

This has actually been a long lived argument among Bible scholars. Some have dismissed it all and say that angels cannot have children because of what the Bible says in Matthew 22: 30; that angels do not get married. Well, this is explained rather simply when we find that there are no female angels, so of course they don't marry one another! In the original Hebrew language that the Old Testament was written in, the word *Mal-ak* means angel and cannot be used in a feminine tense. But Genesis 6: 2 seems to tell us that angels may have sought out human women in marriage around the time of the Flood. This definitely requires further investigation!

DNA AND GENETICS IN THE BIBLE: When the Virgin Mary became pregnant it was through a miracle. Satan is incapable of miracles, acts which violate the laws of physics. He is capable of magic, which is trickery carried out by his unseen agents in the spirit world. So, if an angel were to cause a human female to become pregnant, well, this might involve some sort of genetic manipulation. Surprisingly, there's evidence that this may have been the case.

In the first chapter of the Bible I'm struck by the repetition of simple words. For example, between Genesis 1: 11 and 1: 25 the word *kind* is used ten times!

> Then God said, "Let the land produce vegetation: seed-bearing plants and trees on the land that bear seed in it, according to their various kinds." And it was so. The land produced vegetation: plants bearing seed according to their kinds and trees bearing fruit with seed in it according to their kinds. And God saw that it was good.
> Genesis 1: 11, 12

God created the plant life of the earth *according to their kinds,* which in the original Hebrew means: specific sorts, species or genuses. To this God says "it was good." Next God made the creatures of the sea and all marine life, again according to their kinds, after this he created winged birds, also according to their kinds; and God again says "it was good (Genesis 1: 21)." Genetic organization is apparently very important to God. He next produced the land animals, live stock and creatures that move along the ground, the Bible emphasizing that each had its kind, and that this was good (Genesis 1: 24, 25).

It is not hard to infer that these verses are explaining something akin to genetics here, that each animal kind has its own genetic grouping which we noted God said were *good.* Now consider for a moment how God created Adam's wife Eve, by taking a part of his flesh, specifically a rib bone, and engineered a human being. Surely God is capable of greater miracles, but is this event not akin to modern cloning?

As a Bible believer I believe that the Creator would of course have the most complete and profound knowledge of such things as genetics. When God created all living organisms it seems he used DNA molecules as his building blocks. Scientists often refer to DNA as "the molecule of life" because every life form contains DNA, just arranged in a different fashion than its neighboring species. It was only in 1953 that we came to know the double helical structure of DNA. But in recent years humanity has come to understand genetics enough to start manipulating the traits of various organisms. There has certainly been a backlash against GMOs, genetically modified organisms, in our supermarkets. Mankind has started to breakdown the barriers between species to combine things to make superior products, such as apples that don't rot. But are these *superior* products good for our body's usage?

The Book of Jubilees[3] tells us quite plainly that the boundaries between the kinds somehow fell before the Flood as well... and God was not happy.

---

[3] Don't bother looking in your Bibles for this verse, the Book of Jubilees is considered a pseudepigraphical book, it was found among the Dead Sea Scrolls and exists to this day in the Ethiopian's version of the Bible. We will weigh the pros and cons of Jubilees and pseudepigraphical scripture as we go one.

And lawlessness increased on the earth and all flesh corrupted its way, alike men and cattle and beasts and birds and everything that walks upon the earth, all of them corrupted their ways and their orders... And against the angels that God had sent upon the earth he was exceedingly wroth, and he gave commandment to root them out of all their dominion, and he bade us to bind them in the depths of the earth... they were bound in the depths of the earth forever, until the day of the great condemnation, when judgment is executed on all those who have corrupted their ways.

The Book of Jubilees 5: 2-10

Here it would seem that creatures had corrupted their orders, and when we read further we can also learn that certain angels, called Watchers, were blamed for this. According to the Book of Jubilees this was precisely the reason for the Flood! Something may have gone wrong with the cellular make up and genetics of God's creation.

These Watcher angels can also be found in the Holy Bible (Daniel 4: 13, 17, 23). The prophet Daniel recorded three encounters and each time was sure to mention that the Watcher he met was "a holy one" as the reader would understand that there existed Watchers who were less than holy.

What were the fallen Watchers up to before the Flood, what was their goal in all this? Were they actually tampering with DNA, the very building blocks God had used to create life? How did this start?

THE NEPHILIM: After Satan's fall, it seems a larger rebellion began in the heavenly realms. A group of angels had come to doubt God's authority and gave into their lust for human women. So they came and dwelt with mortals, taking any woman they chose for wives. The Bible says:

When men began to increase in number on the earth and daughters were born to them; the Sons of God saw that the daughters of men were beautiful, and they married any of them they chose... the Nephilim were on the earth in those days, and also afterward, when the Sons of God went to the daughters of men and had children by them. They were the heroes of old, the men of renown.

Genesis 6: 1- 4

Who are these Sons of God? And who are the Nephilim? We must answer these questions as these are among the very few verses in the Bible concerning Noah's lifetime and we're desperately seeking knowledge regarding the days of Noah prophecy.

Let us take a look at these verses from another angle. The *Septuagint* was the first translation made of the Old Testament Bible. This Greek version, the same one that Jesus' disciples used, words Genesis 6 this way:

> And it came to pass when man began to be numerous on the earth, and daughters were born to them, that the sons of God having seen the beautiful daughters of men that they were beautiful, took to themselves wives of all whom they chose... Now the giants were on the earth in those days; and after that when the sons of God were wont to go in to the daughters of men, they bore children to them, those were the giants of old, the men of renown.

Here the Nephilim appear to be giants! How can this be?

Greek mythology is full of giants; can we honestly believe in giants?

There is actually Biblical evidence that supports this notion. In Numbers 13:33, as the Israelites neared the Promised Land, it's claimed that "all the people there are of great size. We saw the Nephilim there." And look at the giant that David fought, Goliath.[4]

That starts to answer the question about who the Nephilim were but who were the fathers of the giants, the Sons of God?

Another source of ancient Biblical history may be found in the so-called *pseudepigraphical* books. I want you to keep in mind that these works are not equal with, or on par with the Bible and its authority in anyway! They might, however, help shed some light on certain issues the Bible may appear to be vague on. These writings certainly show us how the Hebrews of long ago interpreted the Bible, so let's see how the *Book of Jubilees* words Genesis 6:

> "And it came to pass when the children of men began to multiply on the face of the earth and daughters were born to them, that **the angels of God** saw them... that they were beautiful to look upon; and they took themselves wives of all whom they chose, and

---

[4] See the Appendix at the end of this book for *A Brief History of the Nephilim.*

they bare unto them sons and they were giants."
Jubilees 5: 1, 2

In another of the pseudepigraphical books, the *Book of Enoch,* Genesis 6 appears this way:

And it came to pass when the children of men had multiplied that in those days were born unto them beautiful and comely daughters. And **the angels, the children of the heaven,** saw and lusted after them, and said to one another: "Come let us chose wives from among the children of men and beget us children."
...and they were in all two hundred; who descended in the days of Jared.
Enoch 6: 1-2, 6

These sources make it clear that the Biblical *sons of God* are in fact angels, angels specifically known as *Watchers.* Two-hundred of them were apparently led by angels named Azazel and Semjaza. They appeared as very tall men with long white hair and long white robes. The ancient's records also describe them as radiant and glowing godlike beings. Many cultures have accounts, such as in the Egyptian and Sumerians, which describe these beings and it is repeatedly and clearly emphasized that their offspring, sired with human women, were giants!

We might then conclude that the Nephilim spoken of in the Bible are hybrid creatures, part man and part angel, their DNA somehow combined.

Now think about this, angels living among humans would have had powers and knowledge far beyond that of normal people. We can easily imagine them rising to become the rulers, kings and even gods of the populace. A religion would have arisen, instituting the worship of these fallen angels. Many ancient peoples declared that their first kings were in fact "gods."

The first century Jewish historian, Josephus, documented the giant's remains as well.

There were till then left the race of giants, who had bodies so large, and countenances so entirely different from other men, that they were surprising to the sight, and terrible to the hearing. The bones of these men are still shown to this day, unlike to any creditable relations of other men.

Josephus, *Antiquities of the Jews,* 5. 2. 3

Just as there are many legends found around the entire world of the Great Flood there are legends of these giants as well. It is frequently noted they were sired from relations occurring between shining gods and human women. Doesn't the Bible tell us that Lucifer himself can appear as an angel of light (2Corinthians 11: 14)?

THE NEPHILIM: Let's take a closer look at the Biblical/Hebrew term *Nephilim,* pronounced *nef-eel-eem,* the *eem* ending means it is plural. Unfortunately, most scholars differ on the usage of the word. The Hebrew meaning of *neph-el* means something *fallen* or *untimely birth.* The meaning of the word *neph-iyl* is *giant, bully* or *tyrant.* Clearly each meaning can apply to either the fallen fathers or their giant offspring. But when we turn to M. Jastrow's *Dictionary of the Targumim, the Talmud Babli and Yerushalmi and the Midrashic Literature* (vol. 2, pg. 923- 924), we're told that the word *Nephilim* in Genesis 6 comes from the Hebrew word *Naphil* and definitely pertains to "giants" who "caused the downfall of the world." Incidentally, the word is also used to refer to demons.

THE WATCHER'S TEACHINGS: In the Book of Enoch it is written that before the Flood the fallen Watcher angels were teaching mankind "the secrets of heaven." It wasn't bad enough that the fallen Watchers were siring abominations; they were teaching the ways of magic, witchcraft and even greater perversions, maybe even genetics.

And all the others together with them took unto themselves wives, and each chose for himself one, and they began to defile themselves with them, and they taught them charms and enchantments, and the cutting of roots, and made them acquainted with plants. And they became pregnant, and they bare great giants, whose height was three thousand ells.

The Book of Enoch 8: 1- 3

Thou seest what Azazel has done… and on the day of the great judgment he shall be cast into the fire. And heal the earth which the angels have corrupted, and proclaim the healing of the earth, that they may heal the plague, and that all the children of men may not perish through all the secret things that the Watchers have disclosed and have taught their sons. And the whole earth has been corrupted through the works that were taught by Azazel.

The Book of Enoch 10: 6- 8

It seems that the Watchers, who were meant to watch over us humans, in their pride desired to create as the Most High, they created monsters. And they also taught humanity various things, which, from the above statements, seem to have possibly resulted in pregnancies. The Bible then tells us that before the Flood:

The Lord saw how great man's wickedness had become, and that every inclination of his heart was only evil all the time.

Genesis 6: 5

ENOCH: We've been reading from a book supposedly written by this Enoch character, who is he? Well, Enoch was in fact Noah's great grandfather, obviously living well before the Flood, could any of his writings seriously have survived? Did Noah keep his great grandfather's scrolls with him?

The Bible tells us that Enoch was a man of great faith (Hebrews 11: 5), a prophet (Jude 14) and that he even "walked with God (Genesis 5: 24)." But what is most remarkable, and what he is most often remembered for, is that he did not die! He was taken directly to heaven, Enoch was the first being to *rapture*. The story of Enoch is found in Genesis 5: 18- 24, but it is expanded upon in the Book of Jubilees.

Enoch... was the first among men that are born on the earth who learnt writing and knowledge and wisdom and wrote down the signs of heaven... he was the first to write a testimony, and he testified to the sons of men... what was and will be he saw in a vision in his sleep, as it will happen to the children of men throughout their generations until the day of judgment... and he testified to the Watchers who had sinned with the daughters of men; for these had begun to unite themselves, so as to be defiled, with the daughters of men, and Enoch testified against them all. And he was taken from amongst the children of men, and was conducted into the Garden of Eden in majesty and honor.

The Book of Jubilees 4: 17- 23

Enoch gave the Watchers and the people of earth a warning that God's wrath had been stirred and that a great cataclysm was approaching.

PSEUDEPIGRAPHICAL WRITINGS: Throughout the Bible several books are referenced by the writers that were, in some cases, deemed holy writ, but are no longer in existence. For example the Book of Jashar is mentioned in Joshua 10:13 and 2Samuel 1:17, the Book of the Wars of the Lord (Numbers 21: 14), the Book of the Annals of Solomon (1Kings 11: 41) and over a dozen others are mentioned.

The Book of Enoch, which we have been discussing, is quoted in Jude 14 and for a long time was considered a *lost* book. But we can study it today because copies of it were found in 1768, Ethiopia, by James Bruce. To this day the Ethiopians still keep the Book of Enoch in their Bible. Many copies of it were among the Dead Sea Scrolls found in 1947. Also among the Dead Sea Scrolls we find the other important lost record we've looked at, the Book of Jubilees. Some believe that the Dead Sea Scrolls reflect the Bible that Jesus knew in his day.

Parts of the Book of Enoch may have been a book written before the Flood and describes the pre-Flood world. Astonishingly, the writer dedicates the book to those living in the end times! In the first verse of the first chapter it is written "To the blessed the elect and righteous, who will be living in the day of tribulation... not for this generation, but a remote one which is to come (Enoch 1: 1, 2)."

When Jude quotes from Enoch it is also in regards to the end times, to Christ's Second Coming.

> Enoch, the seventh from Adam, prophesied about these men. "See the Lord is coming with thousands upon thousands of his holy ones to judge everyone, and to convict all the ungodly of all the ungodly acts they have done in the ungodly way, and of all the harsh words ungodly sinners have spoken against him."
>
> Jude 14, 15 (in *Book of Enoch* as 1: 9)

Some scholars believe it is too preposterous for the Book of Enoch to have survived from the pre-Flood era, teaching instead that this work is pseudepigraphical, that a writer living in the second century BC wrote it and merely put Enoch's name to it. This may be partially true. It is obvious that the Book of Enoch has been added onto by other writers through the ages. There are roughly five sections, the first, chapters 1- 36, deal with the Watchers and has been regarded as the original pre-Flood portion. We must realize that if any of it was really written by Enoch, then until the time of Moses it may have been the scriptural Word of God to those early generations, containing the history of man and God's earliest commands. Bible scholars know that the Book of Job was written before Moses' time, why couldn't there be others? Linguistic evidence shows that when Moses wrote the Book of Genesis he was really compiling it from several documents that had come into his possession, apparently the records of the patriarchs.

Since these books, Enoch and Jubilees, have been added on to and tampered with they cannot be trusted in the same way as the Holy Bible, whose integrity the Jews guarded religiously (Romans 3: 2). These books do provide insight into ancient beliefs and explain things that we might be vague on otherwise. Some of the history in these volumes certainly warrants our attention.

GOD'S JUDGEMENT: In Enoch's book, we find the author relaying God's judgment to the three groups involved at the time of the Flood: the fallen angels, the giants and mankind.

First, Enoch tells us of God's judgment upon the giants. We're told that God miraculously increased all their nastiness and anger into full-blown rage, forcing them to fight one another to the death as their fallen fathers watched helplessly on (Jubilees 5: 7- 11). The wars must have thundered across the entire planet as many Flood legends speak of their occurrence just before the deluge.

Secondly, and perhaps most importantly, there was no place for the souls of the giants to rest. They were not human, nor were they angels, and God had not prepared a place for them in death. Their souls were destined to roam the earth as demons (Enoch 15, 16)!

For the crimes perpetrated by the 200 fallen angels, they were imprisoned in the dark caverns and volcanic fires within the earth until Judgment Day. The Bible itself tells us that God put...

...the spirits in prison who disobeyed long ago when God awaited patiently in the days of Noah while the ark was being built.
1 Peter 3: 20

God did not spare the angels when they sinned, but sent them to hell, putting them in gloomy dungeons to be held for judgment... he did not spare the ancient world when he brought the flood on its

ungodly people, but protected Noah, a preacher of righteousness.
2Peter 2: 4, 5

In 1909, Louis Ginzberg compiled a volume called *The Legends of the Jews,* which he assembled from the ancient oral legends of the Hebrews, now kept in the Talmud, Haggada, and Midrash. He tells us a similar story:

> Uriel was sent to Noah to announce to him that the earth would be destroyed by a flood... Raphael was told to put the fallen angel Azazel into chains and cast him into a pit of sharp and pointed stones and cover it with darkness, and so was to remain until the great day of judgment, when he would be thrown into the fiery pit of hell, and the earth would be healed of the corruption he had contrived upon it. Gabriel was charged to proceed against the bastards and the reprobates, the sons of the angels begotten with the daughters of men, and plunge them into deadly conflicts with one another. Shemhazai's ilk were handed over to Michael, who first caused them to witness the death of their children in their bloody combat with each other, and then he bound them and pinned them under the hills of the earth, where they will remain... until the day of judgment, to be carried thence to the fiery pit of hell.
>
> Ginzberg, *the Legends of the Jews,*
> Bk. 1, pg 148

BEINGS WITHIN THE EARTH: The Bible does make reference to beings below the earth's surface: "At the name of Jesus every knee should bow, in heaven... and under the earth (Philippians 2: 10, and see Ephesians 4: 9)."

> I bring the ocean depths over you and its vast waters cover you, then I will bring you down with those who go down to the pit, to the people of long ago. I will make you dwell in the earth bellow, as in ancient ruins, with those who go down to the pit.
> Ezekiel 26: 19, 20

Peter tells us that both spirits (1Peter 3: 19) and fallen angels (2Peter 2: 4) were imprisoned there during the days of Noah. Revelation tells us that in the end times these beings will be released, led by Apollyon

(Revelation 9: 11). Let's take a closer look at the history of these inner-earthlings since they seem to play quite a role in the end time's Tribulation.

Throughout the world there are many cultural legends claiming that creatures inhabit hidden caverns and tunnels within the earth. The ancient Romans and Greeks referred to an underworld where beings suffer eternal fiery torment. The Greeks called it *Hades* or *Tartarus*, it was known to the Hebrews as *Sheol,* Christians have called the underworld *Hell* or *the Pit.*

Sir Edmund Halley, who the comet is named after, firmly believed that the earth was hollow and soon his *Hollow Earth Theory* came into mainstream thought. The science fiction writer Jules Verne wrote *A Journey to the Centre of the Earth* in 1864 and Edgar Rice Burroughs wrote *At the Earth's Core* in 1914. John Cleves Symmes petitioned then American President Van Buren to fund an exploratory mission of earth's poles, which Symmes felt were openings into the hollow world bellow. Congress authorized this voyage in 1828.

The Buddhist people of Tibet claim there are secret entrances in the Himalayans where entrance can be attained to a subterranean land called Agarta. Here the capital city is called Shamballah and is ruled by the deity Rigden-jyepo, aka: the King of the World, who is supposedly in close telepathic contact with the Dalai Lama.[5] Agarta was supposedly founded long ago when a holy man was warned of an impending world calamity by the gods. He led his people down through secret tunnels and into the inner lands. During times of turmoil upon the surface the wise ancients from below are said to have communicated telepathically to certain chosen people.

Some people claim to have been contacted by the inner-earthlings, Marquis Alexander Saint-Yves D'Alveydre for one. He documented in his 1886 book *The Kingdom of Agarttha* that the inner earth inhabitants told him they entered the earth about 3200 BC when the surface world faced a terrible catastrophe. Edward Bulwer-Lytton, a prominent member of the British House of Lords, wrote of inner earth beings in his 1871 book *The Coming Race,* and how they are currently awaiting a

---

[5] Rigden-jyepo, who Buddhists also know as Matreiya, is prophesied to return to the earth's surface bringing about a new age, which will be accompanied by global catastrophes. New Agers refer to him as "The Cosmic Christ." Remember, Jesus said to watch out for deceptive false Christs in the end times (Matthew 24: 24).

return to the surface to take over the entire earth! During World War II the Nazis fully believed this notion and searched for "Vril-ya beings in the subterranean land of Thule" in order to make an alliance with these coming conquerors.

These are certainly curious stories, perhaps related to Biblical accounts of imprisoned angels, but no one lends credence to this notion like Richard Shaver does. Richard S. Shaver was working as a welder at the Ford assembly plant in Michigan during the 1930s when he began to hear voices in his head, he believed that these were facilitated and caused by the coils in his welding equipment. The voices were accompanied by visions of a race of "Elder Gods" who explained that they had been forced to take up residence beneath earth's surface. Shaver saw visions of their large cities and interconnecting tunnels and began to carefully document these telepathic interactions.

As an outlet for these writings he approached Ray Palmer, then editor of *Amazing Stories* magazine. In March of 1945 the story entitled "I Remember Lemuria" was published. This was based on Shaver's documentation which Palmer had turned into a fictionalized adventure based on a character living within the earth. Readers and fans of the magazine flooded the Ziff-Davis office with more than 50,000 pieces of mail in that first month, many claiming to have received similar messages and even to have made physical contact, often via abduction, with the inner earth beings. Something strange was occurring across America and Shaver found himself in the middle of it. Over the following years *Amazing Stories* would run many more of Shaver's stories. The circulation of the periodical skyrocketed, climaxing in June 1947 when an all Shaver issue was published. But then *Amazing Stories,* at its all time peak, suddenly and mysteriously pulled the Shaver stories and refused to publish him any further.

Because of this, Ray Palmer quit the periodical claiming that the Ziff-Davis Corporation had been forced by politically powerful people to stop Shaver from telling his stories. We'll see how this fits later, but the day after the Shaver stories were pulled a UFO crashed near Roswell, New Mexico.

What we should notice here is that Shaver said the race within the earth had frequently interbred with humans to create hybrid offspring called deros. Remarkably, he said the demon-like "deros often interfere with civilizations on the surface… to create as much trouble with the outside world as possible. The deros secretly foster wars, crimes and disasters... (causing) illusions, nightmares, hypnotic compulsions and urges to commit crime... (they are) responsible for the strange urge to murder sometimes reported by mad killers." Shaver also said he's heard the screams of humans abducted by the deros, taken down to their underworld.

Shaver said the inner earth races are further made up of Atlans, Teans (which put together equals: *Atlanteans*), giants and other radiant beings known as Titans. David Hatcher Childress would compile some of Shaver's thoughts in 1999 and tell us that:

> Mr. Shaver refers to "ancient" books which have been destroyed, which contained a great deal of Atlan knowledge and history, but points to references in the Bible such as "In those days there were giants in the Earth" as actual truth, recorded memory of the Titans. Especially significant is the definite statement "in the Earth" and not on it!
>
> Childress, *Lost Continents and the Hollow Earth,* pg 27

There are clear similarities between Shaver's stories and Genesis 6, the Books of Enoch, Jubilees and many other ancient sources. We know there are beings within the earth. The Bible tells us so, and God tells us so for a reason: because whatever beings are currently imprisoned within the earth will be freed in the end times (Revelation 9: 1- 11)!

CHAPTER THREE
SURVIVING THE FLOOD

Noah was a just man and perfect in his generations.
Genesis 6: 9 KJV

When the Watcher angels rebelled before the Flood we can perhaps see how they were working with Satan on a part of a larger plan. It seems to be an assault on all mankind. Their goal: to corrupt humanity's genetics, combine us with horrible demons, to breed out and extinguish the human seed. If humans were all genetically corrupt it would be impossible for a Savior to come! Christ would be defeated. It was for this reason that the Great Flood came: to wipe out the fallen angel's genetic tampering.

NOAH'S GENERATIONS: When God decided to flood the earth, he chose to save one man in particular. One man with a particular trait, what was it? The King James Version of the Bible says it this way: "Noah was a just man and perfect in his generations." What does it mean that Noah was perfect in his "generations?" The *New Strong's Complete Dictionary of Bible Words* translates the term as: nativity, offspring in kind. This seems to imply that Noah was genetically pure, without the influence of any kind of genetic impurity!

So Noah was genetically pure, but how far did the genetic tampering go before the Flood? It certainly seems beyond the GMOs we see today. Were animals altered, how about crops and plant life? Remember, God commanded that all life was to be destroyed, even plants (Genesis 6: 17, 7: 4)! And realize it was God who selected which animals were to be brought onto the ark (Genesis 6: 20, 7: 9). And consider the ancients who often sculpted extreme hybrid creatures like centaurs, sphinxes and such. Were they eye-witnesses to the oddities we're discussing here? A cataclysmic flood was needed to undo the Watcher's widespread damage.

But it would seem Satan may have had a provision against this. Genesis 6 does say that the Nephilim would live after the flood as well.

Remember, only about 200 fallen angels are locked away and imprisoned for their crimes, there were fallen angels who were not locked away because they hadn't sired any children yet. One example of a fallen angel who did not father a child before the Flood was Satan. He was waiting for the most opportune moment to unleash his son on the earth! At present there are others such as him, who have fallen and have not been judged yet. Recall the famed giant Goliath who lived centuries after Noah, he had an angelic father and angels like him would still be roaming free.

SURVIVING THE FLOOD: We all know that Noah, his family and a boat load of animals survived the Flood. But very few know that the Luciferians have an interesting story about how their kind prepared for and survived the Flood as well. Satan was surely not ignorant of the approaching cataclysm. Noah was openly warning and preaching to everyone who would listen (2Peter 2: 5).

The following tale makes for an entertaining epic by itself, but I'm not too sure how much of it we should believe. Despite this, we must realize that it is an integral part of the Luciferian's beliefs. We'll see many diverse sources repeat the story especially later when we look at the Freemason's beliefs. I first came across the story in the Book of Jubilees. Here we read that evil Watcher angels inscribed their teachings on a stone structure with the purpose of getting that knowledge through the cataclysm to the people of the post Flood world.

> And Kainam's father taught him writing, and he went to seek for himself a place where he might seize for himself a city. And he found a writing which former generations had carved on the rock, and he read what was thereon, and he transcribed it and sinned owing to it; for it contained the writings of the Watchers in accordance with which they used to observe the omens of the sun and the moon and stars in all the signs of heaven. And he wrote it down and said nothing regarding it; for he was afraid to speak to Noah about it lest he should become angry with him on account of it.
>
> Book of Jubilees 8: 2- 5

So Kainam, who may be the Canaan of Genesis 9: 25 who was cursed by Noah, left home to seize for himself the ruins of a preflood city but apparently found the writings of the Watchers instead.

They had literally left a message written in stone!

When the famed Greek philosopher Plato wrote of Atlantis he may have described a similar concept when he described the Temple of Poseidon where he says all Atlantean knowledge was carved into stone pillars. Manetho, an Egyptian historian who lived during the 3rd century BC, wrote of Siriadic columns which had "the principles of all knowledge inscribed upon them in a sacred language."

The first century Jewish historian Josephus tells a similar story:

> They were also the inventors of that particular sort of wisdom which is concerned with the heavenly bodies and their order. And that their inventions might not be lost before they were sufficiently known, upon Adam's prediction that the world was to be destroyed at one time be the force of fire, and at another time by the violence and quantity of water, they made two pillars; one of brick, the other of stone: they inscribed their discoveries on them both, that in the case of the pillar of brick should be destroyed by the flood, the pillar of stone might remain, and exhibit these discoveries to mankind; and also inform them that there was another pillar of brick erected by them. Now this remains in the land of Siriad to this day.
>
> Josephus, *the Antiquities of the Jews,* 2: 3: 69, 70

There are ancient Hebrew legends that claim Adam was warned by God that the earth would at one time be destroyed by water and at another time by fire. From these accounts it would seem the pre-Flood peoples did not know which was coming, so they began work on two pillars. A stone monument was built to survive a watery flood and a brick one was constructed to survive destruction by flames. Bible believers know that a watery flood did come in the days of Noah,[6] thus the monument of stone survived. But where is it?

Both Manetho and Josephus said that the mysterious monument is in Siriad, this is actually an ancient term for the lands of Egypt, around Cairo and the Giza Plateau. Can we think of any wondrous stone monuments in this region?

---

[6] And prophecy tells us that in the end times the earth is to be scourged by fire (2Peter 3: 6- 12).

Only the Great Pyramids!

Were these monuments constructed before the Flood?

The Giza Plateau has been thoroughly analyzed by John Anthony West, who, in his book *Serpent in the Sky,* says that the obvious erosion seen on the Great Pyramid's nearby neighbor, the Sphinx, could only be caused by very large amounts of water. This kind of erosion can only come from continuous downpours of rain over incredibly long periods of time or during complete prolonged submersion, say, from a flood. Boston University geologist Dr. Robert M. Schoch, who wrote the book *Pyramid Quest,* has also studied the erosion seen on the Sphinx and states that "The current estimated age of the monument, at 2700 BC is out by 2500 years, and that the Sphinx is more likely to have been built about 5000 BC, as no significant rainfall has occurred on the Giza plateau, the site of both the Sphinx and Great Pyramid... This can only mean that both these structures were built more than several thousand years prior to the Egyptians." It has also been documented that salt deposits were found coating many of the inner walls of the Great Pyramid and sea shells were seen around the pyramid's base by Herodotus and other ancient visitors to the site.

Was the Great Pyramid then a repository for sacred knowledge from before the Flood?

The ancient Egyptians certainly thought so! In a manuscript kept in the Bodleian Library one Abou Balkhi wrote in 870 AD that:

> The wise men, previous to the flood, foreseeing an impending judgment from heaven, either by submersion or fire, would destroy every created thing, built upon the tops of mountains in Upper Egypt many pyramids of stone, in order to have some refuge against the coming calamity. Two of these buildings exceeded the rest in height, being four hundred cubits high and as many broad and as many long. They were built with large blocks of marble, and they were so well put together that the joints were scarcely perceptible. Upon the exterior of the building every charm and wonder of physic was inscribed.

Another manuscript attributed to a fellow named Masoudi says that:

> Surid, one of the kings before the flood built the two great pyramids and ordered the priests to deposit within them the written

accounts of their wisdom and acquirements in different arts and sciences, that they should remain on record for the benefit of those who could afterwards comprehend them.

Masoudi,
Akhbar al Zaman Manuscript

The Great Pyramid is definitely a mysterious construct enthralling generations. The Bible never specifically mentions the Great Pyramid, but there is reference to the coming of an Egyptian monument that would someday be "a monument to the Lord in the heart of Egypt (Isaiah 19: 19)." This may imply that any great monuments currently there are not good or Godly.

Where are these writings? Nothing today is visible on the Great Pyramid or in it.

In 1179 AD, the Arab historian Abdul Latif recorded that "the stones were inscribed with ancient characters, now unintelligible. I never met with a person in all Egypt who understood them. The inscriptions are so numerous that copies of those alone which may be seen upon the surface of the two pyramids would occupy above six thousand pages." He was one of the last historians to see and document the existence of the inscriptions upon the Great Pyramid because in 1222 and 1301 AD earthquakes leveled many of the mosques in the area around Cairo and the casing stones of the Pyramid, more than 22 acres worth, were removed, cut smaller and reshaped and used for the rebuilding projects. Since that time, all but two of the inscribed casing stones have disappeared.

William of Baldensal, a wealthy European tourist who travelled in the early fourteenth century, recorded that he saw the stones that had been taken from the Great Pyramid were now visible on the exterior of the Grand Mosque and that of Sultan Hassan, the two most beautiful Mosques in Cairo, and that these recycled stones were covered with strange symbols arranged in careful rows.

The great Egyptologist Sir Flinders Petrie (1853- 1942) reported that some of these markings were still visible during this time, noting that he also saw the inscribed stones at Cairo's smaller Mosques as well. The Arab masons smoothed out the writings, eradicating them, as they reworked the stones. Petrie saw one of the inscribed stones in the Bulak Museum. He remarked that there was a lot of later graffiti on the pyramid's casing stones in the common languages of his day, Greek,

Phoenician and Cypriote, but the original writings that the pyramid's builders had inscribed were not a recognized language.

The noted Western occultist and 33rd degree Masonic scholar Manly P. Hall agrees, his sources also speak of inscriptions written upon the Great Pyramid's outer casing stones. Hall tells us he had learned this from a mysterious "Egyptologist and authority Mr. Gab," who apparently also found "Sea shells at the base of the Pyramid, which advances the evidence that it was erected before the Deluge, a theory substantiated by the Arabic traditions (*The Secret Teachings of All Ages,* page 109)."

Hall's source was Godfrey Higgins who wrote the *Anacalypsis* in 1874. Higgins tells us that this *Mister Gab* was actually a learned Catholic priest. Abbe Gab had concluded that "It evidently appears that this pyramid must have been erected by the Antediluvians before the universal deluge called Noah's Flood." Gab also tells us he found "Shells and portions of loam, which more immediately covered the sides of the Pyramid near the rock... petrified oyster and other sea-shells." These shells are a still a curiosity. Jennifer Viegas reported for *Discovery News* on April 28, 2008, that sea shells are still being found on the Giza Plateau, near the Great Pyramid and Sphinx.

The belief was shared throughout the known world, in Rome the historian Ammianus Marcellinus wrote in 380 AD that the monuments of the Giza Plateau were constructed before the Flood by certain *Elders* who had a certain foreknowledge that a catastrophic deluge was coming. Marcellinus reported that the "Inscriptions which the ancients asserted on the walls of certain underground galleries of the pyramids were intended to prevent the ancient wisdom from being lost in the flood." He said their primary aim was to preserve the Elder's knowledge of secret ceremonies known as "Acts of Creation."

What could this mean, *Acts of Creation?* The ancient historian Manetho similarly mentioned in his work *Aegyptika,* that the message left on the pre-Flood monument by the Elders was, more specifically, the acts "to create gods!"

This is the biggest key to the mystery regarding the Days of Noah.

How exactly could the ancient Egyptians create a god?

Could the genetic component that we've been discussing have anything to do with this?

CHAPTER FOUR
NIMROD AND THE TOWER OF BABYLON

Here's a summary of what we've found so far.

We've just seen how the Great Pyramid may be a monument that survived Noah's Flood. Many legends claim it was engraved with sacred writings that were somehow the instructions to *create gods.*

We've studied the time before the Flood and found that there were strange creatures living on the earth; creatures that were likely thought of as gods by the locals. The Bible calls these creatures the Sons of God and Nephilim. The Bible clearly says that the Nephilim lived during the days of Noah... and afterward (Genesis 6: 4)!

Jesus told us to watch for a sign before his Second Coming, something that occurred in Noah's days would happen again in the end times. We know that in the end times Satan's son will appear, the Antichrist. The offspring of angels are the Nephilim, Satan is a fallen angel; therefore the Antichrist will be of the Nephilim.

I've also spent some time trying to show how genetic manipulation may play a role in the end time's scenario. In this chapter it will become clearer when we examine various myths and see how pagan gods have already risen from the dead! Genetic manipulation has a surprisingly long history.

GENETICALLY MODIFIED CROPS: Scripture tells us that the Hebrews encountered the Nephilim after the Flood in the Promised Land and it also seems to indicate they were genetically modifying their fruit crops!

After Moses led the Hebrews out of Egypt, and upon coming to the Promised Land, scouts were sent ahead to check things out. The spies reported that "All the people we saw there are of great size. We saw the Nephilim there. We seemed like grasshoppers in our own eyes, and we looked the same to them (Numbers 13: 32, 33)." The Bible also tells us that "when they reached the valley of Eschol, they cut off a branch bearing a single cluster of grapes. Two of them carried it on a pole between them (Numbers 13: 23)." A single bunch of grapes so big that two men were needed to carry it? It had to be much larger than anyone was used to. At no other time is such a thing mentioned in Scripture. What were the Nephilim doing to get such fruitful results?

When I first considered Jesus' days of Noah prophecy I only associated Noah's life with the ark, the animals and the cataclysmic Flood. But after learning of the Great Pyramid's inscriptions I realized that, like it, Noah really passed through two worlds. He saw the corrupt world before the Flood, but Noah lived in the world after it as well. With this story of the giant grapes it's easy to see that the subject of genetic manipulation appeared in both.

The riddle of the days of Noah prophecy will be answered here, in the world immediately after the Flood.

THE DAYS OF NOAH: What was the world like after the Flood? There would have been terrible, soggy destruction all around. It would have taken years for things to really dry out. Rebuilding would be slow and it would have taken many seasons before any forests or crops would mature. It would have been a very different world for Noah and his family. Our ancestors were literally starting over in a stone age.

Right after the story of the Flood in the Bible we see a number of verses detailing the family trees of the survivors, Noah's sons and their offspring, and after this we come to the famed story of the Tower of Babel. Although the story is rather brief here, Hebrew traditions tell us that two individuals were in charge of the construction of the tower, Cush and Nimrod. Josephus, a Jewish historian who lived a few decades after Christ's death, had this to say:

> Now it was Nimrod who excited them to such an affront and contempt of God. He was the grandson of Ham, the son of Noah, a bold man, and of great strength of hand. He persuaded them not to ascribe it to God as if it was through his means they were happy, but to believe it was their own courage which procured that happiness. He also changed the government into tyranny, seeing no other way of turning men from the fear of God, but to bring them into a constant dependence upon his power. He also said he would be revenged upon God, if he should have a mind to drown the world again; for that he would build a tower too high for the waters to be able to reach! And that he would avenge himself on God for destroying their forefathers.
>
> Josephus, *Antiquities of the Jews,* 1.4.2

Nimrod sounds like a rather nasty fellow, desiring to have revenge upon God for the Flood, and all. What did he think he was going to do, climb up to heaven and punch God in the nose? There is really very little about Nimrod in the Bible, the only source we can really trust. What it does say, however, reveals a lot.

We know that Cush was the father of Siba, Havilah, Sabtah, Raamah and Sebteca (Genesis 10: 6, 7). In the next verse the Bible lists the descendants of Raamah. But, later in Genesis 10: 8, we find one more child allotted to Cush: Nimrod. Now, why was Nimrod granted such an auspicious spot all his own and not included with the rest of Cush's family? And why, in the original Hebrew language is Cush not listed as the father of Nimrod, but more the *co-creator?*

NIMROD: Let us examine the meaning of the name Nimrod. In Hebrew it is pronounced *marad,* which is a verb, an action word, meaning *we rebel.* Can you imagine a mob of his followers chanting his name; the roar of the crowd would literally say *let's rebel ...let's sin!* Theologians teach that the construction of the Tower of Babylon was an organized rebellion against God. Remember, this was the same goal that Lucifer had in the Garden of Eden, to rebel against the Lord.

But there's more, something was different about this child's birth, why was Nimrod not included in the Bible with Cush's other children? Who was Nimrod?

Genesis says:

> Cush was the father of Nimrod, who grew to be a mighty
> warrior on the earth. He was a mighty hunter before the Lord; that
> is why it is said "like Nimrod, a mighty hunter before the Lord."
> Genesis 10: 8, 9

Three times we're told that this fellow, Nimrod, was mighty, and we're repeatedly told he was a hunter. At first this is understandable. The animals were likely weary of humans after their confinement on the ark, and wilder, possibly even attacking humans. Nimrod may have come to the rescue with his apparent skills and was something of a hero, defending and feeding a community. But why the emphasis, why the repetition? I had to check with the original Hebrew to see the absolute correct meaning, I was wondering if the Bible was repeating itself for a reason or were terms changed?

First off, it is noted that the word *before*, as in the phrase "a hunter before the Lord," is the Hebrew word *el,* or *liphnei',* which could perhaps be better translated as *against* or *one opposing.* With this, we can see that Nimrod wasn't just hunting animals, he was against or opposing the Lord! He was hunting, or battling against, God and his people.

Next we note the repeated use of the word *mighty.* This was certainly done to emphasize something important about Nimrod. Sure he was mighty and strong, but in Hebrew the word used is *ghib-bowr,* meaning Nimrod was: powerful, a tyrant warrior, champion, chief, a mighty man, a strong man and a giant man! Like Nephilim, *Ghib-bowr* is another Hebrew word for giant!

Of the potential meanings for the words representing the original Hebrew we find that Nimrod could have been a Nephilim giant.

WAS NIMROD A NEPHILIM GIANT? Remember earlier we looked at the Septuagint version of the Old Testament Bible. It came about in 280 BC when a group of seventy Jewish scholars in Alexandria, Egypt, translated the Hebrew into Greek, hence the nickname LXX, Roman numerals for *seventy.* Many scholars today refer to this translation when examining a difficult topic. Sometimes it's a better representative of the Hebrew language and meaning, likely because the translators were Hebrew! In this instance it reiterates what we have been discussing.

> And Cush begot Nimrod: he began to be a giant upon the earth. He was a giant hunter before the Lord God; therefore they say, As Nimrod the giant hunter before the Lord.
> Genesis 10: 8, 9, Septuagint translation

This was a version of Scripture that Christ and his disciples were familiar with, and it makes it clear that Nimrod was a giant!

There is another thing that is very interesting regarding this verse which further connects Nimrod to the Nephilim. In Hebrew the wording of Nimrod's description includes the phrase; *hayah erets,* meaning "in the earth." This same term was used in the earlier mention of the Nephilim in Genesis 6: 4:

> There were giants **in the earth** in those days...
> Genesis 6: 4 KJV

> Nimrod… began to be a mighty one **in the earth.**
> Genesis 10: 8 KJV

Why was there this association if the scenario was not one in the same? Apart from the Bible, Hebrew legends make it clear that Nimrod was a monster. Louis Ginzberg compiled a volume appropriately entitled *The Legends of the Jews*, and we learn that Lucifer himself is reported to have met with Nimrod to advise him[7] and that he was:

> …the first among the leaders of the corrupt men… he chose Shinar as his capital. Thence he extended his dominion farther and farther, until he rose by cunning and force to be the sole ruler of the whole world. The first to hold universal sway… Since the flood there had been no sinner such as Nimrod… not satisfied to lead a godless life himself, he did all he could to tempt his subjects into evil ways… Men no longer trusted in God, but rather their own prowess and ability, an attitude to which Nimrod tried to convert the whole world… not enough to turn men away from God, he did all he could to make them pay divine honors to himself. He set himself up as a god.
> Louis Ginzberg, *Legends of the Jews,*
> Book I, pg 177, 178

Nimrod is obviously a nasty and evil being. He not only wanted to take vengeance upon God, he wanted to be a god! Remember these are Satan's goals as well. Nimrod also seems to be a Nephilim hybrid, half man, half angel, the same as the Antichrist is destined to be. Perhaps the Great Pyramid did contain some message to cause the Nephilim to be sired again after the Flood and Nimrod was preeminent.

NIMROD IN OTHER CULTURES: Remember how most cultures have similar flood legends? Well, many cultures also have similar recollections of Nimrod. Some of these various names we may be familiar with as enemies of God in the Bible. As we look at a few of their legends note how many mention that he was murdered and was to somehow have been resurrected.

To the Canaanites he was the dreaded **Baal** (Numbers 25: 3, 5). As a son of Dagan he battles Yam, a being associated with the sea and

---

[7] *The Legends of the Jews,* Louis Ginsberg, book I, pg 192, 200

floods. Baal dies and everyone mourns his passing. His wife Anat descends to the underworld to retrieve his corpse, she kills Mot, the god of the underworld and Baal's life is restored.

The Phoenicians knew him as **Attis** who the Phrygian Greeks and latter Romans adopted as **Adonis.** His mother was supposedly a virgin who conceived by putting a ripe pomegranate in her bosom. Attis grows to become a mighty hero but dies when hunting a wild boar that gores him in the genitalia. In another version of the story he castrates himself and bleeds to death under a pine tree. He is then resurrected from the grave by his wife named Aphrodite, Venus, Persephone or Cybele depending upon the culture seen. Every spring in frenzied bloody rituals his priesthood and devout followers mutilate and castrate themselves as well.

To the Ancient Sumerians he was **Marduk**, son of the god Enki who, as we'll see later, bears a striking resemblance to Lucifer. The Sumerians actually had fifty other names for Marduk: Kan, Dumuzi, Bakus *the libator of ale,* Lord Mukhla, or Azag *the mighty handed.* Azag means "Son of the Shining One."[8] He was known as a great warrior who formed an empire and is religiously called upon and associated with the resurrection of the dead. In the Sumerian legend of Dumuzi and Inanna, Dumuzi dies and Inanna descends down seven levels into the underworld to rescue him. After she returns, coming back up the seven levels, a religion is formed teaching that all humanity is trapped in the flesh, and for people to be free they must re-ascend these seven levels.

The Sumerians also had **Gilgamesh** who crossed over the waters of death searching for immortality. Here he comes across Utnapishtim, the Sumerian Noah, who gives him a sacred plant. Gilgamesh returns to the living, but a serpent steals the plant of immortality.

To the later Babylonians Nimrod was **Ningishzida** "Lord of the Tree of Life," or **Nimirrud** "The first born son of Zag, the king of the lands of Zag (the shining one)." In their historical records he is also sometimes known as Anshar or Zernebogus, meaning, "Son of the great prophet Cush," depicted wearing horns and leopard skins. He became widely known as **Tammuz** or Tahmurs, "The one who built Babylon." Upon his death his wife undergoes a period of wailing and lamentation. Annually, adherents of the religion weep and wail ritually as well,

---

[8] L.A. Waddell *Makers of Civilization in Race and History,* 1929.

which is mentioned in the Bible, Ezekiel 8: 14. The wife of Tammuz, Ishtar, eventually seeks him out in the underworld and secures his release with the provision that he will only come to the surface during the summer months, during the winter he must return to the underworld. As the sun god descends the whole world cools, winter begins and the weeping and wailing begins anew.

To the Assyrian and Chaldean peoples he was known as the great king **Ninus.** When the archeologist Austin H. Layard found the lost city of Nineveh he uncovered inscriptions stating it was Ninus who had built the city. The name Nineveh itself means *habitation of Ninus.* This agrees with Genesis 10: 8- 11 which states Nimrod built Nineveh.

The Persians called him **Mithras,** a great earth god who died and rose from the grave bringing wondrous teachings. The Romans took him as **Mitras**, the Hindus knew him as **Mitra.** In Phoenicia he was known as **Melqart** but he is remembered in the Bible as Moloch the "detestable god of the Ammonites (1Kings 11: 5)," whose rituals involved terrible child abuse and sacrifices (Leviticus 20: 2- 5).

Besides Mitra the Hindu people believe in several gods who died and rose from the grave, but **Shiva** the destroyer, a god of agriculture and fertility is the most recognized. He is depicted wearing the skin of a tiger that he had slain and with serpents hanging from his waist and neck. Shiva's symbolic representation is the lingam, a phallic shaped stone, as legends say he lost his ding-a-ling in battle. Hindus believe Shiva will come to earth as *the destroyer* at the end times to lay waste to the earth.

To the Assyrians he was **Assur,** who their land was named after. In the King James Version of the Bible Asshur is a direct alias for Nimrod in Genesis 10: 11. The Assyrians also immortalized him as the giant Hercules. **Hercules** set the earth free from many hideous monsters and was thought of as a kind of savior as he descended to the underworld at one point but returned to life. He was depicted as a muscular giant.

To the Greeks he was **Heracles,** greatest of the heroes. Legends say his father, Zeus, needed a flesh and blood mortal champion for his battle with the giants, so he copulated with the mortal Alcmene, queen of Thebes. For some reason Hermes played an intermediary role in the conception. In the legend *the Twelve Labors of Heracles,* Heracles is said to have slain the lion of Nema with his bare hands and wore the skin as a trophy. He subjected all the animals of the earth to his rule, all except the serpent. Instead he welcomed this being's enlightenment and subjected himself unto it. The Greeks also believed in the giant Orion, the handsome god of hunting. This son of Poseidon was eventually raised to the stars as a god to form the constellation that is also known as *the Hunter.*

Zeus had many human wives and a few immortal as well. With Leto they sired the child **Apollo.** He is also known as Apollyon who is mentioned in Revelation 9: 11. **Dionysus,** another Greek version of Nimrod, was Zeus' son conceived with the mortal Theban princess Semele. He was known as the *Bull horned god,* and was torn to pieces. All the pieces were eaten except for the heart, which Zeus was able to use to impregnate Semele again in order to bring Dionysus back to life, he then became known as the "twice born." His followers reenacted the process of finding his lost parts in *Mystery plays* and believed personal salvation could be attained through further secret rituals and drunken orgies in his name.

The later Romans also adopted Hercules, still a giant with divine ancestry, and they have **Bacchus,** the god of drunken revelry whom they admitted was a version of the Greek god **Dionysus.** The Romans similarly took Zeus, but called him Jupiter and with Juno he sired Mars the god of war. Now, here is something very scary, Nimrod was also later associated with the Roman sun god Saturn. He was worshipped on the winter solstice, around December 25, where there would be a feast, drunkenness and the exchange of gifts left under a pine tree!

The Germanic peoples saw him as **Balder,** *the bleeding god,* a son of Odin/Wotan. He died and went to Hel, and could only be released if all creatures wept. He is to return to earth in the days of *Ragnarok,* when the gods will fight in the last battle. This sounds like the Hindu's Shiva, returning just in time for the end of the world. Christians call this the battle of Armageddon (Revelation 16: 16).

In the Eddas, the holy writings of the Norse, he was known as **Thor,** who dwelt in the *Innstane,* a monumental stone building.

To the Minoans of Crete he was known as *the Bull man* **Minos,** the son of Zeus. He was the first high priest of Zeus and scribe of his words. He is also often known in legend as the Minotaur, half man, half bull.

The Irish and Scottish called him **Cuchulainn,** son of the god Lugh and Dechtire.

There is the British legend of King Arthur and Guinevere. Arthur was the son of Uthur Pendragon, the head dragon, and Igraine, wife of

Gorlois, Duke of Cornwall. Apparently Uther and the wizard Merlin were able to trick Igraine into the union with her thinking she was with her husband. Arthur became a giant hero and hunter of boars. Mortally wounded in battle his last words, as he sailed off on a magical boat headed to the mystical land of Avalon, were that he would return to lead his people again.

Anglo-Saxon's remember him as Zernebogus, which means in Chaldean *seed of the prophet Cush.*

The Arabic legends refer to him as "Nimrod al-Jabar," meaning Nimrod the giant-king. There is also the legend of the phoenix where a brilliant bird dies in flames and is later reborn out of the ashes.

THE LEGEND OF OSIRIS: Many of the legends dealing with Nimrod describe him similarly, primarily as the offspring of a god and a human. Many also say he was a hunter and wore a crown of horns and a lion skin. The majority also claim he died and rose again. A few mentioned that he was torn to pieces or had issues with his ding-a-ling, but when we examine the Egyptian's legend of Nimrod all these aspects will come together.

In Egypt he was known as Osiris and also as Khons, God of the Hunt, he was of course depicted wearing leopard skins and a crown with bull horns. In all the ancient Egyptian art depicting Osiris, he towered over his people. He was the child of Nut and Geb, but in the Egyptian legends for earthly Geb and heavenly Nut to conceive an intermediary, Thoth, was required to break the curse of the highest god. Recall in the Bible, Cush was the co-creator of Nimrod, not the father. As intermediary for the conception was it Thoth's roll to combine the genetic materials? It is curious that his symbol was the Caduceus, similar to the double helical appearance of DNA; very curious indeed.

Like many of the previous gods described, Osiris was often referred to as *the horned god.* Incidentally, the Egyptian bull god, Apis, whom the Hebrews worshipped while Moses was up on Mount Sinai receiving the Ten Commandments, was a version of Nimrod.

The most complete legend of Osiris comes from the ancient historian Plutarch and here we find that the most incredible event in Osiris' life occurred after his death!

Plutarch tells us that Osiris met his demise at the hands of a character known as Typhon, or Set. The meaning of the name Typhon in Egyptian is *Deluge.* Typhon, who ended the reign of Nimrod/Osiris, was someone the ancient peoples associated with the deluge, the Flood of Noah. Remember, Flood survivors like Noah and his son Shem were still alive at this time.

We know that Shem, the oldest son, carried on the priestly traditions of his father (Luke 3: 23- 37). Without a doubt Noah and Shem would have become aware of the rebellion occurring at the Tower of Babylon. They had full recollection of the preflood world teaming with Nephilim. With the advent of Nimrod they would have understood that somehow the monsters had returned.

So it seems this Shem/Typhon character sought out Nimrod/Osiris.

Plutarch's version of this encounter between them goes like this: It was decided that Typhon was to appear before the giant king. A banquet and celebration were arranged.

Typhon brought a gift, a very large and eloquent jeweled chest. After the feast the chest was shown. Everyone admired the eloquent box. Typhon declared that it was meant to be awarded to whoever could fill it. Everyone at the feast climbed inside, one after another, but everyone there was far too small. No one came close to filling it. Isis warned Osiris, her husband, not to go in it, but he laughed and said he had nothing to fear from his weak brother. Osiris climbed into the sarcophagus and suddenly the lid was slammed shut by Typhon and his conspirators! It was nailed down and then sealed shut with molten lead (Plutarch, *On Isis and Osiris,* 13)!

After Osiris was locked in the sarcophagus it was thrown in the Nile River and Osiris, trapped inside, drowned. The chest came to rest on a riverbank and legend has it that a tree rapidly grew to encompass it. A local king eventually had that great tree cut down and taken to his home to use as a supporting pillar. Isis, who had been searching for Osiris' corpse retrieved the tree, which had Osiris within it. Isis and Thoth then embalmed Osiris' body in the first mummification. Were their hopes like that of all other ancient Egyptians; that a perfectly embalmed corpse could somehow be later brought back to life?

After Osiris was mummified Typhon discovered that something peculiar was going on with Osiris' body. If there was any possibility Isis and Thoth could be correct in their hopes for a bodily resurrection he had to stop it. He cut the mummy up into fourteen pieces and sent a piece to each of Osiris' kingdoms to show the people they were free from this abominable tyrant.

It does not end here, however. Isis again goes in search of her husband. Piece by piece she collects all his parts, but one. The one piece she could not find was the male part, the genitalia. Why was this one piece so conspicuously absent? Legend has it that a fish ate it. But consider that Shem may have discovered that a resurrection was hoped for. Perhaps he purposefully destroyed the genitalia to prevent such a thing from happening. If he had burned that part and scattered the ashes into the sea, the ancients might have been apt to consider this as feeding the fish.

Here comes the really weird part.

Still hoping to somehow bring Osiris back to life, Isis reassembles the body, and with the help of Thoth they "fan the corpse," "warm it to life" and are able to retrieve the "essence" of Osiris.

The *essence* not the *seed,* as there are no genitals.

Legend tells us Isis next makes a gold replica of Osiris' missing member. She attaches the phallus to Osiris and somehow conceives a child, later named Horus.

The weirdest and most important part of the Egyptian legend just described is the manner in which a child is conceived with the seed-producing member of the male absent. Instead here the male's *essence* is obtained and a pregnancy then achieved. If the term *essence* here really pertains to DNA, which it seems to, then this is entirely like modern genetic cloning!

This is the event we've been looking for in the days of Noah prophecy! Osiris was dead, Shem/Typhon had delivered a fatal wound, and yet Nimrod/Osiris' DNA was isolated and a child conceived. This cloning-like procedure to restore Osiris occurred in the days of Noah!

Will Osiris rise again to become the final Antichrist? Was the knowledge of genetics necessary for this relayed from the writings on the Great Pyramid? Does this knowledge come from fallen Watcher angels? There are still many questions, but the legend of Osiris isn't over yet.

While mourning the loss of her husband, the pregnant Isis buried the golden phallus at Mendes. Here a great temple was built in honor of Osiris and his ding-a-ling. She then instituted nationwide worship of her husband's penis. Similar edifices were built in every land; the obelisks in Egypt and Asherah poles of the Bible are these phallic symbols (Deuteronomy 16: 21, 1Kings 15: 13, 2Kings 13: 6, 2Chronicles 15: 16). The term obelisk originats from the term "Baal's shaft."

Pagan religions around the globe have celebrated fertility rituals for millennia paying homage to these objects (Romans 13: 13, Galatians 5: 21, 1Peter 4: 3). In the Bible, the stone phalluses' were named for the Canaanite goddess Asherah, an alias for Isis. Moses later commanded all the Asherah poles destroyed (Exodus 34: 13, Deuteronomy 7: 5). He also told the Israelites not to take part in the pagan's sexual frenzies (Leviticus 18, Deuteronomy 12: 30, 31) and later when the Israelites did take part they were severely punished. On one occasion 24,000 died from the wrath of God (Numbers 25)!

HORUS POSSESSED: For hundreds of years afterward, religious Egyptians all knew that the legendary baby Isis had given birth to, Horus, was in fact the reincarnation Osiris! She was his wife, and now she was his mother and Horus was now the *Widow's Son,* which, incidentally, is the name of the Freemason's deity.

Egyptian lore tells us that Isis kept her pregnancy a secret, hiding out in the marsh-lands until the child's birth. She and Thoth shelter the child, raising it in secret, awaiting the day Horus is ready to avenge Osiris' death.

The preparation of Horus is the last piece of the puzzling days of Noah prophecy. At this point Horus was just a genetic duplicate of Osiris, just a kid raised in the back woods of Egypt. He would have had his own memories, none of those experiences that Osiris had would have carried on into his life.

But this may not be entirely true.

Consider this: Osiris was a Nephilim, and Nephilim do not die as normal people do. Their souls are destined to roam the earth full of hunger and malice. These are the demons we're familiar with from the New Testament. And most often when demons are mentioned Biblically it is when they have possessed someone, taking control over someone's body thus making it their own.

So Osiris would have been fully capable of possessing and inhabiting the body of Horus, thus fully coming back from the dead!

This is the Beast who once was.

This is key to understanding the days of Noah prophecy and understanding how a long dead individual could *rise from the dead* to become the end time's Antichrist, the Beast who yet will come. If any mummified genetic trace of Osiris were found he could be cloned and his spirit could easily return to a duplicate body.

The Bible tells us that Nimrod's spirit will rise up from the pit of hell in the end times. Revelation 9: 11 says that the Greek sun god

Apollo, or Apollyon, will rise from the Abyss, the underworld. Interestingly, the Egyptian Book of the Dead repeats this when it says Osiris is the "Governor of Abydos" which means *the Abyss* in Greek. Another alias for Nimrod was Tammuz: child of the Abyss.

Every Egyptian pharaoh had to under go certain rituals before taking the throne. These rituals were said to bring the spirit of Osiris into them so he could continue his rule. It would then be said that that pharaoh had become a god on earth, a reincarnation of Osiris. Was Nimrod really the reigning monarch over Egypt for hundreds of years, perhaps incarnating in the Pharaohs that Abraham and Moses encountered?

It wasn't just the pharaohs and kings, the common people in the surrounding lands were soon taking part in rituals where they too could be bonded with demons. Known in the Bible as pagans, God commanded the Israelites to fight against them and more specifically these rituals.

THE TOWER OF BABEL: Panic likely set in with every rain storm, Noah and his family who were on board the ark had told the tales of destruction well. Cush and Nimrod planned a refuge from any future flood. They would build a tower... a tower so high they could *become gods.*

Today, many ruined cities in Mesopotamia still have the crumbling remains of towering brick temples known as Ziggurats. These are stepped pyramids with a temple on the top. These can be seen in Ur, Assur, Akkad, Uruk, Borsippa, Aqarquf, Khorabad, Eridu, Nimrud and Kish. The Tower of Babel was one of these. R.A. Boulay, expert on Sumeria, wrote that "atop the ziggurat there was a sacred temple. In its centre was an antechamber or cella, the "Holy of holies," and was reserved for the gods to rest when they were on earth. It was here that they mated with selected human females in order to produce a race of demigods to serve as the kings, generals, and other intermediaries. These acted as a buffer with mankind. All the great heroes of Mesopotamia claimed to be issue of a god and a mortal." With fallen angels regularly visiting lovely young maidens atop the towers, the Ziggurats became Nephilim making machines.

The ruins of the Biblical Tower of Babylon are located where the Tigris and Euphrates rivers meet in modern day Iraq, about 85 km south of Baghdad. Babylon had the largest of all the Ziggurats, today the tower's remains are named Etemenanki. These ruins are found to be 91 by 91 meters square at the base and were apparently 91 meters tall.

It was made up of seven steps leading to a temple on top called *the House of the Bed,* where the centre piece was, of course, a very large bed. This sanctuary was dedicated to the god Marduk, whose name means *Lord of the Air.* This should remind us that the Bible refers to Satan as "the Prince of the Power of the Air (Ephesians 2: 2 KJV). *The Zondervan Pictorial Bible Dictionary* by Merrill C. Tenney also says of Etemenanki that "this great staged tower of Babylon may have been the original Tower of Babel... a seven-story building of sun-dried mud brick faced with kiln-dried brick. An eighth story probably consisted of a small shrine dedicated to Marduk." Stone is exceedingly rare in this region, whereas mud and clay are everywhere. The Ziggurats are made precisely as the Bible says, of kiln-baked bricks, jointed with bitumen (Genesis 11: 3, 4).

There is further evidence outside of the Bible which validates the story of the Tower of Babylon. Archeologist George Smith, while excavating the Etemenanki tower ruins in the mid 1800s, found some very interesting clay tablets. Upon these it was written "The building of this illustrious tower offended the gods. In a night they threw down what they had built. They scattered them abroad, and made strange their speech."

Another similar Assyrian tablet was found in Nineveh by Austen Henry Layard, it is now in the British Museum and seems to be speaking of Nimrod, "His heart was evil against the father of all the gods... Babylon was brought into subjection, small and great alike. He (God) confounded their speech... their strong towering palace and all the days they built; to their strong place in the night He completely made an end... In his anger His word was poured out... to scatter abroad He set His face, He gave His command, and their council was confused... Bitterly they wept at Babel."

Sometime after Nimrod's death God thwarted the Babylonian's efforts to restore elements of the pre-Flood world. God forced the people to scatter as their languages were confused. But as they dispersed each language group took with them some memory of sinful Babylon's teachings.

NIMROD AS ANTICHRIST: The goal of Nimrod and Cush at Babel was to unite the world into a one world religion against God. Nimrod can be compared to the Antichrist because he is prophesied to do the exact same thing. He will succeed in deceiving and uniting the world under a government bent on rebellion against God; just like the pre-Flood world and just like Babel. Nimrod's name meant *let us rebel,* the Bible describes the end time's Antichrist as a rebel and a master of deception.

> Don't let anyone deceive you in any way, for that day will not come until the rebellion occurs and the man of lawlessness is revealed, the man doomed to destruction. He will oppose and will exalt himself over everything that is called God or is worshipped, so that he sets himself up in God's Temple, proclaiming himself to be God… the coming of the lawless one will be in accordance with the work of Satan displayed in all kinds of counterfeit miracles, signs and wonders, and in every sort of evil that deceives those who are perishing.
>
> 2Thessalonians 2: 3- 4, 9, 10

MELCHIZEDEK: Hebrew traditions suggest that Nimrod died a violent death, that Shem was forced to kill him because he had led the people into the worship of Baal. These legends say Shem then became king.

In Genesis 14: 18 there is an individual mentioned named Melchizedek. He is said to be both a king and a "Priest of God Most High." It is a pretty rare individual that is both a priest and a king. He is mentioned again in the book of Hebrews where it presents him as a mysterious and unknown person. He did not appear in any of the Hebrew's genealogical tables, "Without father or mother, without genealogy, without beginning of days or end of life (Hebrews 7: 3)." Of course Melchizedek did not have any birth record because that was not his name, it was his title. It meant "king of righteousness," priest-king.

Shem is the only historical individual who could attest to be this Melchizedek and identified both as a king and a priest. He was of Noah's priestly lineage and as the slayer of the evil king he would be deemed worthy of his crown, hence the old adage "to the victor go the spoils." Melchizedek mirrored Christ with offerings of bread and wine, and Abram later offered him a tithe, recognizing him as a priest of God before the Levitical priesthood of Aaron even existed, before Abraham even begat the Hebrew nation.

Jesus of course fit the bill two thousand years later as priest and king, so it could be said that Shem foreshadowed, or prophetically emulated Jesus. And just as Shem killed Nimrod, Jesus is destined to crush the head of the Serpent's son as well.

NIMROD'S WIFE FOUND IN VARIOUS CULTURES:
Versions of Nimrod appear in the mythology of many different cultures and since his wife was essential in his resurrection wouldn't we expect to see traces of her as well? Maybe we can get a little insight into the Antichrist's character from understanding his wife.

The ancient Assyrians called her Ninlil. The Greeks remember her as Aphrodite, the wife of Dionysus, Apollo or Adonis depending on the source of the legend. Both Dionysus and Adonis have legends where they died and rose again with her help. She is also Rhea, the wife of the Greek horned god Kronos. As Athena, the goddess of war and wisdom, it is her statue that sits atop the Capitol building in Washington. She also was exalted by the Jacobins in France during the revolution and was later a gift to America as the Statue of Liberty with seven solar rays upon her crown.

In Sumeria she was known as Ningizzita or Inanna and legends there tell us that she once descended to the underworld. Later Babylonians called her Ishtar; she too had made a trip to the world of the dead to retrieve her husband Tammuz. She was the goddess of harlots and alehouses, prostitution formed part of her cult. All Babylonian girls had to have sex with a stranger for money in order to enter into adulthood. She was personified as the planet Venus and was the daughter of the moon god whose name was Sin.

The Romans remember her as the goddess of fertility, Venus. The constellation Virgo is her astronomical representation.

The Phoenicians and Chaldeans knew her as Astarte. Known as "Our Lady of Heaven," temple prostitution was also practiced among her devotees.

Dagan's son, Baal was rescued from death by his wife Anat in the Canaanite traditions.

To Phrygians she was Cybele who restored Attis back to life after he was gored by a wild boar. The Vatican in Rome was built upon the ruins of the central Temple of Cybele and Attis.

When Lady Diana, Princess of Wales died in 1997, it was coincidentally at the exact location where the Temple of the Roman goddess Diana, the huntress once stood.

The Germanic peoples knew her as Nanna, the wife of Balder, who is destined to rise from the grave. The Nordic peoples have a goddess of the underworld named Niflheim, a word phonetically similar to

Nephilim. The Irish called her Aoipa, wife of Cuchulainn. The Hindu people have a Mother Goddess named Uma, the wife of Shiva. She has many other names, Artemis, Minerva, Demeter, Cers, Gaea, Terra, Hera, Juno, Hestia, Vesta, Europa, and Fortuna. In fact she has been called Myrionyma, "The goddess of a thousand names."

NIMROD: SON OF LUCIFER: In all the cultures that have a mythological record Nimrod we've seen there is a wife by his side. In these cultural tales Nimrod has a father as well, a father who has an uncanny resemblance to a certain fallen angel.

Some refer to the land of Babylon as Sumeria. Surprising amounts of information have been discovered by archeologists about this ancient land. The most important god here was **Enki,** whose name means Lord of That Which is Bellow, or Lord of the Abyss. In Babylon he was humanity's champion. When the highest god sought to drown and destroy humanity with a flood, just because we're *too noisy* and disturbed his rest, it was Enki that told Atrahasis to build an ark and save all life on earth. The highest god was thereafter despised. Naturally, Satan would attempt to glorify himself by twisting about the story of the flood.

In Sumerian lore Enki was the father of Marduk, who we refer to as Nimrod. Inscribed clay tablets document the process whereby Enki fathered his hybrid son, or *Adapa.* First, Enki required a "survivor of the deluge" to become a human ovum donor and a surrogate womb. He then delivered "repeated incantations" during a procedure where the surrogate's navel or bellybutton "was opened." This sounds similar to modern day in vitro fertilization, but without the ritual incantations. This was all performed in Enki's "creation chamber." Images of Enki depict him with two wavy lines, which some say represent rivers or trees, but the ancient records tell us these are the male and female aspects of the "life essence," which "Enki would mix to create different beings!" There's that word again, *essence,* which we concluded was DNA in the story of Osiris and certainly seems to imply the same thing here. Wouldn't two wavy lines become a double helix when added together? Enki was considered the god of life and semen, his symbol was the Caduceus, the DNA-like symbol. Enki certainly appears to have used genetic manipulation when creating his *Adapa,* who Sumerian scriptures say was Marduk, a "mighty man," and Enki's first priest, ministering between the Serpent Lord and humanity.

In the descriptive phrases that represented Enki in the Sumerian literature we can easily see he fits the characteristics of Satan: Dragon Lord of the Earth, Serpent Lord, Shaitan, God of Light, Lord of the Abyss and Lord of the Sacred Eye, another of Enki's symbols was a triangle with a radiant eye shining in it; just like the one on the American dollar bill, a symbol meaning *doorway to illumination.*

Enki was considered the god of crafts. This is interesting because Freemasonry refers to itself as the Craft. He was depicted with horns coming from his head, as we traditionally imagine the devil, and he is credited for the confusion of languages in Babylon: In the Babylonian story *Enmerkar and the Lord of Aratta* it is written that there was "one tongue" until "Enki changed the speech of their mouths."

The Sumerians also had a curious deity named Tiamet. Tiamet was a *chaos monster,* a giant dragon that mated with the Abyss to bring about a hybrid race of Mer-people and Scorpion Men. Something similar to these Scorpion Men will come from the Abyss in the end times (Revelation 9: 7- 11).

Over in Egypt, Osiris is the son of **Ptah** or Geb. The similarities with Enki are unmistakable; he is known as the Father of Serpents and often depicted as a horned bull, he is associated with the subterranean world, the Abyss, and his symbol was again the Caduceus.

According the ancient Greek historian, Hesiod, in his work *the Theology,* the Egyptian Geb was **Kronos** in the Greek pantheon. Kronos was a horned god who envied his father's power, so he lead the giant Titans to over throw the god of the universe and reign in his place; which sounds like something Satan just might desire. The Greeks also have the story of Prometheus who, again allied with the giant Titans, battled against the highest god to bring mankind the secrets of heaven, namely illumination. For this crime, which some see as similar to that perpetrated by Lucifer in Eden, Prometheus was to face eternal torment but he was rescued by Heracles, the Greek Nimrod.

The Romans knew him as **Saturn** whose holy day was Saturnalia, celebrated on December 25 with private gift giving. In his legend he too envied his father, the ruler of the universe, and led his brothers against him to bring about a *Golden Age.*

The Amorites knew him as Dagon and the Canaanites called him El, father of Baal. To the Phoenicians he was Ea, and the Norse and Germanic peoples knew him as Odin or Wotan, father of Balder. He has been called Uranus, Saturn, Jupiter and Neptune. Plato said Poseidon was the highest god worshipped in pre-Flood Atlantis.

CHAPTER FIVE
THE BABYLONIAN MYSTERY RELIGION

Mystery
Babylon the Great
the mother of prostitutes
and of the abominations of the earth.
Revelation 17: 5

The Bible tells us that Nimrod ruled from the city of Babylon (Genesis 10: 10). We also know that at this place a great rebellion against God occurred. The ancients tell us that here Nimrod wanted to avenge the deaths of those who died in the flood! It is very important that we understand what happened in Babylon because, like Nimrod, his ancient city and the religion taught there are destined to be reborn! The Bible clearly tells us that Babylon will again become a mighty city in the end times (Revelation 14: 8). The city that once rebelled against God and earned his wrath will again revolt against the Most High. And at the heart of the rebellion is a religion, the religion of Satan and Nimrod. It is the same religion that will gain world wide prominence in the end times (2Thessalonians 2: 3)!

LUCIFERISM: The Luciferian religion is active today and has been since the days of Noah when Babylon was built (2Thessalonians 2: 7). It survives within certain bloodlines and small secret societies. It is not to be confused with common Satanism. It is a very old and very sophisticated system designed primarily to deceive; to mislead both those within, and those on the outside of the cult. They primarily target and recruit those with influence. They hook them like fish with offers of power and slowly reel them in.

In the pages ahead it will be shown that Freemasonry is one denomination of many that follows Lucifer as a god. My research into Masonry confirms what the Bible told us millennia ago: Luciferians study the means of deception and use it as a tool. The Bible told us that Satan and his followers try to act like the good guys; they will even masquerade as Christians (2Corinthians 11: 12, 13). Brainwashed, they honestly believe they are righteous in their war against the Creator.

> Satan himself masquerades as an angel of light. It is not surprising, then, if his servants masquerade as servants of righteousness.
>
> 2Corinthians 11: 14, 15

Luciferism is an ancient system of control surrounded by a curtain of temptation. Because it is full of secrets and mysteries, revealed only to the *elite* who have worked their way up through the ranks and degrees, those who have proven their *worthiness,* it is widely known as the Babylonian Mystery Religion (Revelation 17: 5).

Over the next pages we're going to see secrets revealed that men have actually lived and died for. Over the past four thousand years there have been secrets that men have died to keep, and given up their lives to learn. Here they lay fully uncovered. It is time that the followers of Jesus Christ know what is occurring *behind enemy lines.*

SOME SUMERIAN RELIGION: What we refer to in the Bible as Babylon is referred to by academics as Sumeria. The original name that they called their own land was Shumer, which meant the *Land of the Guardians,* or Land of the Watchers. When the Egyptians looked to Babylon in the east, they referred to this land as "Ta Neter," also meaning the *Land of the Watchers.* Babylon was a sinful and fallen land; wouldn't we expect the fallen Watchers to reside there?

What was it like to live in a land where Satan and his followers had united the people under a solitary government and religion? It may surprise you, but we can know exactly what was on the mind of the average person! In 1843 archeologists began to uncover Nimrod's great cities and have unearthed some amazing artifacts. The prized treasure of it all has been the massive library of Nineveh.

The library last belonged to the Assyrian King Ashurbanipal who died in 627 BC. Here hundreds of thousands of baked clay tablets with ancient Sumerian cuneiform writings were found. These tablets have revealed to us the common, daily affairs of the people. We can tell, for instance, the prices paid for house hold goods and necessities like the cost of flour and oil, but the biggest discoveries were of the religious nature.

Being that this land was ruled by those with a definite hatred of the

Biblical God, the stories on the clay tablets have a blatant spin on them and bias, it is incredibly obvious that evil ruled there. Do you remember in the last chapter we saw how the Highest God, the one who brought the Flood, was considered evil and Enki the Serpent Lord was worshipped? This stems from the Luciferian premise that claims Satan freed Adam and Eve from a hateful and controlling God. Otherwise man would be like a brain-damaged, micro-managed, robot. They say that Lucifer is now our rightful god and savior and that Our Father in Heaven should be destroyed for dealing out unjust punishments and suffering. Just as Prometheus stole fire from heaven to bestow upon humanity, they claim Satan did a good thing when he *enlightened* or *illuminated* our ancestors in Eden with the knowledge of good and evil. Biblically, we know that what transpired with the serpent in Eden was a horrendous disaster, death came into existence!

Scholars agree that the tablets found at Nineveh show that the lives and attitudes of the Sumerian people were depressed and pessimistic, which is exactly what we would expect if one were ruled by Satan.

THE MYSTERY RELIGION: Religion can work as a control system and no place models this better than Babylon. To control their people Cush and Nimrod gave different sets of teachings. For the elite priesthood there was the hidden means to commune with the Watchers, but for the public masses there was another staged set of doctrines beginning with the worship of nature and the sun.

Their religion was set out in grades to be advanced through. As individuals living in the pagan communities achieved certain requirements, they climbed through the grades, learning an answer to a mystery at every level. Outsiders, mentally sloppy or otherwise ignorant individuals were not allowed to know the higher teachings; they were considered *profane,* so secrecy was very important. This in effect helped maintain the control and drive within Lucifer's Mystery schools, a student at one level was forbidden, under the penalty of a violent and gory death, from revealing what he was learning to anyone but those he knew as his equals or superiors. There were many secret handshakes, phrases and symbols for members to identify each another with and communicate by; the religion earned its name, *The Mysteries*.

The Mysteries worked because people generally want to solve riddles but even more so because people feel empowered to belong to a group whose secrets put them above others. As part of our sinful nature people have an innate desire to have power over their fellow men.

Satan's strategy is to offer power via occult, or hidden, knowledge, which is precisely what he did to Eve in the Garden of Eden (Genesis 3: 4). A secret or a mystery of a religious nature might create a void in the sub-consciousness and people often hunger for anything that is kept from them. The Bible clearly says that we're best off without these things, God protects us from these dangers for a reason; he loves us. "The secret things belong to the Lord our God (Deuteronomy 29: 29)." But at the same time the Bible also tells us that through God's true light the enemy's secrets can be safely revealed (Daniel 2: 21, 22, 28, 1Corinthians 4: 5).

The secrets the pagan priesthood would allow junior initiates to know were some seemingly empty symbol, rhyme or ritual. Often, lower level members would have no concept whatsoever of what was before them because they were not given the key to unlock the allegories and metaphors their priesthood used. The actual understanding of their regular practices was only bestowed upon an initiate after several years of proving himself worthy of *the honor*. Only then would all the accumulated teachings make sense.

This is similar to a carrot on a pole, held out in front of a beast of burden, to keep it moving ever onwards with the poor beast never knowing the goal or destination. This was all carefully planned and systematic brainwashing.

The Christian religion has no secrets; it's all in the Bible, literally an open book, because God keeps no secrets (John 18: 20). Luciferism, on the other hand, is entirely hidden and completely kept from the initiate (Revelation 2: 24).

THE SECRET OF INITIATION: According to Plutarch it was the widow of Osiris/Nimrod who founded the Mystery religion. In every land that kept the Mysteries there were regular rituals, like somber funerals, celebrating the mystical death and resurrection of their god and every candidate who entered the religion went through a dramatized ritual reenacting the deity's life, death and resurrection.

Initially, in what are known as the Lesser Mysteries, the candidate was tempted with offers of occult knowledge and if eligible could begin the process of purification. This consisted of ritual washings and copious meditative exercises. They next had to somehow prove themselves worthy of entrance unto the Greater Mysteries where initiation would occur. If deemed worthy the candidate would be invited by the priesthood into the temple, usually on a specific and sacred night to stand before peers who had already initiated into the religion. The priests lead the candidate through the reenactment of their god's death with the candidate in the role of their god.

Next in the drama the search for the body is acted out. When discovered the candidate is *resurrected*. At this point any bonds or blindfolds are removed, and out of the darkness, the first thing the initiate sees is the radiant symbol of the cult before them. Through this process, imitating death and rebirth, the priesthood hopes that a mental and spiritual process begins.

Many were initiated and programmed with this effective psychological device which is used to open the doors of the consciousness. In this subtle psychological phenomenon, combined with the previously mentioned meditative training, minds can be placed into a receptive state and reshaped, awakening something else within the individual. They become contactees in a sense. In an altered state of consciousness they make contact with another spirit, and this entity begins to over shadow them. They are then said to have: seen the light, been illuminated, self actualized, become at one with the universe, found their higher-self, become enlightened or even… become a god.

The initiate will mistakenly think they have reached whatever false mental goal their priest, guru or teacher has set for them. Many have even been under the impression that this demonic entity is their own, suppressed, higher and more intelligent self! The great psychiatrist Carl G. Jung claimed that the urging and thoughts of his own demon, who he claimed was named Philemon, was his own *higher self* from deep within his consciousness. Jung referred to initiation as "individuation," and as part of his therapies he guided his patients and others to bond with their own "subconscious self (C.G. Jung, *Memories, Dreams, Reflections*)." It is at this point, when an individual allows the demon to have control over their lives that they become truly initiated and the real answers to the mysteries they were searching for are finally revealed unto them.

The priesthood then gives the individual a seemingly insignificant secret to hold onto, often just a simple gesture or a single incomprehensible word. The priests, however, would strongly avow that this information was of the utmost importance. What they were given was, in fact, the secret of all secrets. It was encoded information; so completely veiled in symbolism that the initiate could never understand it! All they could do was continue to blindly pass it on to other aspiring and deserving candidates.

Some mistakenly report that this great secret has, through the passage of time, degenerated and the meaning behind its symbolism been forgotten and misunderstood.

By the end of this book we will know that secret.

THE THREE LIES: Satan is not very original in his thinking, he frequently tries to copy God, and if he does get an original idea he uses it over and over again. In the Garden of Eden he offered Eve three things when he deceived her. These same three things are offered to every one of his followers in the Mystery religion! The Bible accurately reveals the inner workings of Satan's Mystery religion so none should be led astray.

The first lie: In the Lesser Mysteries everyone worshipped the sun. It brought warmth and life to all things, but it was hinted at that there was more to it. There was always secret knowledge to be had. In the Garden of Eden Satan also offered Eve secret knowledge "the serpent said to the woman "when you eat of it your eyes will be opened" (Genesis 3: 5)."

The second lie: Those deemed worthy in the Mysteries were taught that just as the sun dies every night and is reborn every morning so can humanity be reborn, to live eternally via reincarnation. Eternal life was another lie first told by Satan in Eden "You will not surely die" the serpent said to the woman (Genesis 3: 4)".

The third lie: As an individual rose through the teachings in the Mysteries they were eventually taught that the sun was really a symbol for a higher element.[9] As the sun illuminates the earth with its life giving radiation, the mind and soul of the believer could also be illuminated, and through this illumination one could be a god! This incredible lie reflects back to Eden as well, Satan told Eve "you will be like God (Genesis 3: 5)."

THE SEVEN SPHERES: The Mysteries taught that godhood could somehow be attained by passing through *the Seven Spheres*. The ancient Hymn of Orpheus begins to explain this with a concept called the "Doctrine of the Unity of God." It was believed that whatever

---

[9] The name Lucifer means *light bearer* so it should go without saying that the sun-god worshipped in the pagan Mysteries is none other than Satan (1Corinthians 10: 20). "And no wonder for Satan himself masquerades as an angel of light (2Corinthians 11: 14)."

mysterious substance human souls are made of, and whatever God is made of, they are the same thing. The surviving lore of the Egyptian Mysteries of Isis and the Greek Mysteries of Eleusis tell us that parts of a solitary and united god were tempted and decided to come down to earth. The elements that broke away are now trapped in individual bodies of flesh where they are tormented by the passions and weaknesses of their humanity. The pagans called the larger all encompassing deity the *One* or the *Universe,* and of course the symbol for these teachings was the serpent.

Earlier when were examining the various cultural myths of Nimrod we saw the Sumerian story of Dumuzi and Inanna. Dumuzi died and Inanna descended down seven levels into the underworld to rescue him. As she returned she had to come back up through the seven levels. It was the belief that mankind's godly souls could be freed from the flesh, like these heroes, if we too could ascend these seven levels. The secret taught to the elite in the highest Mysteries was the route back, how to ascend through the Seven Spheres through which the soul once descended, to reclaim one's *godhood.*

A Neo-Platonic philosopher named Porphyry described the route by which souls can escape the world. Each of the Seven Spheres is represented by a planet, and each sphere has a marked gate and each one has its own intelligence! The secret was the specific system of meditation by which to encounter these intelligences and petition them to let one pass by and on to the next sphere.

These spheres can like those Russian dolls, where you take a top off of one to find a slightly smaller one inside, take the lid off of that one and there will be one inside that one, and on and on until you come to the smallest solid piece in the center. The Mysteries essentially taught that man is that small piece in the middle, striving to get out of the flesh and become the god he was originally.

We all know that man cannot become a god, but something is happening in this process. As a man's soul passes through each of the *living spheres,* a little more of the man is stripped away and a little more control is acquired by the spirits! The deceived individual just hands their soul over.

Sallust the Philosopher wrote that parts of god once separated into generative matter and that humanity's goal is to reunite ourselves with the deity and thus *perfect* the soul. The Mysteries all taught that the soul could be "perfected" and reminded of its noble origin and immortality. Christians might be more apt to use the word *possessed* rather than *perfected.*

This might be a belief that came down from the pre-Flood peoples. Remember, when discussing the inscriptions on the Great Pyramid, the Arabic historian Masoudi wrote that "The Great Pyramid was inscribed with the heavenly spheres, and figures representing the stars and planets." And remember that the instructions to create gods were there too, weren't these people trying to recreate themselves as gods?

In the Mithraic version of the Mysteries they symbolized the passage through the spheres as climbing a simple ladder. In their temples before them was a color coded ladder with seven steps, each one representing a gate. With meditation and ritual chanting man figuratively climbed the ladder to deliver their soul from the flesh. Each sphere had a planet and a metal symbolically represent it. The first they encountered was Saturn, represented by lead.

Saturn---lead
Venus---tin
Jupiter---brass
Mercury---iron
Mars---copper
The Moon---silver
The Sun---gold

Did you notice how we started with Saturn, whose metal was lead, and finished with the sun, represented by gold? This is how alchemists claimed someone could turn lead into gold! They were not trying to alter the actual metals to get rich by literally turning lead into gold; they were messing with their souls! The first thing an alchemist learned was the saying "As Above, So Bellow." Which means: as there is a god above, so man can be a god bellow.

WHAT HAPPENED AT BORSIPPA? Teachings similar to the Mithraic ladder were given at the Tower of Babylon, which was a towering temple referred to as a Ziggurat. Every city had one. All were built to have seven stories, and each level was painted a different color symbolic of the spheres.

While we're discussing the Ziggurats here, let's draw our attention to the one in the ancient city of Borsippa for a moment. Borsippa was also called Birs Nimrud, meaning *of Nimrod,* and is in Babylon Province of Modern day Iraq. The name given by the Greeks was *Tongue Tower.* Why would the towering Ziggurat here earn that particular distinction?

The tower was erected as a tribute to the Sumerian god Nabu, the son of Marduk. If Marduk is Osiris to the Egyptians, then Nabu is the cloned Horus. Among the ruins of Nabu's Ziggurat there is an anomaly that science just can't explain. Some of the bricks used to construct it are currently found in a very odd state. They are twisted, discolored, melted and deformed. They were not made this way, this happened after they were set in place. The heat required to do this has been calculated at 1100 degrees. That is equal to an atomic blast, which can be ruled out because it would not have been as selective, decimating the entire region and not just the bricks in the tower.

Something very strange, or miraculous, happened here.

BABYLON ETERNAL: Babylon itself is mentioned in Genesis, the first book of the Bible, and the last, Revelation. It has seen many ages and dominated man's attention nearly as much as Jerusalem. Its history apart from that in the Bible is worth our attention.

Hammurabi was king of Babylon from 1792 to 1750 BC. Many of his writings remain and show that he was a meticulous ruler. Centuries after Nimrod he chose to restore the glory to the city and primarily the tower "whose top" he said "is sky high."

From 605 to 562 BC Nebuchadnezzar was king of Babylon and also restored the tower; he wrote that he "raised the summit of the Tower in stages at Entemenanki so that its top rivaled the heavens."

Years later the Persian king Artaxerxes is known to have restored the Tower during his day, being contemporary with the Biblical Ezekiel during the Israelite's captivity in Babylon.

Even later Alexander the Great did restoration work on Entemenanki after he conquered Babylon. A few years later Herodotus wrote that the city "surpasses in splendor any city in the known world."

In 1898 German archeologists found the old ruins of Babel in modern day Iraq. Many artifacts were taken to the Berlin Museum where they still reside today.

In 1978 Iraqi dictator Saddam Hussein embarked on a $500-million joint Japanese and Korean rebuilding project. The bricks used in the rebuilding of the Tower are engraved "To king Nebuchadnezzar in the reign of Saddam Hussein." Saddam Hussein claimed that he was the reincarnation of the ancient Babylonian king. He went so far as to post giant billboards along the highways showing the two leading the Iraqi people together.

In 2003 the United States sent thousands of troops into this area and captured Iraq. When the Americans invaded, they promptly placed one of their first bases among the ruins of ancient Babylon and turned the Ziggurat Hussein had reconstructed, called "Saddam Hill," into a headquarters for the U.S. Marines, called "Camp Alpha," ensuring that this one site was to be the safest and most stable region in the war torn country.

Is it only a coincidence that the grave of Nimrod was reportedly found just days before America invaded Iraq? The BBC News reported on April 29, 2003, that Jorg Fassbinder of the Bavarian Department of Historical Monuments found the "Lost tomb of King Gilgamesh." After the invasion no further word has been uttered of this discovery in the mainstream media. There are rumors that the artifacts retrieved from the site near Camp Alpha were taken from the archeologists by American men in black suits. It's also interesting to note that the night America attacked, the Baghdad museum was raided by professionals stealing only artifacts related to Nimrod. *National Geographic* did a documentary entitled *Nimrod's Treasure* showing the 613 pieces stolen. Locals say Americans working in conjunction with the military are to blame for this.

It would seem that this area is the most fought over piece of land on the planet. Have world leaders understood the significance of the Tower of Babel and the ancient revolt against God staged there?

The New York Times reported on April 21, 2006, that "UNESCO Intends to Put the Magic Back in Babylon." The United Nations Educational, Scientific and Cultural Organization pumped millions of dollars into the ancient center hoping to create a world renowned theme park! There are to be "restaurants, gift shops, long parking lots and even a Holiday Inn." Pamphlets have been circulated seeking wealthy donors knowing that "one day millions of people will visit Babylon."

The Bible clearly tells us that in the end times Babylon will be a great and wealthy centre where the kings of the earth and the wealthiest businessmen will soak in luxury and sinfulness (Revelation 18). If the end is truly near, wouldn't we fully expect the city to be rebuilt as prophesied?

KUNDALINI: At some point, after Nimrod's death and his wife set the Mystery religion in motion, God decided to disperse the Babylonians by mixing up their languages (Genesis 11: 1- 9). Tribal groups were formed by those who could understand each other and they went off in different directions. The Mysteries spread with the Babylonians to all they lands emigrated, they retained their inner secrets but the outer rudimentary lore was sometimes changed slightly.

In India, the Hindu's means of attaining union with god is said to occur by stimulating the body's so-called Kundalini. This term means *Serpent Energy* and is supposedly a natural energy located coiled near the genital region of every human. The Hindu scriptures, the Vedas, tell us it is everyone's task in life to further evolve into gods and that this is done by elevating the Kundalini up through the seven chakras into the cranium. The chakras are said to be seven energy centers located at the base of the spine, the navel, spleen, heart, throat, between the eyes and the top of the head. These are each thought to be related to certain glands. They believe that when the pineal gland is stimulated enlightenment occurs and individuals are said to see via the third eye, supposedly in the centre of the forehead, which is roughly where the pineal gland sits. The Serpent Energy is actually said to travel up the spine via two channels that weave around one another, similar to a helical strand of DNA.

The power of the Kundalini experience has been described by only a few Western writers. Philip Gardiner and Gary Osborn wrote in *The Shining Ones* that in "the Kundalini awakening... one will feel an awesome, powerful vibration begin in the body, oscillating back and forth and ascending rapidly in frequency. It is said that often this activity along the spine will end with the consciousness separating from the body and other paranormal effects... sometimes painful... if not handled properly, could bring insanity or even death."

Lilian Silburn, director of Research at the National Scientific Research Institute in Paris, tells us in her book *Kundalini: the Energy of the Depths* that "The mysterious energy aroused by the Kundalini yoga manifests with violence beyond belief and cannot be manipulated without incurring certain risks. Some deviations are termed 'demonic,' as they lead to depression and insanity... the arousal of Kundalini will have disastrous results."

The story of Gopi Krishna's enlightenment is also worthy of discussion here. Gopi Krishna (1903- 1984) wrote several books regarding the Kundalini which were aimed at the Western audience, such as his autobiography *Kundalini, the Evolutionary Energy in Man.* He wrote that on Christmas morning, 1937, "Suddenly, with a roar like that of a waterfall, I felt a stream of liquid light entering my brain through the spinal cord... the illumination grew brighter and brighter, the roaring louder, I felt a rocking sensation, and then myself slipping out of my body." Over the following days he began to suffer terrible burning pains and other negative effects. He found "a hidden intelligence" from within was trying to communicate with him, telling him exactly what to do, his mind was flooded with new information and knowledge. He battled the voices, the strange urges and compulsions until he felt all was utterly hopeless and gave up, at which point he suddenly "stabilized." His life became tolerable only after he gave himself over to these powers. He knew he would be insane as long as he battled them, but once he allowed them to have control, he claims he "became a god." The story of Gopi Krishna is a typical story of Eastern enlightenment. One of the famed fathers of psychiatry, Carl Jung, spent a great deal of time exploring the relationship between Kundalini's effects and schizophrenia.

Stories such as these essentially describe people becoming demon possessed. The dangers are well known in the East where many practice yoga and tamper with the Kundalini. In the West the practitioners of yoga and meditation are completely ignorant of the risks involved. Kundalini Syndrome, known as *Wind Illness* in Tibet, will last more than twenty years and have symptoms such as: anxiety, depression, dissociation, altered perceptions and agitation.

Disciples of the higher Mysteries have been warned from the beginning not to attempt the development of these (chakra) centers... Woe to the unhappy mortal who raises Kundalini permanently to the brain! The sting of the fiery serpent is most deadly, as those know who have witnessed the results of her being raised before her time. She will burn her way to the brain and destroy the rational qualities of the mind. The spiritual, twisting force is not an illuminating agent but, like the serpent which is its symbol, can prove a deadly poison. Hints of Eastern occultism are constantly being brought to the Western world, but in too many cases disaster has resulted. When esoteric knowledge or doctrine is committed to individuals incapable of understanding and rightly using it, the forces liberated by such discipline are almost certain to result in tragedy. The warning cannot be too strongly emphasized.
Manly P. Hall, *Man, the Grand Symbol of the Mysteries,* pg 298, 313

Since the hippy era in the 1960s and 70s, many Eastern traditions have caught on here in the West, such as yoga. A top Freemason just warned us about the Serpent Energy associated with it. As we learned from Gopi Krishna; the individual must be willing to completely give themselves over to the spirits, anything less will result in madness or insanity. Possession or lunacy, once this path is taken, it is a no-win situation. The account of Krishnamurti, of the Theosophical Society, who activated the Kundalini in 1922, is but another testimony of many that verifies this Kundalini-demonic possession hypothesis.

> Krishnamurti was undergoing fits of shivering and trembling, and complained of intense heat. He was in great pain, seemed only half conscious, and began to have out of body experiences... at that point, the entity that Krishnamurti called "the elemental" took over and did what it liked; he became semiconscious... "I toss about, groan and moan and mutter strange things, in fact almost behave like one possessed. I get up, thinking somebody is calling me and collapse on the floor; I rave considerably, see strange faces and light... all the time, I have a violent pain in my head and the nape of my neck... I may become clairvoyant when it is all over or merely that I am gradually going mad!!!" ...the personality known as Krishnamurti would recede into the background and the elemental would take over the bodily functions, including communicating bits of mundane information... the perception that unseen presences were working on his body, opening it and preparing it for greater spiritual service... the process continued year after year... "Krishnamurti started saying that he was very hurt inside that they had burnt him inside."
>
> Darrel Irving, Serpent of Fire, a
Modern View of Kundalini, pgs 27- 32

Another similar case is that of Hiroshi Motoyama of Japan.

> I could hear a sound something like the buzzing of bees... and saw there a round blackish-red light like a ball of fire about to explode... my body levitated... my whole body was burning, and a severe headache... a feverish state continued for two or three days. I felt as if my head would explode... hitting myself was the only thing that brought relief... during the process I encountered a

horrible devil-like being. It was an indescribably terrifying experience.

Hiroshi Motoyama, *Theories of the Chakras, pgs* 240- 250.

Manly P. Hall tells us more of the Freemason's use of Kundalini.

Among nearly all these ancient peoples the serpent was accepted as the symbol for wisdom or salvation... the serpent is true to the principle of wisdom... the tree that grows in the midst of the garden is the spinal fire; the knowledge of the use of that spinal fire is the gift of the great serpent. Notwithstanding statements to the contrary, the serpent is the symbol and prototype of the Universal Savior, who redeems the world by giving creation the knowledge of itself and the realization of good and evil... the accepted theory that the serpent is evil cannot be substantiated... it is the symbol of reincarnation... which was common to many of the ancient Mystery schools... the initiates of the Mysteries were often referred to as serpents, and their wisdom was considered analogous to the divinely inspired power of the snake. Sufficient similarity exists between the Masonic Hiram and the Kundalini of Hindu mysticism to warrant the assumption that Hiram may be considered a symbol also of the Spirit Fire moving through the sixth ventricle of the spinal column.

Manly P. Hall, *the Secret Teachings of All Ages,* pgs 272, 273, 241

We know that the serpent was no savior in the Garden of Eden. Therefore, we can trust that working with the Kundalini, as Manly P. Hall and his fellow Luciferians do, would be detrimental.

THE RETURN OF THE DJEDHI: Now that we understand the concept of the Kundalini we can see similar doctrines in other pagan traditions. Recall the Asherah poles and obelisks encountered by the Israelites?

Let us refer for a moment back to the Egyptian Djedhi priesthood. We're told by Egyptian occultists that the Obelisks, which symbolized Osiris' famed phallus, are in fact a metaphor for the spine in a similar Kundalini-like process (Lewis Spence, *the Mysteries of Egypt,* pg 114). The Egyptians called the coiled serpent at the base of the spine the

Mehen. As the phallus would erupt with semen, the Mehen would rush up the spine into the cranium bringing illumination. The Egyptian's thought that cerebral spinal fluid is the same substance as semen. Gopi Krishna tells us that Hindu traditions teach this as well (*The Awakening of Kundalini,* pg. 35).

The ancient Egyptian *Book of the Dead* says that the back bone of Osiris is called the Djed. The epithet of *Dj* pertains to the *fiery serpent* and the hieroglyph of the ascending serpent represents the Dj sound. For example, the Serpent King of Abydos was known as Djt and Thoth was also known as Djehuti. The magician priests of Egypt were known as the Djedhi, meaning *priests of the serpent.* They were regarded as holders of Thoth's wisdom and the Mysteries of his temple, the Great Pyramid. Remember, the Djedhi called the Great Pyramid the Djedhu, which then means *the sacred monument of the fiery serpent.*

We can learn of the Egyptian Mysteries from the hierophant priests Iamblichus and Plutarch, but Apuleius of the second century A.D. reveals the most in his book *Metamorphosis,* better known as *The Golden Ass.* On odd name, but we'll see why in a moment. The Egyptian initiate was taught that all men were once gods who fell into fleshy forms, but there is a secret way of escape, a means to once again become a god. One could wait several life times and through metempsychosis, aka: reincarnation, they could evolve toward this godhood, but there was a faster way, using secret magical knowledge. In the Mysteries of Osiris one can pass through seven gates and bring the soul back to godhood.

THE SEVEN GATES OF THE BOOK OF THE DEAD: The Egyptians believed that as the soul of the deceased went from life to death and on to a pleasant afterlife, to await resurrection, certain spells were needed to get past seven gatekeepers. If these gate keepers were not appeased the soul would suffer eternally. These spells were written on their tomb walls and even on the interior of sarcophagi so that the dead person could find them handy, kind of like a kid taking tiny cheat notes in for a test. In later ages these spells were collected into the volume we know as the Book of the Dead.[10]

The Egyptian's route through the spirit-world was not just taken by the souls of the dead. Via meditation and ritual the Egyptian initiate

---

[10] The Tibet Buddhists have their own Book of the Dead, the *Bardo Thol,* which is also a guide through the spirit world.

was thought to traverse these regions in search of godhood as well. In the 144th chapter of the Egyptian Book of the Dead we're introduced to the notion of Seven Gates. In E.A. Wallis Budge's translation he tells us that at each gate there is a Watcher who must be addressed and given a password, or spell, in order for the spirit to pass by on its journey through the spirit world, the Egyptian Duat.

At the last stage of the journey, the soul passes through a serpent, in its bottom end, through its body, and out its mouth. This may be where the "Golden Ass" adage originates. As the soul emerges from the serpent's mouth, it is as a god. Osiris himself is said to have taken this journey to become the god he is.

After Osiris' death we know that obelisks were erected throughout the land to symbolize his penis, but these also represented his Mysteries. A document that Egyptologists refer to as the *Magic Papyru* tells us that these pillars were also associated with the spine, or Nemma, of the god Ptah! A prayer to him reads "O Nemma of the great face, of the long backbone, of the deformed (serpentine) legs! O column which commences in both the upper and lower heavens." Esoterically, one end of Ptah's spine dwelled on earth, the other in heaven and by entering the serpent's tail end, and its spine ascended, illumination could be acquired.

There is evidence that Egyptians were initiated by spending three days entombed. Facing dehydration and sensory deprivation, they were to meditate and maybe ponder their entrapped status in the flesh, their god's time in the grave before resurrection, or consider themselves within the body of a serpent, struggling to emerge a god. Once released from their stone coffins, they were referred to as an Arisen One, a Kheper. When a pharaoh achieved this spiritual feat, the people celebrated what is known as the Raising the Pillar ritual. The pharaoh then became chief of the Djedhi and wore a serpent tiara called a uraeus, the divine asp. This is seen on many ancient Egyptian sarcophagi, where a snake protrudes from the pharaoh's forehead: the seat of enlightenment.

OPHIOLATREIA: The Kung tribe of the Kalahari Desert referred to the serpent energies that travel the spine as *Num.* As they entered an altered state, referred to as *Kia,* the energies could be harnessed and directed. Joseph Campbell taught that these Kundalini-like philosophies can be found in all cultures: Sumeria, Mesopotamia, Egypt, Ireland, and among the Navajos, Mayan and Aztec peoples (Joseph Cambell,

The Inner Reaches of Outer Space).

Opiolatreia, the worship of the serpent... there is hardly a country in the ancient world, however, where it cannot be traced, pervading every known system of mythology, Babylon, Persia, Hindostan, Ceylon, China, Japan, Burmah, Java, Arabia, Syria, Asia Minor, Egypt, Ethiopia, Greece, Italy, Northern and Western Europe, Mexico, Peru, America, all yield abundant testimony to the same affect, and point to the common origin of pagan systems wherever found.

Hargrave Jennings, *Opiolatreia,* pg 1

Throughout the Book of the Dead are dozens of Hymns to the serpent god Osiris, most of which claim he will rise again from the grave. Remember, it is his example that millions of Egyptians were following as they were mummified. However, the truth is a different matter, untold mountains of mummies were transported to the U.K. to be crushed and turned into fertilizer in the 1940s.

CHAPTER SIX
FREEMASONRY

Now that we have an understanding of who Nimrod was and how his religion works, let's look at the Freemasons. Is Nimrod really their deity? Do they follow his religious teachings? Most importantly, are they preparing for his resurrection?

The Mason's own writings will say it all; however the majority of Freemasons have no clue what they are apart of. Most teachings are deceptive and cryptic, surrounded in layers of Metaphor and symbolism. The lower level members are completely ignorant of their fraternity's ways and most have never taken the time to read their own books. Albert Pike, author of the Masonic Bible, *Morals and Dogma*, wrote that:

> Freemasonry has two doctrines, one concealed and reserved for the Masters… Fictions are necessary to the people, and the Truth becomes deadly to those who are not strong enough to contemplate it in all its brilliance. In fact, what can there be in common between the vile multitude and the sublime wisdom? The Truth must be kept secret, and the masses need a teaching proportioned to their imperfect reason.

This text actually says that the Freemasons deceive even their own members! But here we will examine their most sacred writings where their historians have documented everything. They tell us of the origins of the Craft, a term the Masons use to describe their fraternity, keep in mind some claim that the term *Craft* may merely be a short form of the word *witchcraft*, and earlier we saw that Ptah was god of crafts.

NIMROD AND THE FREEMASONS: One of the Freemason's oldest documents is the Cooke manuscript which speaks of the pre-Flood family of Lamech, who appears in Genesis 4: 19- 22:

> And these four brethren knew that God would take vengeance

for sin, either by fire or by water. And they were much concerned how to save the sciences they discovered, and took counsel together and exercised their wits... fortunately knowing of the vengeance that God would send the brethren knew not whether it would be by fire or water. They knew by a sort of prophecy that God would send one or the other, and therefore they wrote their sciences on the two pillars of stone. And some men say that they wrote on the stones all the seven sciences, but this I affirm not. As they had it in mind that a vengeance would come, so it befell that God did send vengeance, and there came such a flood that all the world drowned and all men died save only eight persons. There were Noah and his wife and his three sons and their wives, of which sons all the world is descended, and they were named in this wise, Shem, Ham, Japhet. And this flood is called Noah's flood, for he and his children were saved therein. And many years after the flood, according to the chronicle, these two pillars were found, and the chronicle says that a great clerk, Pythagoras, found the one, and Hermes the philosopher found the other, and they taught the sciences that they found written thereon.

Every chronicle and history and many other writers and the Bible especially relate the building of the Tower of Babel; and it is written in the Bible, Genesis 10, how that Ham, Noah's son, begat **Nimrod, who grew a mighty man upon the earth and waxed strong, like unto a giant. He was a great king and the beginning of his kingdom was Babylon proper... and this same Ham began the tower of Babel taught his workmen the Craft of Masonry and he had with him many masons... And in this manner the Craft of Masonry was first instituted and charged as a science.**

Matthew Cooke Manuscript,
Speth translation, 1861

Did Cooke just say that Freemasonry began in Babylon?
From the *Dowland Manuscript* of 1500 AD, we can see *The Legend of the Craft*:

Good Brethren and Follows: Our purpose is to tell you how and in what manner this worthy science of Masonry was begun... Before Noah's flood, there was a man named Lamech, as it is written in the Bible in the 3rd chapter of Genesis... (he had) four children... and these children knew well that God would take vengeance for sin, either by fire or water; therefore they wrote their science that they found in two pillars of stone, that they may be found after Noah's flood... Our intent is to tell you truly how and in what manner these stones were found that these sciences were written in. The great Hermarynes... afterwards was called Hermes, the father of wise men; he found one of the two pillars of stone, and found the science written there, and he taught it to other men. And at the making of the Tower of Babylon there was Masonry first made much of. And the King of Babylon that height **Nimrod was a mason himself; and loved well the science.**

Nimrod was a Freemason? Albert Mackey, referred to by Masons as *the historian of the Craft,* wrote in 1898 that Nimrod wasn't just a Freemason... he was their first *Grand Master!*

> The traditional history of Masonry now begins... before the Flood there was a system of religious instruction which, from the resemblance of its symbolic character to that of Freemasonry, has been called by some authors "antediluvian Masonry."... this idea is well exemplified in the American ritual... in this ritual, this symbolic journey is supposed to begin at the Tower of Babel.
> **Their "first Grand Master"... Nimrod, the King of Babylonia... in the ancient chronicles he was represented as of gigantic stature, ten or twelve cubits in height.** To him was attributed the invention of idolatry... to have persuaded the inhabitants to become fire worshippers. He built a large furnace and commanded that all who refused the idolatrous worship should be cast into it... Nimrod was a mighty leader, a man of great prowess in war and hunting.
>
> Albert G. Mackey,
> *The History of Freemasonry,*
> Pt 1, *Prehistoric Masonry*

Mackey says Nimrod was ten or twelve cubits high. That is tall. A cubit is roughly the distance from a man's elbow to the tip of his middle finger, about eighteen inches. This means Nimrod may have been eighteen feet tall! He would be very hard to miss.

Mackey then summarized his research:

> The Legend attributes to Nimrod the creation of the Masons into an organized body and he was the first who gave them a constitution or laws for the government. Masonry, according to the legendary account, was founded in Babylon, whence it passed over to the rest of the world.
>
> Albert Mackey,
> *The History of Freemasonry*, ch. 19

Freemasons claim to be carrying on the sciences of the pre-Flood world, clearly the dogma and rituals of the Luciferian religion. They've also claimed Nimrod is their founder. Masonic scholars have revealed these secrets and we now see them in the light of Biblical truth.

THE RELIGION BEFORE THE FLOOD: Earlier Albert Mackey called the pre-Flood religion *Antediluvian Masonry. Diluvian* refers to a flood, and *ante* means before, so Antediluvian means before a flood, the Flood of Noah is what is indicated. Mackey has implied that the religion before the Flood was Freemasonry. This would be the religion of those messing with genetics, those who forced God to bring a cataclysmic flood upon the earth, and the Masons are calling it their own! And the Masonic historians have made it pretty clear that they are also following the religion of Nimrod and Babylon. Can't we then conclude that Nimrod was reviving the pre-Flood religion at Babylon?

When the Flood came it momentarily halted this horrible religion but it was reinstated at the city of Babel by Nimrod. With the confusion of languages its spread slowed and was forced to mutate. This will be the same religion a tyrant will force upon the world in the end times. This religion in itself is a horrible affront to God and his people that few understand. In the Book of Revelation more time is spent describing the end of this religion than the end of Satan himself!

Masons deny the Biblical position regarding Babylon, claiming it is erroneous in its presumption that Nimrod's Babel was "a place of intellectual darkness." Mackey claims that the Babylonians were righteous and "in possession of a wonderful literature... the *Legend of the Craft* vindicates its character and correctly clothes in historic fact... when it portrays Babylonia, which was undoubtedly the fountain of all science and architecture, as also the birth place of Operative Masonry."

The Mystery Religions were vile and disgusting. They enticed with offers of bliss and peace or with secret knowledge and power, but at the core they were blacker than black. They were designed to leave the practitioners with less than nothing, dependant and in constant discomfort. God does not want his children to ever take part in the ways of the pagans. The practitioners of these ways understood this and went underground and hid with the emergence of Christianity.

LOCATING THE MYSTERY RELIGION TODAY: Most people have never heard of the ancient Mystery Religion. And many more would scoff at the idea that any ancient Luciferian Religion lives on in secret societies today. This chapter includes a great deal of shocking information regarding the latest link in the chain of the Mystery Religion; its first link was cast before the Flood and later it was reestablished in Babylon. It may be a surprise for some to learn that the most recent link in that chain is the Masonic fraternity, but Masonic scholars admit it. W.L. Wilmshurst (1867- 1939) wrote in his book *The Meaning of Masonry* that not only is Freemasonry a descendant of the ancient Mysteries, but the pagan doctrines of evolution and becoming a god are still paramount!

> This; the evolution of man into supermen, was always the purpose of the ancient Mysteries, and the real purpose of modern Masonry is, not the social and charitable purposes to which so much attention is paid, but the **expediting of the spiritual evolution of those who aspire to perfect their own nature and transform it into a more godlike quality.** And this is a definite science, a royal art, which it is possible for each of us to put into practice; whilst to join the Craft for any other purpose than to study and pursue this science is to misunderstand its meaning... **the conscious realization of our divine potentialities.**
> W.L. Wilmshurst,
> *The Meaning of Masonry,* pg 47

Albert Mackey spoke of the Mystery Religions in his 1896 seven volume *History of Freemasonry,* where he declared:

> The mind was to be gradually purged of many errors, by prepatory steps, before it could bear the full blaze of truth, both the Mysteries and Freemasonry have obeyed a common law of intellectual growth... the fact that there existed in both institutions

secret modes of recognition presents another analogy. It is known that in the Mysteries, as in Freemasonry, there was a solemn obligation of secrecy, with penalties for its violation, which referred to certain methods of recognition known only to the initiates... I have traced the analogies between the ancient Mysteries and modern Freemasonry... 1. The Preparation, which in the Mysteries was called the Lustration. It was the first step of the Mysteries, and is the Entered Apprentice's degree in Freemasonry. 2. The Initiation, which in the ancient system was partly in the Lesser Mysteries, but more especially in the Greater. In Masonry it is partly in the Fellow Craft's, but more especially in the Master's Degree. 3. The Perfection, which in the Mysteries was the communication to the aspirant of the true dogma, the secret symbolized by the Initiation. In Freemasonry it is the same. **The dogma communicated in both is, in fact, identical... Freemasonry is a lineal and uninterrupted successor of the ancient Mysteries,** the succession being transmitted through the Mithraic initiations which existed in the 5th and 6th centuries.

The great Masonic philosophers all wrote about the ancient Mysteries which they regard as the beginning of their own religious history. Wilmshurst said that anyone seeking enlightenment...

...in the form of new enhanced consciousness and enlarged perceptive faculty... must be prepared to divest himself of all past preconceptions and thought habits and, with child like meekness and docility, surrender his mind to the reception of some perhaps novel and unexpected truths... men were once in conscious conversation with the unseen world and were shepherded, taught and guided by the gods... in the remote past the gods walked with men and... they chose the wisest and the truest... with these specially ordained and illumined sons they left the keys of their great wisdom... they ordained these anointed and appointed ones to be priests or mediators between themselves, the gods, and that humanity which had not yet developed the eyes which permitted them to gaze into the face of Truth and live... these illumined ones founded what we know as the Ancient Mysteries.

W. L. Wilmshurst;
The Meaning of Masonry (1927)

The legend of the columns, of granite, and brass or bronze... which survived the flood, is supposed to symbolize **the Mysteries, of which Masonry is the legitimate Successor.**

Albert Pike, *Morals and Dogma*

MASONIC INITIATION: As with the Mysteries, the Masons believe in evolution into godhood and that through their initiation process this can be facilitated.

Man who has sprung from the earth and developed through the lower kingdoms of nature to his present rational state, has yet to complete his evolution by **becoming a god-like being** and unifying his consciousness with the Omniscient, to promote which is and always **has been the sole aim and purpose of initiation.**

W.L. Wilmshurst,
The Meaning of Masonry, pg 95

Few Masons know what real initiation involves... real initiation means an expansion of consciousness from the human to the divine level... man has that in him enabling him to evolve from the stage of the mortal animal to being immortal, superhuman, godlike... can this slow process of human evolution be expedited? ...transform the sensual human animal into an illuminated godlike being? To this the answer of the Ancient Mysteries was "Yes, there is. Human evolution can be accelerated in suitable individuals."

W.L. Wilmshurst, *Masonic Initiation,*
Ch 1

THE HISTORY OF FREEMASONRY: Masons insist they're a legitimate heir to the original Babylonian Mystery Religion. This is correct, but the name *Freemason* has had a shorter life span. The oldest document with the name Freemason attached is from 1450, but most Masons claim their organization was officially born in London on June 24, 1717, when the first Grand Lodge organized and decided to set up similar lodges throughout the world like hamburger franchises, only evil... and without the burgers.

Just a few years prior, in 1666, there was a terrible fire in London which destroyed much of the city. As part of its recovery stone masons from all over Europe converged on the city. It is believed some of these transient laborers brought the Mysteries with them, leaving their religion to be remembered by their occupational title, Masonry.

In the following years Freemasonry would be altered. No longer did you have to be an actual stone worker to join the group. And no longer would there be as much mention of Osiris or Nimrod; they would say their founder was Hiram Abif. In Masonic lore Abif would be the one who died to later rise from the grave. Later we will see that, Biblically speaking, Abif was an appropriate, and sinister, choice for their needs.

Over the years the Mysteries remained very secretive, but with the Renaissance and the so-called Age of Enlightenment, the Masons came out of the shadows. All lodges now answered to superior lodges and ultimately to a world wide Masonic Parliament overseen by an annually elected Grand Master.

Today there are many Luciferian secret societies. Elite Masons intermingle with the heads of the other Luciferian cults and families around the world, even amongst covens of witches, Rosicrucians and neo-pagans. Just as Christians have many denominations and occasionally jostle about, so do Luciferians. These different groups have even staged wars against one another and have frequently and angrily denied any relationship with one another. However, the truth is they have been related. They share the common origin at Babylon and the common lord Lucifer.

THE LEGEND OF HIRAM ABIF: Remember how various lands have different versions of Nimrod? The Egyptians had Osiris, the Greeks had Dionysus. Well, the Freemasons formed their own version with the tale of Hiram Abif. The story of Hiram actually has its start in the Bible so he was a real person, and maybe a nasty one at that, but the Masons take his story in a whole other direction.

Both David and Solomon had an alliance with the king of Tyre, Hiram. In the Bible it says this man thought he was a god (Ezekiel 28: 2)! According to Ginzberg's *Legends of the Jews* he was a follower of the Luciferian religion (Book IV, pg 335). When it was time to build the Lord's Temple in Jerusalem, King Hiram was to supply the wood for the construction, he also sent along eighty thousand stone cutters, commonly known as masons (1Kings 5). The Freemasons say the master mason assigned to the job was Hiram's best craftsman, and referred to as Hiram Abif. The Masons claim Hiram Abif is the individual mentioned in 1Kings 7; 13, who is referred to as "the widow's son,[11]" This may or may not be so, but this is where anything Biblical about the story ends.

The Masonic legend says Abif's workmen were divided up into three different classes, with differing pay scales. When payday came, each group had a different secret pass word to tell Hiram that determined how much they were to be paid. One day a trio of men wanted to have their passwords promoted for the higher salary without laboring in the various degrees to achieve it. So they planned to meet separately with Hiram and force him to divulge the secret. Each met him at a different part of the Temple and attacked him with a different tool: a ruler, iron square and a mallet. Each struck a different part of his body, eventually killing him. They then hid the body. When Solomon learned of his master mason's murder he sent out agents to find the body.

What follows is the most important part of all Masonic rituals: those seeking their master's body find it and resurrect it with... a secret handshake!

Hiram's experience is lived out in the Masonic ritual for the initiate entering the third level, or third degree. The third degree is the highest of the Blue Lodge, that of Master Mason. Everyone entering this level must participate in a dramatic reenactment of the death and resurrection of Hiram Abif, taking center stage in the role of Abif. Upon the initiate's resurrection their blindfold is removed and they are shown a symbol and receive a sacred word.

The legend of Solomon's Master Mason, Hiram Abif, is eagerly declared by Masons as the number one most important of all their allegorical tales to explain their Mysteries. This is their version of the story of Osiris, including Biblical figures to give it all some validity. But there are some very good reasons the Freemasons selected this individual.

The Mason's selection of Hiram Abif as their version of Nimrod is actually quite fitting. Masons tell us that Hiram wasn't just the best craftsman in Tyre; he was actually the son of the king. If we turn to the Bible, Ezekiel 27 used the king of Tyre as a metaphor for Lucifer. So if he is Lucifer, who is his son?

Hiram Abif is a metaphor representing the Antichrist.

WHAT GOD THINKS OF THE MASONS: There is actually

[11] Remember Horus was also referred to as the "widow's son."

evidence in the Bible that God doesn't care for masonry. For example, God told Moses to never make any altar for him out of cut stones. God said the stones themselves could be defiled if they were shaped with a mason's tools (Exodus 20: 25).

This sentiment was repeated in the construction of Solomon's Temple. God ordered that the actual cutting of the stones, which were ultimately necessary for such a large building, occur far away at the quarries, no hammer, chisel or any other iron tool was to be heard at the temple site while it was being built. The Bible also tells us that inside the Temple none of the cut stone was to be seen, it was covered in wood or precious metals (1Kings 6: 18).

MORALS AND DOGMA: In the late 1800s Albert Pike was a very prominent figure. Not only was he Brigadier General in the Confederate Army, a lawyer, and a founding member of the Klu Klux Klan, but he also wrote a book called *Morals and Dogma of the Ancient and Accepted Scottish rite of Freemasonry:* "The Masonic Bible."

Modern Masons refer to him as "the Prince Adept, Mystic, Poet, and Scholar of Freemasonry." This sounds nice but Pike himself was literally a beast of a man. Often appearing in photographs unkempt and very obese, he was known to make an annual pilgrimage into the forest taking with him every prostitute in town. He took a wagon load of whiskey and food and did not return until the wagon was empty. They would return at the end of the week. The women spoke of a wooden throne in a clearing and said that certain ritualistic acts were carried out when the *stars were right.* What is odd is that in Washington DC there is a statue commemorating this monster. The only national memorial dedicated to anyone or anything related to the Confederacy.

Morals and Dogma is the guide for the Scottish Rite branch of Freemasonry. Inside the front cover it is written in bold characters "Esoteric book, for Scottish Rite use only; to be returned upon withdrawal or death of recipient." The book is written in a way that kept most secrets rather vague, giving many references to the verbal teachings members would have received in the Lodges. Still, within its pages we can discover many subjects and secrets us *profane* outsiders should not be aware of.

Most Masons will deny they are a religion. This is of course is nothing but a lie. If one were to read any single page of Pike's thousand plus page epic, they could easily see the esoteric, spiritual and religious nature of this volume. It contains the teachings that are to be bestowed upon the initiate within every one of the first thirty-two levels of Scottish Rite Masonry. In the beginning levels they are constantly taught to "seek the light." But when an initiate reaches the highest levels, they find *the light* isn't what they thought it would be.

> The first born is the Creative Agent, Conservator, and animating Principle of the Universe. It is the Light of Light... the Light, the object of our labors, appears as the creative power of the Deity.
>
> Albert Pike,
> *Morals and Dogma*, Level 17

> Light, as contradistinguished from darkness, is Good, as Eternal Good, for which Masons in all ages have sought. Still Masonry marches steadily onward toward that light that shines in the great distance, the Light of that day when... Life and Light be the one law of the Universe, and its eternal harmony.
>
> Albert Pike,
> *Morals and Dogma*, Level 18

"Seek the light!" Freemasons are taught that the light is the source of knowledge and all things desirable. Every pagan sun-worshipping denomination has *sought the light*. A secret is finally revealed to the initiate, after they have been worshipping this light for some time, in level nineteen when they attain the rank of Grand Pontiff, that they have all along been worshipping...

> Lucifer, the light-bearer! Strange and mysterious name to give to the Spirit of Darkness! Lucifer, the Son of the Morning! Is it he who bears the light, and with its splendors intolerable binds feeble, sensual or selfish souls? Doubt it not!
>
> Albert Pike,
> *Morals and Dogma*, Level 19

> The Devil... for the initiates, this is not a person, but a force created for good... it is the instrument of Liberty or free will. They represent this force... the He-goat of the Sabbat, brother of the ancient serpent, and the Light-bearer or Phosphor... Lucifer.
>
> Albert Pike,
> *Morals and Dogma*, pg 102

We shall unleash the Nihilists and Atheists, and we shall provoke a formidable social cataclysm which in all its horror will show clearly to the nations the… most bloody turmoil. Then everywhere, the citizens… disillusioned with Christianity… will receive the pure doctrine of Lucifer, brought finally out into public view… which will follow the destruction of Christianity.

Albert Pike, August 15, 1871,
Letter to Grand Master Guiseppie
Mazzini, Archives British Museum,
London, England

We worship a God, but it is the God that one worships without superstition.

To you, sovereign Grand Inspectors General, we say, so that you can repeat it to the Brethren of the 32nd, 31st and 30th degrees: the Masonic religion must be, by all of us initiates of the high grades, maintained in the purity of the Luciferian doctrine.

If Lucifer were not God, Adonai, the God of the Christians, whose deeds prove his cruelty, perfidy and hatred of man, his barbarism and repulsion of science, if Lucifer were not God, would Adonai and his priests not slander him?

Yes, Lucifer is God.

Albert Pike, 23rd Supreme Council,
June 1889

It wasn't just Albert Pike, a top thirty-third degree Mason, that was preaching the Luciferian doctrine among the Freemasons, but many other Masonic writers have subtly tipped their hats to their infernal lord. Manly P. Hall, another 33rd degree Mason, wrote in *The Lost Keys of Freemasonry* that:

The day has come when Fellow Craftsman must know and apply their knowledge. The lost key to their grade is the mastery of emotion, which places the energy of the universe at their disposal. Man can only expect to be entrusted with great power by proving his ability to use it constructively and selflessly. When the Mason learns that the key to the warrior on the block is the proper application of the dynamo of living power, he has learned the mystery of his Craft. The seething energies of Lucifer are in his hands, and before he may step onward and upward, he must prove his ability to properly apply energy.

Manly P. Hall, *the Lost Keys of Freemasonry,* Ch. 4: The Fellow Craft

"Lucifer himself masquerades as an angel of light... his servants masquerade as servants of righteousness (2Corinthians 11: 14, 15)!" By the time the Mason understands that they have been following a false-light, they are in too deep to get out, their businesses, lives, and even family's safety is on the line and they cannot escape. They have made deadly vows of secrecy that if they tell what they have learned they will suffer torture and death. Or worse yet, many have been successfully duped, which is most often the case, believing the lies.

MASONIC PROGRAMMING: Members are programmed with a rather subliminal method. First off, they agree not to use the name of Jesus Christ in their functions in anyway. They say that they are not a religion and they would prefer not to upset anyone of another belief. In Lodge prayers, they agree to instead pray to the great creator and "Architect" of the universe, "whoever that may be to them."

After praying to the Masonic Architect for some time, they are encouraged to question God and the Bible. In the Garden of Eden Lucifer also had Eve question God: "Did God really say 'You must not eat from any tree in the garden?'" The Masons work in the same way, getting the initiate to question God's truth.

Soon the questioning of God moves to another easier target, the Church. We know that the Christian Church is made up of believers who are not without their faults. Then they have the Masonic initiate question themselves as a sinful and unworthy person. While in this position, it is easy to start to dislike a god who you think is displeased with you.

Sadly we look around us, and read the gloomy and dreary records of the old dead and rotten ages (the Bible). More than eighteen centuries have staggered away into the spectral realm of the past, since Christ, teaching the Religion of Love, was crucified, that it might become the Religion of Hate... The God of Nineteen-twentieths of the Christian world is only Bel, Moloch, Zeus or at best Osiris, Mithras or Adonai, under another name, worshipped with the old pagan ceremonies and ritualistic formulas... it is the

Statue of Venus, become the Virgin Mary... God seems to have abdicated, and Moloch to reign in His stead... Faith is always satisfied; and it has been a great source of happiness to multitudes that they could believe in a Devil who could relieve God of the odium of being the Author of Sin... man is a free agent ...he must be free to do evil. The light necessitates the Shadow... O, ye initiates, ye whose ears are purified, receive this in your souls, as a mystery never to be lost! Reveal it to no Profane One, Keep and contain it within yourselves, as an incorruptible treasure... Masonry... her traditions reaching back to the earliest times, and her symbols dating further back than even the monumental history of Egypt.

Albert Pike, *Morals and Dogma,*
Level 18

These are very evil words from men who tell new members, families, friends and the media that they are not a religion.

ANTIMASONRY: Masons refer to those of us who point out the truth of their Order as Anti-masons. In 1826 Captain William Morgan became the premier Anti-mason when he wrote a book called *Illuminations of Masonry.* He was kidnapped, tortured and drowned by the Freemasons. His grave, in the cemetery in Batavia, New York, has a forty ton marker bearing this inscription:

Sacred to the memory of William Morgan, a native of Virginia, a captain of the War of 1812, a respectable citizen of Batavia, and a martyr to the freedom of writing, printing and speaking the truth. He was abducted and murdered from near this spot in the year of 1826, by Freemasons, and murdered for revealing the secrets of their Order. The court records of Genesee County, and files of the Batavia Advocate, kept in the recorder's office, contain the history of the events that caused the erection of this monument, September 13, 1882.

"The bane of our civil institutions is to be found in Masonry, already powerful and daily becoming more so. I owe to my country an exposure of its dangers" Captain William Morgan.

After Captain Morgan was murdered by the Masons for divulging some of their secrets, the United States government investigated the

Order. The Joint Committee investigating the event in Massachusetts declared in 1834 that "A distinct government exists within our own government, and is beyond the control of the laws of the land by means of secrecy." Soon a successful political party was formed called the Anti-Masonic party. John Quincy Adams said "I do conscientiously and sincerely believe that the Order of Freemasonry, if not the greatest, is one of the greatest moral and political evil."

Consider the testimony of James D. Shaw, a former 33rd degree Freemason. He achieved the level of Grand Master of all Scottish Rite Bodies.

> 'Oh it's all in fun,' I was told as I impersonated a character named Hiram Abiff in the initiation of the third degree... I didn't know, and neither does one in one hundred thousand candidates for the Third Degree know that they are impersonating Osiris of Egypt, or Baal of the pagan Canaanites and Phoenicians, or Bacchus sun-god of the Greeks, who was slain annually by the principle of darkness represented by the three winter signs of the Zodiac. And is portrayed in the Masonic Lodge by three ruffians, called Jubela, Jubelo, and Jubelum. How Satan must have laughed at me as I served him diligently as priest of the Lodge for so many years. I was not willing to be just a 'card carrier,' I was too eager for that. So I served in all the chairs and ultimately became Worshipful Master of the Lodge. I pursued the degrees of the Scottish Rite and joined the Shrine in my quest for pre-eminence in the eyes of men. In time I became Past Master to all Scottish Rite Bodies. And finally was selected for the 33rd Degree, and was made a 33rd Degree Mason in House of the Temple in Washington, D.C.
>
> C.F. McQuaig, *the Masonic Report*

After leaving Freemasonry James D. Shaw became a Christian Pastor.

THE ILLUMINATI: Most people have probably heard of the Illuminati associated with conspiracy theories. Online they've been linked with everything from the death of Jesus to the attacks of September 11, 2001. I had heard of them but never took the idea very seriously until I saw references to the Illuminati in that mountain of Masonic books I had obtained. If the Masons took this group seriously I thought I should do a little research into their history.

It seems a great terror arose in Bavaria in 1784. Dangerous publications were circulating that called for a rebellion against the Church and every government. These were traced back to the Masonic Lodge Theodore. These writings were dangerous enough for the Bavarian government to place a ban on all secret assemblies and locked down all the Masonic Lodges on June 22. In 1785 four professors at the Marianen Academy were summoned before a court of inquiry. These men had once been members of this secret movement but had quit once they discovered its secret and horrible plans. They claimed that the ancient Mystery Religion was taught here, sensual pleasures were more than advocated and that evil was promoted "if it was used for a good purpose."

A further judicial inquiry in 1786 ordered that Counselor Xavier Zwack's home be raided and searched on October 11 and 12. Secret documents were found belonging to an Order called the Illuminati. A further search of Baron Bassus' Castle of Sandorf in 1787 found an even larger collection of papers.

Among these documents were volumes from one Adam Weishaupt (1748- 1830), a professor of law at the University of Ingolstat. It could be seen that Weishaupt himself had founded the Order on May 1, 1776, which is curiously the date that now appears on the American dollar bill. Weishaupt was raised by his godfather Johann Adam Baron von Ickstatt, professor and rector of the University of Ingolstadt. It is known that Ickstatt secretly kept certain books the censor of the University library had rejected as inappropriate, dangerous and blasphemous. Apparently his young charge Weishaupt was also very attracted to these forbidden works.

In 1774 Weishaupt come into contact with the Egyptian Mysteries of Memphis via a Count Cagliostro who claimed he was guided by "secret superiors" who later "vanished." Following Cagliostro's advice Weishaupt entered into Freemasonry in 1777 and learned all he could within two years. He soon found Masonry was rather impotent and craved greater things. So he formed his own secret society, the Order of Perfectibilists. Its emphasis was primarily on the possibility of human perfection, ie: becoming a god. He later changed the name of the Order to the *Illuminati*. He saw that the Church stood firmly in the way of universal human initiation and enlightenment and taught that it must be destroyed. The goal was to convert every human to their religion, to have every human illuminate.

In his contempt for Christianity and its adherents, Weishaupt, while writing of Christ's disciples, said that:

> What these men have done for the Altar (the Church) why would not I do in opposition to the Altar? With legions of Adepts subject to my laws, and by the lure of the Mysteries, why may not I destroy under the cover of darkness, what they edified in broad daylight? What Christ did for God, why shall not I do against God, by means of adepts now become my apostles?

Weishaupt revealed that he produced the code of the Order while in an altered trance state using automatic writing, "I am ignorant of the author; but they appear exactly as they flowed from my pen; that is to say, as I compiled them." Members all swore an oath of loyalty to Weishaupt's secret superiors.

The student of the Illuminati was to study meditation and antichristian philosophers such as Voltaire and Plato while the more elite members were taught the art of manipulation. They were to infiltrate the Bavarian and foreign governments in order to begin earth's transformation into an enlightened utopia. The wealthy and socially prominent were recruited and soon Masonic leaders were specifically targeted. It was Zwack's strategy that the Masonic Lodges be infiltrated and hijacked to serve the Illuminati's greater goals.

At Willemsbad, in 1780, a great Masonic congress was held. Deputies came from all corners of the globe to debate the Illuminati's new ideas which had already been accepted by many Lodges. The proceedings lasted more than six months and the final conclusion was that Masonry should open its doors to the new Order of Illuminism.

Manly P. Hall has referred to the Illuminati's present position imbedded within Masonry as "a fraternity within a fraternity."

In 1781 an ex-Jesuit named Ignatius Franck was the first to publicly attack the Illuminati. In a sermon he called the members "Masonic traitors, brothers of Judas" and claimed the Order was preparing the way for the Antichrist!

In Edinburgh, Scotland, John Robison, a physicist, a professor of philosophy and a Freemason had watched as this subversive element infiltrated his Lodge and others that he had contact with. Until then he was under the impression that Masons were not to speak of religion or politics, but the new Illuminism more than allowed this, they openly demanded the Church's downfall. In 1798 he wrote a book with a long-winded title: *Proofs of a Conspiracy against all the Religions and Governments of Europe Carried on in the Secret Meetings of the Freemasons and Illuminati* in an attempt to alert the world to the Illuminati and its goal to destroy Christianity and all forms of government.

Early in 1785 Weishaupt was dismissed from his position at the University for utilizing his position there to procure "ungodly books."

With concern and suspicion mounting, the Bavarian government published the seized papers in 1786 and Weishaupt was forced to flee to Gotha where he received asylum from Ernest Lewis, the Duke of Saxe. Here he lived out his days writing further works on Illuminism, including *A Complete History of the Persecutions of the Illuminati in Bavaria, an Apology for the Illuminati,* and *a Picture of Illuminism.*[12] The remaining members either fled, were fined or jailed.

The current accepted notion is that the Order of the Illuminati then came to an end. There is, however, ample historic evidence that this is not so. The Illuminati was certainly not destroyed, merely driven further underground to become reading societies and *Jacobin clubs.* In fact it can be seen that zealous members such as Friedrich Munter, J.J.C. Bode, Weishaupt's number two man, and Carl Reinhold continued the activities of the Order and recruited even more vigorously.

THE FRENCH REVOLUTION: Just three years later, in 1789, the French Revolution occurred and the Bourbon monarchy was toppled. It was widely known at the time to have been manufactured by the Jacobins; who were Masons Illuminated by Weishaupt and Zwack. Incidentally, the symbol for this movement was the All Seeing Eye.

The Illuminati first put down roots in France when a Jacobin chapter was started by Count Honore Gabriel Mirabeau. This Lodge, Club Breton, would be home to the most influential of the soon-to-be revolutionaries. From here a group of rich men were organized, led by the Duke of Orleans, the Grand Master of the French Masons, who was initiated by none other than George Washington, bought up all the grain in the land. It was secretly hoarded and caused a famine which was blamed on the French King, causing the uprising now known as

---

[12] Reinforcing the notion of a continuing conspiracy is the fact that these works have never been translated into English.

the French Revolution.

In April of 1793 Maximilien Robespierre, the head of the Jacobins, took power and became dictator over France. The old pagan Mystery Religion was immediately implemented. A sacred and mysterious "Tree of Liberty" was erected at Cathedral Square. On the entrance to every town or city "Liberty Poles" were erected. *The Religion of Reason* was then founded and the famous Notre Dame Cathedral in Paris was made The Temple of Reason. Mission Deputies were sent out to enforce the new religion and ensure all Christian Churches were shut down. Christians who did not convert were executed. The paranoid Jacobins rounded up all their perceived enemies and had 40,000 of them beheaded with a device invented by a Freemason named Guillotine. This machine was designed especially for the purpose of executing large numbers of people in a very short period of time.[13]

As the state was eager to finalize the de-Christianization of the people a new holiday was introduced. On November 10, 1793, the Festival of Reason was first celebrated. A ballet dancer, Therese Momoro, had claimed she was the reincarnation of the Greek Goddesses of the Mysteries, Athena. She was selected to personify the Goddess of Reason, the symbol of the new religion. A procession was led through the streets of Paris with her carriage as the focal point. A drunken mob scene ensued; sex and violence filled the streets as she reached her Temple at Notre Dame. The Freemasons, in their full regalia, met her and lifted her high upon the altar and she was worshipped by the masses.

The nation soon collapsed into anarchy. Immorality filled the streets and people clamored to turn in their enemies for execution, claiming they were dissidents against the new state. Disgruntled workers turned in supervisors, students turned in teachers and the debt ridden turned in those who had lent to them. Civic services collapsed and the surrounding nations manned their boarders to ensure the crisis did not spread. In 1799 Napoleon Bonaparte, an ally of the secret societies, would seize power, stabilize the situation and declare himself Emperor of France. Interestingly, Napoleon's name means "New Apollyon."

As emperor, Napoleon secured his position and power and then headed for Egypt, the ancient home of Osiris. As an initiate he was

---

[13] Revelation 20: 4 seems to refer to this instrument being used against Christians during the reign of the Antichrist.

searching for the lost god, perhaps hoping to be witness to his resurrection. He took along a team of scholars who actually performed the first archeological assessment of the ancient region. He even spent a night in the Great Pyramid! When he emerged in the morning he was visibly shaken and would not comment on what had occurred, even to his closest men who begged to know what happened. On his death bed he still refused to answer, saying they would not believe him if he told them.

In 1797 Abbe Augustin de Barruel would write in his third volume of *Memoirs Illustrating the History of Jacobinism* how the network of Masons and secret societies had played a prominent role in the French Revolution and that the Illuminati had further planned to repeat their successful formula and bring down every monarchy, freeing the way for the perpetration of their ultimate goal, the destruction of the Church. History firmly shows that within a few years many Monarchs did lose control over their nations, such is the case in the American and Russian/Bolshevik revolutions. The key revolutionaries were, in both cases, members of secret societies.

Albert Pike admits to Masonry's involvement in bringing about the French Revolution (*Morals and Dogma,* page 24). The Freemason's have always had the Illuminati's principles at their core. Why else would the French Lodges freely take in Illuminati members, an Order that was banned in most of Europe? If they were a simple fraternal organization why would the Masons risk their very lives to hide and later fund and support these outlaws? Albert Mackey tells us quite frankly in *The Encyclopaedia of Freemasonry* that Adam Weishaupt was a Masonic reformer, much like Martin Luther, who had brought their religion back to its roots. Kenneth Mackenzie's *Royal Masonic Cyclopedia* tells us that the Masons of that era were in a state of chaos until Weishaupt came to "purify Masonry."

A last curious incident occurred in 1876 when the French gave America a giant centennial birthday present. It was an enormous statue of the Goddess of Reason to remind their fellow nation of the glories of their revolutions. Today this statue stands in New York Harbor holding aloft the *Eternal Flame of Enlightenment,* with the broken shackles of Christianity lying at her feet, she is now called the Statue of Liberty.

ILLUMINED OR SCOTTISH RITE MASONRY: So far in our examination of the Luciferian religion we have seen more quotes from Albert Pike than any other pagan scholar. He compiled the teachings for the Scottish Rite branch of Masonry thus creating the "Masonic Bible" *Morals and Dogma* in 1871. Where did Pike get this mountain of data from? He certainly did not live in the information age. Some of the sources he quotes have been lost to history for some time. The Scottish Rite itself has a very interesting history.

The Scottish Rite's Mother Lodge was established in Charleston, South Carolina in 1801. It was planted in America by the French, not the Scottish as many would think. In Bordeaux, France, there existed a branch of Weishaupt's Illuminati called the Masonic Rite of Perfection, similar in title to Weishaupt's Order of Perfectibilists. In French they pronounced it *Ecossais,* phonetically similar to the word *Scottish.*

Most Masons are unaware that Scottish Rite Masonry has nothing to do with Scotland whatsoever, it's French! The French word *Ecossais* sounded like the word *Scottish,* so it stuck.

These Illumined Masons came to America led by Comte Auguste de Grasse-Tilly, the son of one of Napoleon's Admirals. De Grasse himself served as a Captain under General Leclerc, Napoleon's brother in law. When the Illumined Masons came to the New World they brought their library of documents.

Albert Pike (1809- 1891) was brilliant, born in Massachusetts he learned Greek, Latin and Hebrew in his teens. In Harvard he completed two years work in half the time. He became a lawyer and later Supreme Court Justice. In 1851 he entered Freemasonry. In 1861, Jefferson Davis, president of the Confederate United States, appointed him to the rank of Brigadier General. At the end of the Civil War he retired to the Ozark Mountains and immersed himself in the occult. He had been assigned by the Illumined Masons to be part of a team to organize their library of fragmented documents. He was the only one of the team to take an interest in the task. In his remote cabin he mastered Kabala, alchemy, Hermeticism, philosophy and the Eastern arts. He dwelt frequently on Elias Levi's works, especially *Dogma and Rituals of High Magic* (1855).[14] Pike revered this work so much he frequently plagiarized portions of it in his own work. Mostly isolated, except for the annual pilgrimage into the forest mentioned earlier, where he took the wagon load of whiskey, food and prostitutes, in 1868 Pike finally came down from the mountains with the completed *Morals and*

---

[14] Levi was an occult philosopher, resultant of the French Revolution. He led the Occult revival of the 1800's.

Dogma.

He lived out the rest of his life in Washington D.C.

As you can see there are many ties here to Weishaupt's Illuminati. The name of the Rite is similar to the original name of the Illuminati. It comes from France, historically the last home of the Illuminati. It came to America in the days immediately after the French Revolution, the Illuminati's most famous action. Its founders were known Illuminati associates.

The top, or thirty-third, degree of the Scottish Rite is accessible by invitation only. It is often hereditary, or due to familial ties that one gets in. It has been said that many of the world's top politicians are Freemasons. This is where they sit in Masonry, the elite thirty-third degree of the Scottish Rite, the fraternity within the fraternity.

It has a long winded name "The House of the Temple of the Supreme Council of the Thirty-Third and Last Degree of the Ancient and Accepted Scottish Rite of Freemasonry," and is the name of the Masonic Lodge in the heart of Washington DC. Its roof is designed to match the truncated pyramid on the American dollar bill and has two large sphinxes on either side of its front door. Pike's body is entombed within this building.

The members of the 33rd degree of the Scottish Rite are the Masons that have the enormous influence that conspiracy theorists warn of.

FREEMASONRY IN CHURCH HISTORY: In the history of the Roman Catholic Church we can see they have come up against the Freemasons many times. Pope Clement XII's 1738 Papal Bull *In Eminenti against Freemasonry* condemned Freemasonry, suspecting a plot to take over the Church and the governments of the earth.

Pope Benedict XIV's 1751 constitution *Provida* again warned of the dangers of Freemasonry.

In 1781 Ignatius Franciscus Franck delivered a sermon in which he was the first to publicly condemn the Order of the Illuminati. He said members were traitors, brothers of Judas and were preparing the way for the Antichrist!

Pope Pius VI (1775- 1819) sent out letters also warning of the dangers of the Illuminati. He said that the Order was incompatible with the teachings of the Church. With the French Revolution, designed and carried out by Illuminated Freemasons, Napoleon deposed Pius in 1799 forcing him into exile in Valence where he would later die.

Pius VII (1800- 1823) warned against Freemasonry in his

constitution *Ecclsiam a Jesu Christo,* issued on September 13, 1821. He was soon exiled, but first he was forced to officiate at Napoleon's Coronation at Notre-Dame. This ended the Vatican's military powers as the Papal States were annexed. Napoleon then had the Vatican archives and library removed to Paris where his men scoured the documents seeking out papal secrets with a special interest in the Knights Templar.

Pope Leo XII warned of Freemasonry in his March 13, 1825 apostolic constitution *Quo Graviora.*

Pope Pius VIII's 1829 encyclical *Traditi* warned of Freemasonry.

Pope Pius IX repeatedly warned of the Freemasons in such works as *Qui Pluribus* (1846) and *Multiplices* (1865).

Pope Gregory XVI condemned Freemasonry in his 1832 encyclical *Mirari.*

Pius IX (1846- 1878) published Masonic documents from the Alta Vendita Lodge which clearly showed their goal was to infiltrate the Catholic Church and take control!

On April 20, 1884, Pope Leo XIII issued the encyclical *Humanum Genus* severely condemning Freemasonry. He also republished the Masonic documents confiscated from the Alta Vendita Lodge which showed the Masonic goal to infiltrate the Vatican and put their own man on the throne. Leo also demonstrated that the Masons had begun to put in place mechanisms "to control the education of youth, and mold it to their godless pattern."

After the death of Pope Leo, in 1903, at the conclave to elect the next pope, the Cardinal Mariano Rampolla Del Tindaro, Pope Leo's second in command, appeared to be easily sweeping into power. But, at the final moment of the last vote the Cardinal Puzyna of Cracow, Austria, applied a never before used veto to halt the process. This veto, known as the "Right of Exclusion," was put in place to ensure unworthy candidates could not take power. It had never been applied before, or ever again. One Monsignor Jouin had found out that Rampolla was a Mason. Perhaps the Mason sent to infiltrate the Church. Not only was Rampolla a Mason, but he was found to have come from the diocese of Caffeol, home of Aleister Crowley's Luciferian Abbey of Thelema. A few years prior, Crowley's elite secret society, the OTO, the Ordo Templi Orientis, had issued a list of members and associates in the OTO's journal *Oriflamme.* Rampolla's name was on that list. He was also noted to be an initiate of the

Catalonian Balearic Grand Lodge in Barcelona. This Masonic Lodge was implicated in the practice of Black Masses.

In 1978 Pope John Paul spent only 33 days as pontiff. His sudden death led many to believe he was poisoned. Oddly, in the days just prior to his death, Vatican laws were passed forbidding any deceased pope from ever having an autopsy. Sources inside the Vatican revealed that John Paul was investigating problems within the Vatican Bank and that he was about to enforce Canon Law 2338 and excommunicate one-hundred top Vatican officials for being Freemasons. It should be then seen as ironic that he was murdered specifically on the thirty-third day, a number significant to Masons.

In 1981 the scandal finally broke involving the Vatican, organized crime and the Freemasons. Creditors were threatening to sue so Pope John Paul II finally had to explain how the Vatican had been caught up in all of it. The Vatican Bank was the main share holder in Italy's Bank Ambrosio when it collapsed in early June 1982. It was discovered that between 1.5 and 2.4 billion in U.S. dollars had been secretly removed through the Vatican Bank. As part of the ensuing police raids the home of the international banker and P2 Mason member, Michele Sidona, was searched. The police were looking for any information on those involved embezzling the nation's money. They found a list of nearly a thousand P2 Mason members, European and American politicians, big business men, military officers of every degree and nation and many members of Vatican clergy, including Bishop Paul Marcinkus of the Vatican Bank. These police raids then found that the Vatican Bank had been used for money laundering stemming from prostitution and drug trade. Assassinations were paid for as well as huge donations to the U.S. Republican Party!

Just after this, Robert Calvi, known as *God's Banker* and the head of Bank Ambrosio, was found dead, hanging by the neck under Blackfriar's Bridge in London's financial district on June 17, 1982. His death was originally deemed a suicide, but two ensuing coroner's inquests confirmed it was a homicide. Calvi had been a member of the Italian branch of Masonry known as P2; members referred to themselves as Frati Neri, or the Blackfriars, leading many to presume that Calvi's body hanging from London's Blackfriar Bridge was a sign of Masonic involvement. Before his death he had written a letter to the Vatican claiming he was about to incriminate those responsible for the money laundering.

In 1982 Canon Law 2338 forbidding Catholics from being Freemasons was reversed. Some say that this alone proves that the Freemasons have infiltrated the Vatican.

Soon after becoming pope, Benedict XVI began claiming that the world needed a New World Order. On December 3, 2012 at the Pontifical Council for Justice and Peace he called for the "construction of a world community, with a corresponding authority." Remember, such a one-world government has always been the goal of Luciferians.

THE WOMAN WHO RIDES THE BEAST: Could the Luciferians have really infiltrated the Roman Catholic Church?

Bible prophecy seems to tell us we should expect it to happen. With the infrastructure of the Catholic's organization it would be a brilliant move, strategically. In the Revelation of John we're told of a very important end time's event where a religious body, symbolized as a woman, will cause the greatest strife ever for God's people. "I saw that the woman was drunk with the blood of the saints, the blood of those who bore testimony to Jesus (Revelation 17: 6)." Who could this woman be?

The Bible gives us several hints. This woman is in fact a city and verse 17: 9 tells us the city claims to be of a religious nature and sits on seven hills. Only two cities in the world have historically sat on seven hills, Rio de Janeiro and Rome. Rio has never been considered a religious city. This leaves us with only one more choice. *The Roman Catholic Encyclopaedia* says "It is within the city of Rome, called the city of seven hills, that the entire area of Vatican State proper is now confined."

The Bible gives us further hints. Revelation 17: 4 tells us that the woman will be dressed in purple and scarlet. Cassocks, the ankle-length robe worn by Catholic Bishops are purple, and the Cardinals wear scarlet, these are the official colors of the Catholic clergy. The Bible says that in the woman's hand will be a golden chalice (Revelation 17: 4). *The Roman Catholic Encyclopaedia* tells us that the chalice "is the most important of the sacred vessels," this is where the sacred wine is poured. Revelation describes this woman as excessively rich; the Catholic Church has been one of the wealthiest organizations ever.

ROME, THE NEW BABYLON: The Bible refers to this religious movement brought by the woman on the beast as *Babylon* many times (Revelation 17: 5, 18: 2, 10). Are there any indications that Nimrod's *Babylon* may be another name for Rome? When the disciple Peter travelled to Rome while spreading the gospel he referred to it as Babel, "She who is in Babylon sends you her greetings (1Peter 5: 13)!" Peter never went to Babylon. When did Rome become Babylon? It wasn't just Peter, but the ancient Roman historians Tacitus and Juvenal both indicated that Rome was considered a New Babylon. Both these men went so far as to claim that Babylonian blood was flowing in the veins of Rome's senators and knights during Nero's day. How did this happen?

During Rome's conquests into the Mediterranean many Babylonian slaves were claimed and taken back to Rome. According to Roman law, slaves were set free immediately after their master's death. Through these individuals, now freemen, the population of Rome became largely Babylonian. Making matters worse for the Roman population, their young men all went off to various wars. Former slaves became the dominant part of the population, and remember, they would have certainly brought with them their Babylonian customs and religion. The Mysteries became deeply rooted in Rome.

MYSTERY BABYLON: When Constantine legalized Christianity throughout the Roman Empire in the year 313 a certain trend began. To ease the transition from the Mysteries to Christianity, several pagan customs were *Christianized.* Former pagans perhaps found it easier to transition into the Church with their old traditions and beliefs relatively intact, but Christianity was never meant to include anything of the Mysteries of Nimrod, especially a celebration of his birth.

Most Westerners, whether Christian or not, celebrate Christmas. Once a year I love to spoil the kids with a pile of gifts and treats. But who knew we weren't really celebrating Jesus' actually birthday? There's plenty of evidence that December 25 is Nimrod's birthday, and none to suggest it relates to Jesus Christ. In fact all the evidence points otherwise. Remember the famous phrase "the shepherds were watching their flocks by night (Luke 2: 8)?" In December it's too cold to do such a thing in Israel.

In 1853 Reverend Alexander Hislop wrote of these things in *The Two Babylons, the Papal Worship Proved to be the Worship of Nimrod and his Wife* and Martin Luther as well in his book *the Babylonian Captivity of the Church:* "I now know of a certainty that the papacy is the kingdom of Babylon and the power of Nimrod the hunter."

THE POPES AND 666: We must consider what prophecy seems to indicate: the Antichrist will take over the Catholic Church. There is indication that he will even claim the papal throne!

The popes have been called by various names and titles. The most curious is *Vicar of Christ.* The 1993 *Catholic Dictionary,* by Peter M.J. Stravinskas, tells us that this term is a "title used almost exclusively of the Bishop of Rome as successor of Peter and, therefore, the one in the Church who particularly takes the place of Christ; first used by the Roman Synod of A.D. 495."

Did he say someone who takes the place of Christ? Another way to say this might be *substitute* or *false* Christ. Anyone calling themselves a Vicar of Christ may as well be calling themselves an antichrist!

There is something else very interesting about the phrase, Vicar of Christ, in its original Latin. *Vicarius Filii Dei* literally translates as "in-place-of son-of God" and when you apply the old Hebrew system of substituting letters for numbers, and adding the numbers together, the phrase Vicarius Filii Dei totals 666!

This discovery was first published by Andreas Helwig in 1600, in his book, with the long winded title: *Investigating Proof that a Name of Antichrist Exists that Exactly Corresponds to the Apocalyptic Number 666; Incontrovertibly Handled.* Helwig published another book on the same topic in 1612, *Antichrist Romanus,* and one more in 1630. It has been whispered about for centuries that a pope will become the Antichrist. In the November 15, 1914, edition of the Catholic Publication *Our Sunday Visitor* it was written: "The Pope's title is Vicarius Filii Dei and is inscribed on his mitre and that the letters add up to 666." And again in the April 18, 1915 edition "The letters on the Pope's mitre are Vicarius Filii Dei." The Mitre is the pope's head piece, some of these hats look like a fish head, others a triple crown. In the November 24, 2011, issue the Vicarius Filii Dei topic is still being discussed. The title means antichrist, and the numbers say antichrist. The only trouble is these currently belong to the head of a Christian organization!

How is the number 666 associated to Osiris?

Sure, he will take the Vatican as a seat of power; he's destined to take over the entire earth! But there is more to the number. If you take the name Nimrod, the NMRD letters in Hebrew, and add his last name, which would be "Son of Cush," *ben Cush* in Hebrew, or BN CSH. NMRD BN CSH in Hebrew adds up to 666.

How does this compare in Nimrod's home land, in his own language? The name Saturn, in Chaldean, STUR, also adds up to 666.

Saturn is the name of the "hidden god," that is, Nimrod.

MALACHI MARTIN: One of the most famous exorcists to work within the Catholic Church, Malachi Martin, was a priest from 1958 until 1964, when he asked to be released from his vow of obedience. In his 1990 book he reveals why he felt forced to do this.

> Most frighteningly for pope John Paul II, he had come up against the irremovable presence of a malign strength in his own Vatican and in certain Bishop's chanceries. It was what knowledgeable churchmen called the 'superforce.' Rumors, always difficult to verify, tied its installation to the beginning of Pope Paul VI's reign in 1963. Indeed Paul had alluded somberly to 'the smoke of Satan which has entered the Sanctuary' ...an oblique reference to an enthronement ceremony by Satanists in the Vatican. Besides, the incidence of satanic pedophilia, rites and practices, was already documented among certain bishops and priests as widely dispersed as Turin, Italy and **South Carolina,** in the United States. The cultic acts of satanic pedophilia are considered by professionals to be the culmination of **the Fallen Archangel's rites.**
>
> Malachi Martin,
> *The Keys of This Blood,* pg 632

Occurring barely a week after the election of Paul VI, the ceremony called "The Enthronement of the Fallen Angel Lucifer" was held in St. Paul's chapel on the grounds of the Vatican on June 29, 1963, in conjunction, via telephone, with Satanic rites also practiced in South Carolina. The only way Malachi Martin could describe the ceremony was in fictitious form in his 1996 novel *Windswept House,* which would be his last before he died mysteriously from a "fall" in 1999. What Martin maybe did not know, or did not tell us, is that in Charleston, South Carolina, is the Headquarters for the Scottish Rite branch of Freemasonry! The number one top Lodge of Illumined Masonry, the "Mother Supreme Council of the World!"

The Freemasons may have been involved with the Luciferian enthronement ceremony at the Vatican. The Catholic's records point to the fact that the Masons were certainly attempting such a feat, and it was the stated goal of Weishaupt's Illuminati, after all.

Malachi Martin disclosed to Art Bell on the radio show *Coast to Coast,* on October 18, 1996, while discussing exorcisms, that some of the wealthiest and oldest American families are under the influence of generational curses. That these families purposefully demonize their children to ensure their *familiar* demons will live on in the familial bloodlines. He also indicated that this was done ultimately in preparation for the Antichrist. As the end time draws near, he also mentioned the fact that the number of exorcisms being performed has grown 800% since 1975.

Just before Martin died, sensing trouble, as he had spoken out regarding the hidden roots of Luciferism, he gave another writer all his documentation to carry on his work. William H. Kennedy reviewed Martin's yet unpublished manuscript and followed down several leads. But he was not convinced and unbelieving… he sat on things. However when the Boston Globe broke the story on January 6, 2002, of a ring of Satanic pedophiles working within the Roman Church he realized Malachi Martin's work was all true. He rushed back to the leads and witnesses Martin had provided and put together the book *Lucifer's Lodge Satanic Ritual Abuse in the Catholic Church.*

CHAPTER SEVEN
THE ANTICHRIST AND LUCIFERIANS IN THE BIBLE

The concept I had of the Antichrist was not scripturally based when I started researching Flood legends several years ago. It was formed more on the ideas presented by Hollywood with films such as Rosemary's Baby and The Omen. We've already seen that more accurate knowledge of the Beast can be found in the writings of secret societies such as the Freemasons as well as the ancient records of the Egyptians, Sumerians, Babylonians and others who followed the Mystery religions. But most Christians will look to the Bible, the most reliable of all sources. Many go straight to the Book of Revelation for information regarding the Antichrist but he actually appears throughout both the Old and New Testaments! You just have to know what you're looking for. In this chapter we will thoroughly examine the Word of God to see what we can of Satan's seed.

ASSUR: Remember the first prophecy in the Bible, in Genesis 3, where it is prophesied that Satan would have seed, a son? There is mention of Nimrod a few chapters later in Genesis 10: 8. In Genesis 10: 11 the original Hebrew and the King James Bible seem to indicate that he had a nickname, Asshur, which means *successful*. As Asshur, Nimrod is mentioned many more times in the Old Testament, and always in the context of being the opponent of the Messiah.

> When the Assyrian invades our land and marches through our fortresses we will raise against him seven shepherds, even eight leaders of men. They well crush the land of Assyria with the sword, the land of Nimrod with drawn sword. He (Christ) will deliver us from the Assyrian.
> Micah 5: 5, 6

> There are Asshur and all his company; all the slain have been laid there: and their burial is in the depth of the pit... laid with the giants that fell of old, who went down to Hades with their weapons

of war: and they laid their swords under their heads, but their inequities were upon their bones... the captains of Asshur, who go down slain to Hades... even Pharaoh, and all his multitude with him.

Ezekiel 32: 22- 32 (LXX Version)

In the Babylonian creation epic, *the Enuma Elish,* is a prayer to Asshur, but pronounced here as "O Asari." Phonetically speaking, this is incredibly similar to "Osiris."

O Asari, bestower of planting, founder of sowing, Creator of grain and plants, who caused the green herb to stand up!

In the Sumerian *Hymn to Asarluhi* we read of him again,

August sage, first born son of Enki... Asarluhi, son of the Abyss, he is Marduk, the bringer of council. Tall in stature, he can survey all.

DANIEL: In the Old Testament the prophet Daniel has the most to say regarding the end times and the Antichrist. Daniel describes the physical characteristics of the Antichrist and he certainly sounds as though he could be a Nephilim! The Beast will appear "more imposing than" other men (Daniel 7: 20) and will be "very strong (Daniel 8: 24)." We're also told that he will be a master of deception (Daniel 8: 23) and very successful, in fact he'll be so successful that he "will succeed at everything he does (Daniel 8: 24)!" Nimrod's nickname was Asshur, which means successful, so this may be Daniel telling us that Nimrod is the Antichrist.

Daniel also describes some of the events that the Beast will orchestrate. Firstly he will make a seven year truce between Israel and all her enemies. Later not only will he break the truce and seek to destroy the Jews himself, he will put an end to the Temple rituals, set up an idol to himself there, "the abomination that causes desolation," and declare himself god (Daniel 9: 27)!

ISAIAH: Isaiah 14: 9 speaks of the spirits in the grave, coming forth, one-time kings, and rulers over nations, literally rising up from the dead, which is exactly what has been prophesied for Nimrod. This verse comes just prior to Isaiah 14: 12- 15 which we examined in the first chapter as speaking for Lucifer.

EZEKIEL: When the Antichrist makes the truce between Israel and her enemies that is when the final seven year Tribulation begins. Ezekiel seems to tell us of the events, the attacks against Israel, which necessitate such a truce. The Bible refers to this as the war of Gog and Magog (Ezekiel 38, 39, Revelation 20: 8). The Antichrist will step onto the world stage as a hero, calming a fearful world, declaring peace in a region that has seen no end of strife, never mind the fact that it was God who miraculously stopped the war and saved Israel.

Some strange things are described regarding this conflict. We're told that the Israelites will be able to use the enemy's weapons as a source of fuel for seven years (Ezekiel 39: 9). We're told that it will take seven months to bury the dead and that specially trained men will need to go out onto the battlefield to clean the land. At first markers will be placed to identify the location of the remains of the dead and then gravediggers will dispose of the remains (Ezekiel 9: 12- 16). This should really come to our attention as an anomaly. Why can't anybody just dig a hole and bury the dead? Why would specially trained people have to go out and mark the locations of the dead prior to their burial? And how could the Israelites use the enemy's weapons for fuel... for seven years?

Because of this evidence, it is likely that the Holy Land will be attacked with nuclear weapons. I'm certainly no nuclear physicist, but perhaps the nuclear energy available from a few undetonated bombs could be used to power reactors for seven years. What's important is that from this point on there will only be seven years left before Christ returns!

PSALMS: Psalm 110 is referred to as the Melchizedek Psalm because here the Messiah is called a "priest forever in the order of Melchizedek." Who is Melchizedek? In Genesis 14: 18 he seemed to come out of nowhere.

In the book of Hebrews it is said that Melchizedek was a king of Jerusalem and a priest of God Most High. To be both King of Jerusalem and a priest is a tough distinction to match! But we're told that this exceptional person had no mother or father, he didn't even show up in the Hebrew's genealogical records (Hebrews 7: 3). Of course he didn't, Melchizedek wasn't his name. It was his title. Melchizedek means priest-king.

Earlier we surmised that Shem most likely became known as

Melchizedek when he took Nimrod's kingdom. From Psalm 110 we begin to realize that there are a lot of similarities between Shem/Melchizedek and Jesus.

In the prophecy of Genesis 3: 15 it is said that the seed of the woman, the Messiah, will crush the head of the seed of Lucifer. The Melchizedek Psalm similarly states that Melchizedek "will crush the kings on the day of his wrath… crushing the rulers of the whole earth." So if Melchizedek was Shem, and he killed Nimrod… and Jesus is also coming to kill Nimrod we can see a similarity between the two.

The Antichrist gets to die twice! Once by the hand of Shem and once by Jesus, but the similarities certainly don't stop there. We saw that Shem brought out bread and wine (Genesis 14: 18), this is exactly what Jesus did (Matthew 26: 26- 28, 1Corinthians 11: 23- 26).

Jesus, our savior, is a priest and king. It was so important that this could be shown to the Hebrews, the Bible actually records the lineage of their priests (Luke 3: 23- 38) and kings (Matthew 1: 1- 17) and Jesus is on both lists. Like Jesus, Shem was a priest-king, he was the son of the priest Noah, and he took the kingdom from Nimrod with his death.

Shem's name in Hebrew means "the Name," or "Divine Name." Jesus is said to have an important name as well, the "name above all names (Philippians 2: 9)." This word *name* appears 764 times in the Bible and carries a lot importance, it is a weighty term. In many instances the word appears capitalized. The Masons noticed this as well, "The Jews in their sacred rites often designated God by the word *Name,* but most applied it only to him in the most exalted character… to the Jew this great and holy name was the symbol of all Divine truth. The *Name* was the true name, and therefore it represented the true God (Albert Mackey, *Encyclopaedia of Freemasonry,* pg 685)."

Shem and Jesus have a great deal in common. Like Jesus, Shem, after he took the kingdom form Nimrod, was rejected by the people. Remarkably, Shem was left with Jerusalem, the capital city of the Holy Land.

God works in mysterious ways, the "greatest story ever told" is still being revealed.

THE APOCRAPHA: The Apocrypha, or Deuterocanonicle writings, are a set of books written during the 400 years before Jesus' time. Protestant Christians don't regard them very highly, Catholics do. Here we see the books of the Maccabees, these writings accurately document the history of the Jews in a war against a Greek king of the

Seleucid Empire named Antiochus IV Epiphanes (215 BC – 164 BC). During this time many of Daniel's prophecies about the Antichrist seemed to be fulfilled in the character of Epiphanes!

First of all, Antiochus IV thought very highly of himself, in fact he believed he was a god. He added the word *Epiphanes* to his name which means "god made manifest."

Antiochus began a systematic persecution against Jews who would not turn to his religion. Murdering many, he also turned God's Temple in Jerusalem into a Greek temple. Worship of the Hebrew's God was forbidden and the Jews were forced to worship Dionysus, who we've seen to be a version of Nimrod. Soon after Antiochus had a pig, a very unclean animal to Jews, sacrificed on God's altar.

Prophecy tells us that the Antichrist is incredibly similar to Epiphanes. He will also force his own religion on people, persecute the followers of the true God, take over God's Temple and declare him self a god there. He may not sacrifice a pig there, but he will set up an idol of himself, in the Bible referred to as the Abomination of Desolation.

So did Antiochus IV Epiphanes fulfill the prophecies? Was he the Antichrist?

No. He was not the Antichrist because both Jesus and the disciple John repeated Daniel's prophecies in the New Testament over 250 years later.

THE ANTICHRIST IN THE GOSPELS: Jesus mentions the Abomination of Desolation just as Daniel did (Matthew 24: 15, Mark 13: 14). This is the idol representing the Antichrist that he will have set up in God's Temple. But there may be more appearances of the Antichrist here than most have perceived.

There is a phrase used only twice in the King James Bible, "the son of perdition." It is definitely used to describe the Antichrist in 2Thessalonians but it is also seen when describing Judas (John 17: 12).

Sure, Judas was a traitor and pretty bad, but how could he be the Antichrist?

Consider that the Bible tells us that Judas was possessed! "Then Satan entered Judas, called Iscariot, one of the Twelve (Luke 22: 3)."

This statement may be a bit misleading. No where else in Scripture is there any evidence that an angel can possess a human; that is what disembodied demons do. Why would an angel take on a human's body when they can manifest their own? I believe this to be a figure of speech similar to "Hitler killed six-million Jews during World War II."

Adolf Hitler did not personally kill six million people, but the forces under his control did. So, Satan did not possess Judas, but an agent under his control did.

Who possess people? Demons do.

What are demons? Demons are the spirits of dead Nephilim.

Nimrod, the coming Antichrist, aka: the son of perdition, is the spirit of a dead Nephilim. He very well could have been the spirit that possessed Judas!

This must be so, because it is the only way to explain the prophecy in Genesis 3 where we're told that the son of Satan would bruise Christ's heel. This is the only way Judas, possessed by Nimrod, would then fairly acquire the title reserved for the Antichrist, "son of perdition." Judas had the role of turning Jesus over to the governmental forces of the day thereby leading to his crucifixion where nails were driven through his hands and lower legs, perhaps heels.

Archeologists found an ancient heel bone near Jerusalem with a nail through it and piece of wood still attached, there is no other explanation than this bone belonged to a person who was crucified. The Romans were excellent at what they did, terrorize, torture and execute. They would have been methodical, knowing what bones could take a nail and still support their victim's weight (*Times of Israel,* March 26, 2012).

PAUL: In 2Thessalonians Paul speaks of the end times, but before he does, he, like Christ in the Gospels, warns us to beware of deception (2Thessalonians 2: 3). Paul then says that that time will not come until *the* rebellion comes, remember the meaning of the name Nimrod: rebellion. Then, still in that same verse, the Antichrist is referred to as "the son of perdition" in the King James Script, just as Judas was in John 17: 12.

Paul then indicates that something is keeping the Antichrist away. Undoubtedly that would be the Holy Spirit, "the one who now holds it back will continue to do so till he is taken out of the way." How could the Holy Spirit be taken out of the way? The Holy Spirit lives in every Christian on the planet. When the rapture occurs and all the Christians are taken up to heaven, in the twinkling of an eye (Colossians 15: 52), the Holy Spirit will not be present in the same way he currently is on the earth.

Paul also tells us that the "secret power of lawlessness is already at work (2Thessalonians 2: 7)." I took this to mean the work of Satan and his followers, maybe Paul knew that efforts were being made to prepare the way for Lucifer's son, as they are today. But this may mean something even more. It may also refer to the spirit of the deceased Nephilim Nimrod, whose spirit is undoubtedly still in existence.

THE REVELATION OF JOHN: The Book of Revelation is devoted entirely to end time's prophecy. The Antichrist of course appears here, referred to as the Beast. We're told that Lucifer, the dragon of Eden (Revelation 12: 9), will give the beast his authority to rule earth, his throne and his power (Revelation 13: 2).

> The beast which you saw, once was, now is not, and will come up out of the Abyss and go to his destruction. The inhabitants of the earth will be astonished when they see the beast, because he once was, now is not, and yet will come.
> Revelation 17: 8

John is telling us here that "the beast was alive, right now he is dead, but he will live again." John specifically tells us that the beast will come up out of the Abyss. This prophecy has been ignored for two thousand years! But you and I are of the generation where genetic manipulation and cloning is possible. We are the first to fully understand this! We are the first to positively identify the Antichrist. He will not be the son of some super rich politician like in The Omen movies. He will not be some alien astronaut, or a subversive pope. He is Nimrod.

THE WOUNDED BEAST: In the thirteenth chapter of Revelation we're repeatedly told that the Beast will have had a fatal wound. Fatal means dead. He will not be wounded and recover, he will be dead and gone, but later seen to rise from the grave.

To raise the dead is a miracle. Only God can truly break the laws of physics and perform miracles. Whatever Satan does, it is through the work of his unseen minions: demons and fallen angels. To bring someone back from the grave requires two separate processes. The first is to restore the flesh to life, easy enough… if you are a geneticist. The second part is to get their personality, their thoughts, mind and spirit into the cloned body, easy enough… if you're a demon and can possess people.

SEVEN SATANIC KINGS: John the disciple tells us that the Antichrist is coming and that "even now many antichrists have come (1John 2: 18)." Is there more than one Antichrist? Let's look at

Revelation 17: 8, 11:

> (Of the) seven kings, five have fallen, one is, the other is yet to come, he must remain for a little while. The beast who once was, and now is not, is an eighth king. He belongs to the seven and is going to his destruction.
>
> Revelation 17: 11

This strange verse has always been a mystery. Not only are we told that the final Antichrist will be the "eighth king," but that he was also one of the prior seven. One sure way to explain this is a resurrection from the grave.

Regarding eight kings, well, some have made up lists of seven antichrist-like individuals trying to explain this. There are many tyrannical kings through history to pick from including the likes of Alexander the Great, Antiochus Epiphanes, the Pharaoh that Moses battled, Napoleon, Hitler and others.

Historically, there are indeed seven kings who have definitely stood against God and his people. This is the key element to identifying the satanic kings, to make it on the list they had to have stood against God and his chosen people. Alexander the Great encouraged the Luciferian Mysteries, but he never went directly against God, in fact he made a peace treaty with Israel. Napoleon was of the Masonic Illuminati, but he did not specifically persecute God's people, the Jews, either.

So who are the seven kings?

To discover this we must look at the history of God's people. And since a great deal of Israel's history is in the Bible, most of the satanic kings will be found there.

In a Bible based list of seven satanic kings we could start with Nimrod, king of Babylon, first ruler in the post-Flood world.

Next would be the Pharaoh who Moses battled, apparently Amenhotep II. Remember, according to Egyptians the pharaohs were Osiris incarnate.

Chronologically, the next satanic king would be Sennacherib of Assyria (2Kings 18- 19). While discussing him, the prophet Isaiah compared him to Lucifer himself "How you have fallen from heaven, O morning star, son of the dawn (Isaiah 14: 3- 15)."

The fourth satanic king is the King of Tyre who Ezekiel compared to Lucifer (Ezekiel 28: 1-19); this may be King Ithobaal III.

Next is Antiochus IV Epiphanes whom the prophet Daniel compared to the final end time's Antichrist (Daniel 11: 21- 36).

The sixth king is Caesar Nero. Several Church Fathers tell us that Nero ruled the Roman Empire during the time that John wrote the Revelation at Patmos. Nero persecuted the emerging Christian Church like no other. He is responsible for the executions of the apostles Peter and Paul.

Of more modern times no one can forget Adolf Hitler who had six million Jews murdered, and someday hoped to wipe out the Christians as well.

So let's review the prophecy "They are also seven kings. Five have fallen, one is, and the other has not yet come... The beast who once was, and now is not, is an eighth king (Revelation 17: 10, 11)." Of the satanic kings listed here we see five that had fallen, that had existed before the time John received the Revelation, one that was in existence then, Nero, and one that would come, Hitler.

The eighth king, the missing one, we're told is the same as the very first one, Nimrod. But so far we have no evidence that Nimrod persecuted God's people. There is, however, a very ancient Sumerian document that may reveal that he did; the epic *Enmerkar and the Lord of Aratta*. Enmerkar is the first Sumerian king and easily determined to be Nimrod, *kar* meaning hunter, but who is the Lord of Aratta? The location of Aratta bears an uncanny resemblance to Ararat, where the family of Noah and Shem lived.[15] Enmerkar demanded assistance from the people of Aratta in his construction efforts. His own land was lacking stone so Enmerkar's people had been forced to make their Tower with mud bricks, matching the Biblical account of the Tower of Babel. Enmerkar demanded stone. Obviously we know he was denied. This is likely the occasion when Nimrod began his persecution of God's followers.

From the Sumerian story of Enmerkar and Aratta we can infer some other interesting things. We know that Shem was later able to get close enough to Nimrod to kill him. How? Perhaps Shem acted as if he had

---

[15] At the foot of Mount Ararat there existed the remains of an old settlement named Agouri, which local legends say was the habitation of Noah until his death. The Monastery of St. James was built here and the monks that maintained it would at times display what they claimed were relics taken from the Ark itself. An earthquake and landslide eventually destroyed Agouri on July 2, 1840.

relented to the giant's requests for stone and gems. From Egyptian legends we know that Shem brought Nimrod a huge box completely studded in gems. Shem may have implied that more of this was on the way, "to whoever can fill the box (with their body), we will return it filled with gems!" That could be when he tricked Nimrod to get in the box.

With that it fits that Nimrod was the first of the seven satanic kings, as well as the last.

> The five that "have fallen:"
> 1. Nimrod
> 2. Pharaoh Amenhotep II
> 3. Sennacherib of Assyria
> 4. Ithobaal III of Tyre
> 5. Antiochus IV Epiphanes
>
> The one that "is," during John's life time:
> 6. Nero
>
> The other that "has not yet come:"
> 7. Adolf Hitler
>
> The one that "once was, now is not, and yet will come"
> 8. Nimrod

Further evidence that Nimrod is the Antichrist restored to life is found in Revelation 13: 3 which describes how the final Antichrist will have a fatal wound that will somehow be healed. Could this be the wound delivered by Shem, "The beast who was wounded by the sword and yet lived (Revelation 13: 14)?" The recovery will likely be related to his mummified DNA and the emerging modern science of cloning; the genetic manipulation which the Watchers have long been masters of. Revelation 13: 11 speaks of a beast that will come out of the earth, maybe meaning the grave! And the next verse tells us upfront that he will have the authority of "the first beast," ie: Nimrod. The abomination of desolation, the idol the False Prophet sets up in the Temple (Revelation 13: 14), is again that of "the first beast," and out of the seven, that would be Nimrod.

THE RAPTURE: The word rapture does not appear in the Bible. It pertains to a time when the entire Church, every Christian believer, will be taken up to heaven "in the twinkling of an eye (1Corinthians 15: 52)." This is prophesied to occur in order to save us from much of the suffering of the end times (Matthew 24: 22)." There are actually seven raptures recorded in the Bible, seven occasions where a person, or persons, are taken up to heaven: Enoch (Genesis 5: 24), Elijah (2Kings 2: 11), Jesus (Acts 1: 9), some un-named person, perhaps Paul (2Corinthians 12: 2), the two-witnesses (Revelation 11: 12), those members of the Church who have previously died (Revelation 11: 18, 2Thessalonians 4: 16), and members of the Church who are living at that time (Revelation 11: 18, 2Thessalonians 4: 17).

The timing of the rapture is debatable. Most are of the opinion that it will occur right at the beginning of the seven year Tribulation in accordance with the *Left Behind* series of books. I believe that Scripture indicates otherwise, that the rapture will occur mid-way through the Tribulation. The Bible says that it will happen at the *last Trumpet* (1Corinthians 15: 52, Matthew 24: 31). There are seven trumpets mentioned in Revelation. With the seventh and last trumpet the demon Nimrod seems to rise out of the Abyss, perhaps prepared to possess and take over his genetically cloned and revived body. It is only at this time that the Holy Spirit, living within every member of the Church, will be taken away: when *the lawless one* is revealed (2Thessalonians 2: 7, 8), when the demon Nimrod rises from the Abyss (Revelation 9: 11).

As I said earlier I was a fan of Tim LaHaye's *Left Behind* series of books when they came out. But now my interpretation of prophecy differs. I think the rapture will be in the middle of the seven year tribulation and not at the beginning as LaHaye taught. My concern is, if I am correct, for the Christians who might not see the Antichrist for what he is. Some might think that "he can't be the Antichrist. If he was, I would have been raptured by now."

THE SEVEN TRUMPETS: Living in the end times will be very hard. You'll have the Antichrist running around deceiving and lying and tricking just about everybody, then there is the wrath of God to tend with. The Bible describes three sets of "woes (Revelation 9: 12)." These are seven trumpets (Revelation 8: 6), seven plagues (Revelation 15: 1) and seven bowls of God's wrath (Revelation 16: 1), which will make it rather like hell on earth.

I was taught in the public school system that the dinosaurs were killed off when an asteroid or comet struck the earth. Now I believe in the Bible and that Noah's Flood was probably all started when an asteroid or comet came near the earth and it was in the Flood that the dinosaurs died. The ancient Babylonians say a rogue planet named Nibiru came by long ago and caused all sorts of havoc, but they also say it's coming back in the end times! Could the appearance of a space born object, the cause of Noah's Flood, and its return in the end times be a part of the days of Noah prophecy?

The Book of Revelation seems to indicate this. We're told in Revelation 8: 12 of an object from space, named Wormwood, striking the earth. All the wrath of God's seven trumpets point towards the idea that a comet will hit the earth causing all sorts of destruction, sending smoke up into the sky and blocking out the sun and spoiling the water.

> The first angel sounded his trumpet, and there came hail and fire mixed with blood, and it was hurled down upon the earth... The second angel sounded his trumpet, and something like a huge mountain, all ablaze, was thrown into the sea... The third angel sounded his trumpet, and a great star blazing like a torch, fell from the sky... the name of the star is Wormwood... The fourth angel sounded his trumpet, and a third of the sun was struck, turned dark... The fifth angel sounded its trumpet and I saw a star that had fallen from the sky to the earth. The star was given the key to the shaft of the Abyss. When he opened the Abyss, smoke rose from it...and out of the smoke locusts came down upon the earth... They had a king over them the angel of the Abyss, whose name in Hebrew is Abaddon, and in Greek Apollyon.
> Revelation 8: 7- 9: 11

Apollyon, another name for the Greek god Apollo, who we suspect to be Nimrod, will be freed from the Abyss when the earth is hit by this object from space. Parts of the earth will split open and Nimrod's demon ghost will be free to possess his own genetically preserved and cloned body.

If this is the return of the same object that caused the Flood it would also fulfill the days of Noah prophecy.

FALSE JEWS: In the Bible we're mysteriously told that some of the end time ruling elite will be "those who say they are Jews and are not (Revelation 2: 9, 3: 9)." They will be very rich and they will belong to something called the Synagogue of Satan! The term "synagogue" means a gathering of Jews for the purpose of worship. So, in the end times there will be wealthy men who will be claiming to be Jews, who will actually be worshipping Satan.

There is a Hungarian legend that Nimrod had two sons, Magar and Hunar and that Hunar begat the Huns, most famous of which was Attila the Hun. A group of Huns settled in the region of Khazar. Khazaria was a nation that was forced by their king to convert to Judaism in 740 AD. Those who converted became Jews, in the religious sense, but they were not Jews by blood. They are not Abraham's descendants. These people often refer to themselves as Ashkenazi Jews. There is nothing wrong with being an Ashkenazi Jew! But, like every cultural group, among these good people there may be a few bad apples. Most of the elite families of the world have this familial connection: the Rothschilds and Rockefellers,[16] the Tafts, Morgans, Oppenheimers, DuPonts. There are also the Freeman, Kennedy, Schiff, Astor, Bundy, Collins, Sassoon, and the VanDuyn families just to name a few more (Andrew Hitchcock, *History of the House of Rothschild*).

The Rothschilds are likely the wealthiest family on earth. It is also alleged that they can proudly retrace their lineage to Nimrod himself.[17] According to the prestigious genealogical publication Burke's Peerage, one Rothschild born in 1922 was named Albert Nimrod Rothschild.[18]

Interestingly enough, the Rothschilds were very involved in the process when Israel returned to the Promised Land in 1948, their family symbol can be seen on Israel's national flag, the occult six pointed star. Called the Star of David, it has never had anything to do with old King David. The symbol is made of a triangle pointing down, over a triangle facing up, representing the alchemical adage "as above, so bellow." This is like the Masonic logo with the compass and square, the compass points up while the square points down.

These types all inter breed. Ancient Egyptian gods and royalty certainly did. And many royal families throughout the ages have repeated this pattern to various degrees. Researchers have found that this is a perfect means to exactly reproduce a selected individual's

---

[16] I visited Rockefeller Plaza in Manhattan in 2013 and saw two statues they had erected there, Prometheus who stole fire from heaven and Atlas, the god of the Pre-Flood word.

[17] Joseph P. Farrell, *Babylon's Banksters*, page 288.

[18] *Our Occulted History*, Jim Marrs, page 54

genetics! Egyptian princes usually married half sisters from unrelated mothers, the Pharaoh of course having many wives. In the offspring of such a union, the resulting pair of X and Y chromosomes could make the child an exact match of the original Pharaoh, especially if this pattern followed suit over several generation, then every other generation would see the genetic reproduction of that original Pharaoh. The results of this would be similar to that of cloning.

THE FALL OF FALSE GODS: It seems that after Satan is finally done with, life on the earth will be restored to how it was meant to be, how it was for Adam and Eve in Eden, before the Fall and before the Flood (Revelation 21: 1). The earth was very different before the Flood. The Bible tells us that it did not rain back then (Genesis 2: 6), meaning the barometric pressure was much higher. This is the only way to explain the long necked dinosaurs, their rib cages are too small to house a heart big enough to pump blood up such a long neck, but if the barometric pressure was higher such creatures could live. Because of this our atmosphere may have been more like that on the planet Venus, with a thick vapor canopy. The Bible actually tells us this is so:

> And God said, "Let there be an expanse between the waters to separate water from water." So God made the expanse and separated the water under the expanse from the water above it. And it was so, God called the expanse sky.
> Genesis 1: 6- 8

There was water above the sky! This would explain many things: the inconsistencies with carbon dating, how air bubbles in fossilized tree sap have much higher oxygen content than we are used to, and the extremely old ages people lived to before the Flood. Noah was six-hundred years old when the Flood began. With a water canopy in place what is known as actinic radiation would not hit the earth, the prime cause of aging.

But then some object from the depths of space comes by and things change greatly. The earth was probably knocked off a perpendicular axis; the earth is tilted as we currently spin through space around the sun. The water canopy fell, the oxygen content in the air decreased, the barometric pressure plummeted and the rain fell for the first time.

Plato recorded that the first king of Atlantis was Atlas, of whom the island nation was named (Plato, *Critias,* 114 a). In ancient Greek

imagery he is depicted as holding the world upon his shoulders but
Homer insists that Atlas was actually the deity, the "Pillars,"
responsible for holding up the sky. The Bible tells us that Noah warned
everyone he could that God's wrath had been stirred and destruction
was coming (2Peter 2: 5). So, what did the Atlanteans think when the
sky began to fall with the Flood? Did they realize that Noah's God had
toppled the false god of Atlantis? It would seem that perhaps Noah's
Flood was a direct assault upon the principle god of Atlantis! Did the
Atlanteans recognize that Noah's God was victorious as they panicked
in the chaotic destruction of their world?

Now skip ahead to the time of Moses. When he had his battle with
the pharaoh's magicians God brought about ten plagues. Each one was
a direct assault on the gods of the Egyptians. For example, the serpent
was a primary deity in Egypt, so Moses' rod became a more powerful
serpent that devoured pharaohs. The Nile River was worshipped and it
was seen murdered as it was turned to blood. The sun god Ra died as it
was darkened. Their bull god Apis would have certainly died when the
cattle all succumbed. They worshipped frogs, locusts and flies and were
forbidden to ever kill them, but as these pests invaded how could they
avoid not killing their own gods? These critters were everywhere, in the
cupboards and under the bed covers. In a trip to the market the common
Egyptian would crush and slide about upon dozens of their false gods.
The irony and truth should have been humiliatingly obvious. The final
plague was directed specifically against Osiris, the first born son.

Our God specifically targets false gods that may lead his children
astray. Let's look at the seven trumpets, plagues and bowls of God's
wrath in the end times. These collectively strike one false god we are
all familiar with today: Mother Earth. She was known to the ancient
Greeks as Gaia and to New Agers as the Great Mother Goddess. She
became the god of environmentalists in 1979 when James Lovelock
wrote *Gaia: a New Look at Life on Earth.* Lovelock's *Gaia Hypothesis*
claims that the earth is a living organism with its self-regulating
functions and is threatened only by mankind. She must be nurtured and
loved... even worshipped.

The earth is no god, it is a creation. God, the Creator, will make this
all very clear in the end times.

THE LUCIFERIAN RELIGION IN THE BIBLE: The more I
learned from the Luciferian's own historians, the more easily I could
see their impact on my own life. I do not want to sound paranoid but

they have affected all of us. Even Jesus and his disciples encountered those immersed in Satan's religion.

> You have let go of the commands of God and are holding onto the **traditions of men.**
> Mark 7: 8

In this verse Jesus is scolding a group of Pharisees who had criticized his lack of dedication to their traditions. Jesus always had a hard time dealing with the Pharisees. They were the religious teachers of the day, the holier than thou types. I was always comforted by this, knowing that those who judge you and look down on you are not really God's favorites. But I discovered something else more sinister about this group in the Freemason books I acquired. It turns out these Pharisees' "traditions of men" included secret teachings that really placed them at odds with Jesus. These teachings did not originate from Moses or the Biblical Prophets. Their secret system, known as Kabala, was picked up during the Jew's seventy year captivity in Babylon.

What do the Freemasons have to say about Kabala? It's one of their most closely guarded secrets; it's their meditative route to godhood!

> All truly dogmatic religions have issued from the Kabala and return to it: everything scientific and grand in the religious dreams of the illuminati… is borrowed from the Kabalah; all the Masonic associations owe to it their Secrets and their Symbols.
> Albert Pike, *Morals and Dogma,* pg 744

> The Hermetic science… embodied in certain symbols of the higher Degrees of Freemasonry, may be accurately defined as the Kabalah in active realization of the Magic of Works.
> Albert Pike, *Morals and Dogma,* pg 840

> The Kabalistic doctrine, like Freemasonry, incessantly tends toward spiritual perfection… the Kabala is the key of the occult sciences.
> Albert Pike, *Morals and Dogma,* pg 625, 626

KABALA: Kabala can be spelled in various ways: Cabbala, Cabala, Cabbalah, Kabbala, Kabalah, Qabbala, Qabalah, Qabbalah, etc. The term means "knowledge of the light," which many occultists believe to be an ancient, even pre-Flood, means of attaining enlightenment.

In the East they have the Kundalini, in the West there is Kabala. We'll see that both systems are incredibly similar. The Kabala is key to Scottish Rite Masonry. A female Mason is called a Co-Mason, and the most prolific was Helena Blavatsky, she wrote in her 1888 book *the Secret Doctrine* that Kabala and Masonry are made from the same stuff (page 39). She also admits that Kabala is at the heart of the Luciferian Religion: "the truth, although known to most of the higher Kabalists on the radiant star-god, Lucifer, the Son of the Morning, (is that the) Kabala contains the most complete exposition of the doctrine, including the peculiar version accepted by the Luciferians and other Gnostics (page 238- 239)." Further more, Blavatsky wrote, rather cryptically, that the power behind Kabala is Lucifer himself, "The true and uncompromising Kabalists admit that, for all purposes of Science and philosophy, it is enough that the profane should know that the great magic agent called by the Alchemists the Sidereal Virgin and the Mysterium Magnum is that which the Church calls Lucifer (page 511)."

She goes on to say that the Watchers and the Nephilim gave this teaching to humanity. "The Kabala was first taught by God himself to a select group of Angels who formed a theosophic school in Paradise. After the Fall the Angels most graciously communicated this heavenly doctrine to the disobedient... this shows how the event; of the Sons of God, marrying and imparting the divine Secrets of Heaven to the daughters of men, allegorically told by Enoch and in the sixth chapter of Genesis, was interpreted by the Kabalists (page 284)." Blavatsky claims the Christian Church is merely reading the story of Genesis 6 wrong, that it was all an allegory and that "Lucifer, the light bringer... is a beneficent, generous and powerful god... and the principle of good, not of evil (Helena Blavatsky, *the Secret Doctrine,* page 283)."

In these statements Blavatsky has said that Kabala and Masonry are the same thing, she then admitted Kabala was Luciferian, we must then conclude Freemasonry is Luciferian. She also demonstrates the twisted thought patterns behind their logic. "In the Kabala," she said "the Abstract and Absolute Light is Darkness (Helena Blavatsky, *the Secret Doctrine,* page 37)."

THE ORIGIN OF KABALA: You might be shocked to learn that the Kabala is shared by certain Jewish people and the Freemasons. I certainly was, how did this happen?

Occultists, such as the eminent Freemason, Eliphas Levi, claim that the teachings of Kabala began prior to the Flood, supposedly even with Adam in the Garden of Eden where God is said to have given him the "Mysteries of wisdom." Although I agree that Kabala may have begun before the Flood, it was most certainly not a teaching given by the Creator God. It was more likely delivered by some other being who wishes he were God. This sounds more like the work of Satan.

MacGregor Mathers wrote in 1938's *Kabbalah Unveiled* that the Kabala was the religion of fallen angels and it was known in Egypt where "a portion of this mysterious doctrine oozed out. It was in this way that the Egyptians obtained some knowledge of it... No one, however, dared to write it down, till Schimeon ben Jochai, who lived at the time of the destruction of the second temple. After his death, his son, Rabbi Eleazar composed the celebrated work called the Zohar."

These sources agree that the Kabala was a pre-Flood religion taught by fallen angels, and likely what Nimrod was trying to revive in Babylon. In Adolphe Franck's 1940 book *the Kabbalah* he concluded that the Kabala, as it exists today, originated during the Hebrew's Babylonian captivity where they would have encountered the Mysteries taught directly by the priesthood of the Chaldeans and Magi. They then merged the ancient Babylonian religion with their own. There are statements within the book of Jewish history and lore called the Talmud that support this. They also brought home the names of angels and the means to work with them.

It is ironic that the secret Babylonian form of meditation to "become a god" would survive within the Hebrew community, the very people chosen to destroy it!

Today the Kabala is held as authoritative to many religious Jews, kept alongside the teachings of Moses and the Prophets, but in some cases regarded more highly and therefore its teachings kept secret. Despite this, as of late, many celebrities, such as the pop singer Madonna, have hopped on the band wagon and announced that they have accepted Kabala as their religion. There is a great deal of information now available regarding the subject in bookstores and on-line. This is a sacrilege to the Jewish Kabalists because the only ones allowed to learn it are married men, more than forty years of age who have devoted many years to studying the Talmud. It is within the

Talmud, in the second chapter of Tractate Hagigah, where the teaching protocols are found. There are three main points to Kabala; Biblical interpretation, meditation and magic.

It is believed that by reinterpreting Holy Scripture, twisting it in various ways, the secrets of Kabala can be found, such as the meditative means to follow the "Way of the Serpent up the Sephiroth Tree." We'll see more of this later, but it is nearly identical to the Eastern notion of Kundalini.

THE ZOHAR: Centuries after the Diaspora, when the Romans kicked the Jews out of the Holy Land in 70 AD, exiled Jews brought Kabala's secret lore to Italy in the ninth century. By the year 1200 it appeared in the Rhineland and it was known that the family of Rabbi Judah the Pius was devoted to its secrets. Rumors and superstitions spread claiming that practitioners of this Jewish mysticism had magical powers.

When persecutions in Spain forced the Jews out in 1492 the Kabala could no longer be kept secret, the religion swiftly spread among Europe's alchemists and occultists. It reached its zenith in Spain and exploded across Europe. There was a period where it was a sign of sophistication to have some rudimentary knowledge of such things.

Their holy books are the *Sefer Yetzirah,* the Book of Formation, and the *Zohar,* the Book of Light, which consists of several encyclopedic volumes. The Talmud tells us that while under Roman persecution the Rabbi Schimeon ben Jochai and his son Eleazar fled and lived in a cave for twelve years writing down the teachings which until then had been kept orally, these are likely the traditions Jesus referred to (Mark 7: 8).

THE SEVEN SPHERES: Inside the Zohar we find all the doctrines of the Mysteries. There is the belief in karma, reincarnation, as well as belief in the godlike human soul trapped in the wicked fleshy body, referred to by Kabalists as the "shell." They even give the old Babylonian means to ascend to godhood via the "Seven Heavenly Spheres."

> Above, below…The world below is, in shape and form, the reflection and copy of the world on high… in the invisible world there are seven spheres… six can be apprehended by the human mind and only by those initiated into the highest mysteries… to acquire a state of perfection.
>
> Zohar: Genesis ch17, the Devachanic

The Higher Devachanic tells us that each of the spheres is home to an angel and gives their names. Once equipped with an angel's name the Kabalist can encounter the sphere, harmonize with it and pass through to the next one.

THE WAY OF THE SERPENT: Long ago the Kabalists took the notion of the Seven Heavenly Spheres and reorganized things a bit. The new system is thought of as a tree. The Sephiroth Tree is made up of ten spheres connected by twenty-two channels. Kabalists refer to it as "The Tree of Life" and claim that "man can unite himself with God," and even "reach the magnitude of the Omnipotent God" by "rising through the spheres." The *Sepher Yetzirah* tells us that this system is the secret behind all spiritual works and a means to accelerate human evolution.

This tree obviously bears forbidden fruit. Consider that the method of scaling the Sephiroth tree, passing through the ten spheres, is called *the Way of the Serpent*. Kabalists say that humans can climb this tree by attuning their minds to the specific vibration of each Sephiroth reached. However certain routes may be closed off to individuals because of their sin, which they refer to as *excessive din*. Din is merely *restrictive judgment* which can be eliminated when a person stops feeling judged by it. To a Kabalist, if you do not feel judged or guilt regarding a sin, it is not really a sin. The term sociopathy describes this mind set well. The Bible clearly tells us to stay away from all of this and to "pay no attention to Jewish myths (Titus 1: 14)."

THE GNOSTICS: Few realize it but there are other elements of the Luciferian religion mentioned in the New Testament. The Mysteries existed long before the time of Christ, and Satan's minions were ready to pervert the true gospel immediately after its appearance. Thankfully the apostles were ready to defend the truth.

The Bible records a meeting between Simon, a sorcerer known as the Great Power, and the disciples Peter and John. Simon offers to pay them money to acquire the power of the Holy Spirit (Acts 8: 9- 25). Of course the offer is refused and it is said that Simon's "heart is not right before God" and that he is "full of bitterness and a captive to sin."

There is a sect, known as the Gnostics, whose origin lies in this story. Both Christian and Gnostic sources agree that this mysterious sect did come into existence at this time. They once called themselves a "Christian" denomination and eventually would rise to count one third of the Christian Church as members, rather they were able to deceive one third of the Church.

The Gnostics were definitely not Christians. In accordance with the Mysteries they taught that the Creator did a great evil by imprisoning the spirit of man in the flesh of the body. To the Gnostic, all flesh, and even all physical matter, was evil. The name of their secret teaching that could free mankind from matter was Gnosis.

GNOSTIC GOSPELS: The Gnostics are known today largely for the many false gospels that they had written. Few Christians have taken the time to read them, but these fictitious stories involving Jesus, the apostles and other Biblical personalities actually put forward very evil doctrine. The real apostles were very much aware of the threat and alerted the true Church to it. In the Bible, Paul recorded a warning regarding these writings.

> I am astonished that you are so quickly deserting Christ and are turning to a different gospel, which is really no gospel at all. Evidently some people are throwing you into confusion and are trying to pervert the gospel of Christ. But even if we or an angel from heaven should preach a gospel other than the one we preached to you, let him be eternally condemned... some false brothers had infiltrated our ranks... to make us slaves.
> Galatians 1: 6- 9, 2: 4

John also warned the Church about the Gnostics, primarily for one strange belief they had about Jesus (1John 4: 1- 3). The Gnostics did not believe that Jesus came in the flesh. They had complex theories that explained away his humanity. It has amazed many Biblical scholars that the first and gravest attack on the Christian Church was not an attack on Jesus' divinity, but his humanity.

The Gnostic Gospels say that there was a "Christ Spirit" that overshadowed, or possessed, the man Jesus upon his baptism. They claim that this spirit taught through him and that this same spirit went back up to heaven before Jesus died on the cross. Jesus and the Christ were two different, but for a time symbiotic, entities, according to the Gnostics. At the core of their teaching is the notion that we too may be over shadowed or possessed by a "Christ Spirit" and guided towards godhood ourselves.

And no one shall hinder you in what ye desire and ye shall beget for yourselves aeons, worlds and heavens, in order that the mind-born spirits may come and dwell therein. And ye will be gods.

Untitled Gnostic Apocalypse, Mead,
Fingerprints of a Faith Forgotten,
pg 563

They say the basis for their beliefs is that the "Christ Spirit" returned to earth three days after Jesus died and gave secret teachings to his closest disciples. The teachings this spirit gave were only revealed to certain persons who had *purified and trained their minds* to ready themselves for the awesome presence of this *truth.*

When one reads these false gospels they find that the Gnostic's version of the Christian faith is not about faith at all, it is about experience. A very real experience can occur in the believer who has adequately *trained their minds* to accept the "Christ Spirit's" presence in their own body. This is when testing the spirits becomes very important! John told us: if the spirit denies the Jesus of the Holy Bible, then that spirit is evil and must not be welcomed (1John 4: 1- 3).

Amazingly, many of the Gnostic's false gospels have survived unto today. They were unearthed near Nag Hammadi, Egypt, in 1945. From one called *On the Origin of the World,* we can see the perverse way the Gnostics saw world history.

Death was established over the sixth heaven… then Death, being androgynous, mingled with his own nature and begat seven androgynous offspring… they had intercourse with one another, and each begat seven demons. Their names and their effects you will find in the Book of Solomon (these became the seven *rulers*).

Then came the wisest of all creatures, who was called Beast. And when he saw… Eve he said to her, "What did God say to you? Was it 'do not eat from the tree of gnosis?' …he knows that when you eat of it, your intellect will become sober and you will come to be like gods…" Now Eve had confidence in the words of the instructor… she took some of its fruits and ate it. Then their intellect became open. For when they had eaten, the light of acquaintance had shone upon them.

Then when the rulers knew that they had broken their commandments, they entered Paradise and came to Adam and Eve… "What is this that you have done?" Eve answered and said,

"It is the instructor that urged me on, and I ate.

Then the rulers came up to the instructor. Their eyes became misty because of him, and they could not do anything to him… they were powerless. Thereupon… the rulers were envious of Adam.

Then when Sophia …chased those rulers out of the heavens, and cast them down into the sinful world, so that they should dwell in the form of evil spirits upon the earth… now, when the seven rulers were cast down from their heavens onto the earth, they made for themselves angels, numerous, demonic, to serve them. And the latter instructed mankind in many ways of error and magic and potions and worship of idols and spilling of blood and altars and temples and sacrifices and libations to all the spirits…

When a multitude of human beings had come into existence, through the parentage of the Adam who had been fashioned out of matter, and when the world had already become full, the rulers were masters over it, that is, they kept it restrained by ignorance.

When the blessed beings appeared in forms modeled by authorities, they were envied. And out of envy the authorities mixed their seed with them, in hopes of polluting them.

The craziness of this boggles the mind. God powerless before "the instructor," aka: Satan? Here Satan is a *savior* for bringing the Gnosis which frees mankind from fleshy imprisonment. In this garbage, God is the villain. Remember that this upside-down mindset is the basis of the Luciferian religion. In what the Gnostics refer to as *The Apocryphon of John* is more of the Luciferian dogma and a reverse interpretation of Genesis 6.

But what they call the tree of knowledge of good and evil… it was I who brought about that they ate.

And I said unto the Savior, "Lord, was it not the serpent that taught Adam to eat?"

The Savior smiled and said, "The serpent taught them… and made him more correct in his thinking than the chief archon (the Creator God)… they have tasted the perfect Knowledge… the pure light, that I might teach them and awaken them out of the depth of sleep. For they were both in a fallen state.

And when Yaldaboath (the Creator God) noticed they withdrew

from him, he cursed his earth. He found the woman as she was preparing herself for her husband… and the chief archon seduced her and begot in her two sons … Cain and Abel.

He (the creator God) made a plan… He sent his angels to the daughters of men, that they might take some of them for themselves and raise offspring for their enjoyment… and the angels changed themselves in their likeness into the likeness of their husbands… and they steered the people who had followed them into great troubles, by leading them astray with many deceptions… and thus the whole creation became enslaved forever, from the foundation of the world unto now. And they took women and begot children.

Apocryphon of John, 22- 24, 28- 30

In the Luciferian version, God the Creator is the one who had sex with human women, and the "Savior" has freed mankind via the Tree of the Knowledge of Good and Evil. All is opposite in this Satanic and deceptive world, good is evil, and evil is good.

Because of these "gospels" many meetings of the early Christians fell into debates as to what believers should in fact believe. Lies were creeping into the Church and taking hold in the vulnerable minds of new Christian believers. For the Apostles this became one of their major enemies, this was the one that had infiltrated the Church, the enemy within.

HERMES AND THE GNOSTICS: Even from a quick examination of Gnostic beliefs we find that they were much more related to the Mystery teachings than those of Christ.

When the Gnostic documents were found near Nag Hammadi, other writings were among them. From these we will see a great deal about the character of Gnosticism, and see some of the secret history behind the Masons and allied Luciferian societies. The Greek philosophers were represented in the Nag Hammadi books, like Plato, himself a student of the Mysteries, but we also find here the works of Hermes Trismegistus.

Who was this Hermes?

We can tell he was regarded as somebody special, his name Trismegistus means "three times greatest." The Greeks knew Hermes as the messenger of the gods. He could cross between the lands of life and death to relay messages between the gods and mortal man. The

Greeks tell us that Hermes was their take on the Egyptian god Thoth, the scribe of the gods. Both of them have a similar task, relaying written messages.

Interestingly, the Greek name Hermes means "Son-of-Ham." Noah had a son named Ham! Who was the son-of-Ham?

Ham's son was Cush (Genesis 10: 6).

Cush was the one who built and ruled Babylon alongside Nimrod! So the name Hermes, the *son of Ham*, may well be an alias for Cush!

We've seen how different cultures have Flood legends and different cultures have legends of hybrid giants. We've seen different gods who've died and arose from the grave. We've seen Nimrod's wife and even versions of Lucifer in different cultures. Now we're seeing different versions of Nimrod's step-father, Cush. He was Hermes to the Greeks and Thoth to the Egyptians. In Richard Carlyon's *Guide to the Gods*, he has written regarding Thoth that he is the:

> …great god of wisdom, magic, medicine, astronomy, geometry and writing… He invented all the arts and sciences. His followers said that Thoth had certain books which contained all magic and all knowledge. Not without reason was Thoth called 'Thrice Greatest.' He was responsible for measuring time, historian and scribe. Thoth was called Hermes by the Greeks and is the original of Hermes Trismegistus ('thrice greatest Hermes'), the mystical figure behind many an arcane school of celestial philosophy; and for those who know, the god was the originator of the Four Laws of Magic.

HERMETICS: Cush/Thoth/Hermes wrote 42 books which came to be known among the ancient Greeks as *the Corpus Hermeticum*. Only fragments of 17 of them have openly survived to this day.

These books may be what Cush copied directly off of the Great Pyramid!

When the Graeco-Egyptian city of Alexandria was burned, the great Egyptian archives and libraries that would have surely kept these works were destroyed. Traces of the *Corpus Hermeticum* survive inscribed in the hieroglyphs on the crumbling walls of the 5000 year old Saqqara Temple in Egypt, however. Some Westerners would later rename this lost volume *The Necronomicon* and there have been many faked versions as well, but we are assured by the prominent Freemason Manly P. Hall that the book has been handed down over generations, kept within certain Luciferian families and exists to this day safe and sound.

> While Hermes walked the earth with men, he entrusted to his chosen successors the sacred Book of Thoth. This work contained the secret processes by which the generation of humanity was to be accomplished and also served as the key to his other writings. Nothing definite is known concerning the contents of the Book of Thoth other than its pages were covered with strange hieroglyphic figures and symbols, which gave to those acquainted with their use unlimited power over the spirits of the air and the subterranean divinities. When certain areas of the brain are stimulated by the secret processes of the Mysteries, the consciousness of man is extended and he is permitted to behold the Immortals and enter into the presence of the superior gods. The Book of Thoth described the method whereby this stimulation was accomplished. The book is still in existence and continues to lead the disciples of this age into the presence of the Immortals. No other information can be given to the world concerning it now, but the apostolic succession from the first hierophant initiated by Hermes himself remains unbroken to this day.
>
> Manly P. Hall, *the Secret Teachings of All Ages,* pg 96, 97

Hall admits that it is by a *stimulating of the mind* that they commune with the *spirits of the air*. This is the meditative mind training taught at the first Mystery schools. The most important section of the Corpus Hermeticum is *the Divine Pymander*. This was the section found with the Gnostic library at Nag Hammadi. Hall paraphrases it to show how Cush/Hermes stimulated his mind and met the spirits of the air, to receive teachings from Lucifer himself!

> Hermes, while wandering in a rocky and desolate place, gave himself over to meditation and prayer. Following the secret instructions of the Temple, he gradually freed his higher consciousness from the bondage of his bodily senses; and, thus released, his divine nature revealed to him the mysteries of the transcendental spheres. He beheld a figure, terrible and awe inspiring. It was the Great Dragon, with wings stretching across the

sky and light streaming in all directions from its body... pulsating radiance. The Light was the spiritual nature of the Great Dragon itself... Hermes beheld the spirits of the stars, the celestials controlling the universe, and all those powers which shine with the radiance of the One Fire... (The Dragon spoke) "Those who are saved by the light of the mystery which I have revealed unto you, O Hermes, and which I now bid you to establish among men... shall deliver themselves up to the Light... and they shall become Powers in God... establish my Mysteries... for I am the Mind of the Mysteries." ...Hermes commanded his disciples to preserve his doctrines inviolate throughout all ages.

> Vision of Poimandres, *the Divine*
> *Pymander,* Manly P. Hall translation.
> *The Secret Teachings of All Ages*

Cush practiced what he read from "the Temple," likely the Great Pyramid. He meditated on the seven "transcendental spheres." He trained his mind and he encountered the *spirits of the stars*, and then the Dragon appeared; that serpent from Eden.

Occultists know that among nearly all the ancient peoples, the serpent was regarded as the symbol of wisdom and salvation. It is only among the Judeo- Christians that the serpent stands to been seen as the exact opposite, being the revealer of suffering, beginning at the Garden of Eden. It is because of this that a true savior was required. Gnostic proponents Timothy Freke and Peter Candy reveal in the commentary to their 1997 book *The Hermetica* that the basis of these Hermetic teachings is the same lie told to Eve in Eden, stating:

> Hermes declares that "man is a marvel." With his mind he may not only understand the universe, but even come to know God. He is not a mortal body which will live and die. He is an immortal soul which, through the experience of spiritual rebirth may become a god.

The Poimandres describes the incident where Cush first met up with Lucifer himself. Now, why would the Gnostics embrace this if they were truly a Christian denomination? Willis Barnstone published many of the Gnostic's gospels in a book entitled *The Other Bible*. He writes about the Gnostic's association with the Hermetic *Poimandres* that:

Hermes Trismegistus… the Poimandres is a prime source of Gnostic speculation. The speaker in the Socratic dialogue, Poimandres, proposes a severely dualistic view of life in which the body represents everything dark, deceptive, temporal, and mortal while the mind represents truth, light, timelessness and eternal salvation. The purpose of life is to free the soul from the prison of the body through gnosis, which is knowledge and enlightenment, and to return to the heavenly realm of light. So one leaves the physical universe by embarking on a celestial journey, through seven levels of spirituality, until one comes to the Father of All. There one becomes God.

> Willis Barnstone, *the Other Bible,*
> pg 568

So here we can conclude that the core ideas of the two religions, Gnostic and Hermetic, are indeed one in the same: that of the Luciferian Mysteries. The Gnostics taught the secrets of Hermes by which godhood could be attained. They all believed that the body and flesh are evil and the soul must be set free by a secret method. These religions are dualistic, erroneously believing that the powers of good and evil are equal and opposed against one another.

The Gnostics also subscribed to many other pagan ideas, they renamed the angels as *archons* or *aeons,* and they openly taught that there was a feminine, mother goddess, aspect to God, which they named Sophia. Sex magic, meditation and astral projection (out of body experiences) frequently accompany Gnostic dogma in the past as well as today. Since the discovery of the Nag Hammadi library in 1945, the Gnostic cult has made quite a return.

SOPHIA IS LUCIFER: Plato, the Greek philosopher, played a huge role in planting the foundations of Gnosticism, he even coined the term "Gnostikoi" centuries prior, a word meaning "divinely inspired knowledge." Plato's teacher was Socrates and he had an invisible spirit guide they called a daimon, ie: a demon. In conversing with this demon they would receive its "divinely inspired knowledge," or Gnosis.

Both Socrates and Plato are considered the great philosophers. The root of the word "philosophy" is *sophia,* meaning "wisdom." Sophia is the most important Gnostic god. Although often portrayed as a female, she is actually androgynous, having both male and female body parts.

She is said to be an "emanation of Light" that fell from the heavenly realms for wanting to be a creator herself. She is also portrayed in the Gnostic gospels as a *destroyer.*

As mentioned earlier, an important part of the Gnostic faith is dualism. Everything has two equal and opposite sides. They believe their androgynous god at one time divided into two, becoming a male and a female. The thought was that male and female must reunite into *One* in order for creation to manifest.

They teach that the first human was like this as well. He was named Adam- Kadmon and had both sets of sexual organs. When he metaphorically had a rib removed from his side, he divided and the female, Eve, came into being. Now when the two halves, male and female, unite a pregnancy and new life is created. But the initiated Gnostics took it further. They taught that through strange sexual practices the participants could be restored, made whole again and godlike. They had strange rituals referred to as sex-magic and Sophia was the patron of this.

What do the Gnostic Gospels themselves have to say of Sophia? In the *Trimorphic Protennoia* she claims to have been the first emanation, the first born of the angels. Lucifer is said to be the first of the angels God created. In the *Hypostasis of the Archons* it says: "Then the female spiritual principle came in the snake, the instructor; and taught them saying "What did he say to you? Was it, from every tree in the garden you shall eat; yet from the tree of recognizing good and evil do not eat?" Sophia was the deceiving serpent in Eden! Sophia supposedly became man's true savior when she brought humanity secret teachings to escape the flesh.

Accordingly, the serpent was a frequent fixture within many of the old Gnostic Churches and it seems was at times readily worshipped and referred to as Ophis. Snakes even crawled over the bread of the Lord's Supper. They believed that Sophia sent this holy serpent to free Adam and Eve from God! In their churches they worshipped the idol of Nahustan, a brazen serpent. Church Father Hippolytus wrote that the Gnostics were known in North Africa as the Naaseni, meaning "Serpents."

Epiphanius of Salamis (315- 403 AD) was a Father of the Church who managed to infiltrate the Gnostics and write the *Panarion,* a report of what he had discovered. He tells us that the Gnostics associated the human spine with the serpent and believed that the serpent energies of

Sophia could be persuaded via sex magic to travel upward bringing the initiate illumination. This is very similar to the Eastern system of Tanta.

GNOSTIC MASONRY: As mentioned earlier, Freemasonry and Gnosticism are closely related. Of the Gnostics, Albert Pike tells us in *Morals and Dogma* that there are Gnostic Mysteries and initiation (pg 542), Gnostics worked with the seven Planetary Spirits (pg 254, 255), and that Gnosticism originated with the Kabalists who acquired it as Jews in Babylonian exile (pg 626).

Upon reading *Morals and Dogma* it is easy to see that Freemasonry is dependant upon the teachings of Hermes, Gnosticism and Kabala. Co-Mason Helena Blavatsky also wrote of this in her 1877 book, *Isis Unveiled*. Keep in mind these two wrote long before the Gnostic Gospels were re-discovered. Blavatsky tells us how Jewish Mystery schools, Kabalists, tried to popularize themselves by combining the new teachings of Jesus with their own Luciferian religion, calling it Gnosticism. They believed that Jesus was a normal man, who had merely followed their teaching and fully united himself with the higher spiritual powers, thus becoming overshadowed or possessed. The Gnostics also taught that all people have the potential to do so:

> The Gnostics maintain that Jesus was a man overshadowed... it is from Ephesus that nearly all the Gnosis spread... in Ephesus that flourished in those days the greater college, wherein the abstruse Oriental speculations... were taught in conjunction... the quintessence of Buddhist, Zoroastrian and Chaldean philosophy... which proved to be the hotbed of all the Kabalistic speculations... This is pure Buddhist doctrine. The religion of Gnosis... godlike beings as Gautama Buddha, Jesus, Lao-Tzu, Krishna, and a few others had united themselves with their spirits permanently, hence they became gods on earth... this Wisdom was the Source of Light... from **this eternal and infinite light, which to us is darkness...** preserved a common likeness to one prototype. This parent cult was none other than the primitive "Wisdom Religion..." the Kabala has survived... (despite) Christianity... a most cruel, fiendish superstition.
>
> Helena Blavatsky, *Isis Unveiled*

In the Luciferian's own writings they often refer to themselves as Gnostics. The two words are often interchangable and seem to have the same meaning. Albert Mackey fully admitted in *the Encyclopaedia of Freemasonry* that the famous letter 'G,' often seen in the Mason's square and compass symbol, actually stands for Gnosticism!

DUALISM: Like the Luciferians, the Gnostics see the Creator as evil and the Serpent as good. They also think that both are equal is strength and power. This aspect of *Dualism* underlies all pagan belief systems, the notion that good and evil are perfectly balanced, that light is equal to darkness, that Satan is equal to God. This is a lie. It only takes a little bit of light to dispel a great deal of darkness. Satan is by far inferior to God. Satan is also inferior to Jesus Christ. Satan's equal, many feel, may be the Archangel Michael. Never-the-less, every occult philosophy portrays their god Lucifer as equal with the true God, who, in their lustful minds, is a real party-pooper.

Along with dualism goes the notion that an individual should remain in perfect balance, which often means that every blessing should include a curse, and every act of benevolence should be followed by one of malice!

The Gnostics had a symbol for this kind of dualism, a two headed bird known as Abraxas. Abraxas, like Sophia was androgynous, having both a male head and a female head on one spine. Recall the spinal/serpent energies of the Kundalini; there were two snakes, the female Ida and male Pingala, which together formed a double helix similar to the caduceus with its two heads. The ancient Babylonians had an identical feathered creature represent their god of money and forces, Mammon-Ra. The Russian Romanov Dynasty had a black two headed phoenix as their symbol which is still seen in Soviet motifs. The wealthy Rothschilds have it on their family crest. Albert Pike's *Morals and Dogma* has it on the cover; along with the Latin phrase *Ordo Ab Chao.* What does this all mean?

The famous magic word Abracadabra literally means the cadaver, or corpse, of Abraxas. Do some wait for it to arise from the ashes like the legendary phoenix?

We are now going to look at one of the most import aspects of Luciferism, their mindset. How can people exist in society with backward notions such as up is down, black is white, deceit is truth, and ultimately; good is evil and evil is good?

The two headed Abraxas, in part, represents this double-mindedness. The Luciferians refer to this mind trick as "reconciling opposites." It is taught from birth. Perhaps this is why certain politicians can lie so easily, they can believe in the opposite of what they are saying, to them the lie is true and the truth is the lie. Most can even pass lie detector tests; their belief is that strong. No one has demonstrated this concept better than George Orwell in his book *Nineteen Eighty- Four*. Orwell was brought up among the wealthy elite, learned their secrets and wrote a story in which the main character is trapped among those who model this bewildering Luciferian mindset.

Consider how the floors of Masonic Temples are always covered in alternating black and white tiles, checker-board style. Look at the Yin and Yang symbol, and the alchemical slogan "as above, so bellow," these all model the concept of reconciling opposites. The Latin phrase on *Morals and Dogma* "Ordo Ab Chao" takes it even further. It means "Order out of Chaos."

This refers to the Hegelian Dialectic which is an old form of population control. World's manipulators will stir up all kinds of wars, turmoil and chaos, with the average everyday people dying en masse. When the populations are exhausted and fearful from constant war, poverty and disease, they will happily accept slavery to any system that offers them relief. A population happy with slavery? A disgusting and unthinkable notion to you and me, but this kind of control and social engineering is a science to the power hungry. This is called the Royal Secret of Freemasonry! Albert Pike discusses the concept and refers to the reconciling of opposites under the Kabalistic terms "Mystery of Balance" and "Secret of Universal Equilibrium." Let's read from the very last sentences of *Morals and Dogma:*

> The Royal Secret of which you are Prince is that which the Zohar terms The Mystery of the Balance. It is the Secret of Universal Equilibrium... Of that Equilibrium between Good and Evil, and Light and Darkness in the world, which assures us that all is the work of the Infinite Wisdom and that there is no rebellious demon or Evil, ...by attaining to the knowledge of which equilibrium we can see that the existence of Evil, Sin, Suffering, and Sorrow in the world, is consistent with Infinite Goodness.
>
> And, finally, of that Equilibrium, possible in ourselves, and which Masonry incessantly labors to accomplish in its Initiates... proves to us that our (sinful) Appetites and Senses also are Forces given unto us by God... and not the fruits of the malignancy of a Devil, to be detested, mortified, and, if possible, rendered inert and

dead: that they are given to us to be the means by which we shall be strengthened and incited… to be controlled and… to be made useful instruments and servants. Such my Brother is the true ROYAL SECRET, which shall at length make real, the HOLY EMPIRE of the true Masonic Brotherhood.
GLORIA DEI EST CELARE VERBUM. AMEN.
Albert Pike, *Morals and Dogma,*
pgs 858- 861

This Holy Empire of the Masonic Brotherhood is their long awaited New World Order, which will be established out of the chaos they will send forth. This will be the kingdom of the Antichrist.

THE APOSTLE'S CREED: The early Christians clearly understood the threat posed by the Gnostic's. To combat this, the Apostles started to define which scriptures should make up the New Testament. Next, they designed a creed, or a statement of beliefs, that the Gnostics, those who *appeared* on the surface to be Christian, and many members believed themselves to indeed be Christian, could not agree with or repeat. They had made vows upon their very lives to be true to the Gnostic's secrets. Most of the Gnostics were so deceived they felt they were doing right. The Church had to rid itself of this malignant teaching before others could be deceived, hence the Apostle's Creed. It was recited by believers upon their baptism.

THE APOSTLE'S CREED
I believe in God the Father Almighty; Maker of Heaven and earth;
And in Jesus Christ, His only son, our Lord;
Who was conceived by the Holy Ghost, born of the Virgin Mary;
Suffered under Pontius Pilate, was crucified, dead and buried;
He, descended into hell, the third day He rose again from the dead;
He ascended into heaven,
sitteth at the right hand of God the Father Almighty;
From thence He shall come to judge the quick and the dead;
I believe in the Holy Ghost, the Holy Church;
The communion of saints, the forgiveness of sins;
The resurrection of the body; Life everlasting.
Amen.

**CHAPTER EIGHT
THE PARANORMAL CONNECTION**

Everyone knows we experience this world through our five senses: seeing, smelling, tasting, touching and hearing.

We also know there are many dimensions to this existence. All objects have length, width and height: three dimensions. Everything exists in the dimension of time as well, thus making four dimensions we can easily recognize. But few know that there is mathematical evidence for many more than four dimensions! It would seem we live among parallel worlds that are beyond our senses.

Is it in these strange places that God and the angels dwell? Can they see us while we are unaware? Many Bible stories talk about angels moving in and out of our world at will. These could also be the realms that demons and fallen angels dwell in as well. Since prophecy indicates that these deceptive beings will be busy in the end times, we'd be well off to know something of their nature.

Like most fans of science fiction I've been curious of paranormal things like Bigfoot, swamp monsters, UFOs and the like. For centuries many credible people have reported experiencing incredible things! What can we make of this? Once you remove the hoaxes and frauds and just plain mistaken perceptions, plenty of evidence remains that something strange is happening. When considering such things I chose to use the one true guide and textbook of the paranormal: the Holy Bible.

I've realized something very important about the paranormal. The first I noticed a few years ago when reading the report of a local girl, in her early twenties, who saw a hairy giant beast in the forest not far from my home. The natives have legends of such a creature called a Wendigo. What stood out the most in her story was the absolute, stark terror and fear she felt in the creature's presence. It seemed to grip her very soul. I came to realize that this same thing happens to most people who've had similar encounters, whether they're with ghosts or UFOs.

Along with this terror, I noticed, as well as many paranormal researchers, that Bible believing Christians simply do not have paranormal experiences! Can someone explain to me why aliens and other strange creatures discriminate against people of a certain religion? It has also been frequently noted that when someone is accosted by a paranormal entity that the assault stops instantly when a prayer or plea is made to Jesus!

Let's consider what the Bible has to say about the paranormal. Christians would be foolish to dismiss this subject outright because we are told that angels and demons do exist. The Bible tells us that they have affected our world and since it is clear that God's angels do not mess around deceiving people and the fallen ones do, we must conclude there is a satanic nature to these things. Whatever the paranormal experience, beasts in the forest with red glowing eyes, the Loch Ness Monster, alien astronauts, or balls of light, they all stem from the same source. Some of the brightest minds who've researched the paranormal have concluded that these entities, no matter which façade they present, have an agenda!

JOHN DEE: Outside of the Luciferian families and secret societies there have been a few who have gone it alone and tried to find forbidden secret knowledge. Some of these men succeeded, at the cost of their lives, in opening doors that should never be approached. Paranormal experiences can be brought on, by coveting a desire for their contact, they will come. No matter the mask the entity chooses to wear, they can be summoned.

John Dee was born in London, England, in 1527. He was a brilliant mathematician who worked for the Monarchy from Henry VIII to Queen Elizabeth. A lifelong friendship formed between him and Elizabeth, even as a young princess she was very fond of examining Dee's extensive library and discussing life's curiosities with him.

At the age of 37, while meditating, he entered a trance-like state. Over the next twelve days he would write what the spirits told him, creating a work he entitled *the Hieroglyphic Monad.* In 1581, while following the Hieroglyphic Monad's instructions he came into contact with a mysterious ball of light. That light identified itself as an angel and taught Dee how to communicate further.

The method Dee was to use was called "scrying." Meaning he would enter a trance like state by gazing into a shiny crystal or other reflective object. Dee kept careful records of his experiments. These tell us that his own attempts at scrying were not very successful which led him to use others for the actual crystal gazing. He would ask questions of the angels and document what those under his employ would see. Due to the rather creepy nature of Dee's work he went through many such assistants. After a while Dee came to acquire the services of Edward Kelley. Dee's diary tells us that Kelley was a colorful, yet highly unpredictable character, who bordered between charming and violent. Together they raised many spiritual beings. Hundreds are recorded in Dee's own magical diaries, the *Mysteriorum Libri Quinque*. Like most pagans, Dee really believed that if he could just learn the name of a spirit he could control it. Kelley was not afraid to tell Dee that he thought the beings they were conjuring were in fact "devils in disguise," but Dee was resilient that the angels they worked with were good and holy.

John Dee documented that the angels told him of their history that "in the same instant when Adam was expelled, the Lord gave unto the world her time, and placed over her Angelic Keepers, Watchmen and Princes." The angels told Dee that these "Watchmen" were holy guardian angels sent by God to watch over mankind.

Around that time Dee found in *the Zohar,* the sacred books of the Kabala, that there was once a book written by Enoch. Dee desperately set out to discover a copy. Failing to find any, he tried another method, he petitioned his angels to dictate a copy to him.

The angels never gave Dee the *Book of Enoch.* They gave him something else, a volume known as the *Liber Logaeth.* To do this, these spirits first taught them their language, first known to Dee as *Angelic,* then later, *Enochian.* The angels claimed that this was the original language of Adam and Eve spoken before the Flood. The Liber Logaeth consisted of forty-nine calls to make when summoning the Watchers.

Using the calls, Dee's angels correctly predicted the attack of the Spanish Armada and the execution of Mary Queen of Scots. Leaders from many lands began calling upon Dee to look into the future for them, such as Lasky Rudolf, emperor of Germany. The angels predicted great things for Lasky; that he would become a great hero king over many lands, but this never came to be. The angels caused a faire deal of frustration and embarrassment for Dee. They were unpredictable and couldn't be trusted.

What happened next totally shattered Dee's impression of the angels. Through Kelley, the angels told Dee that the two men were to swap wives. Kelley's reaction to this was complete anger and he now became more insistent than ever that these entities were in fact devils. The wives "disliked utterly this last doctrine," but Dee insisted they commit the act, believing that this was a test of faith and that breakthroughs were soon immanent.

Afterwards the angel's behavior changed, their messages were filled with filthy and perverted talk. Poltergeist phenomenon began to occur, and ultimately a physical attack by the angels!

> There appeared a great flame of fire in the (scrying) Stone... Suddenly one (angel) seemed to come in at the fourth (floor) window of the Chapel... the stone was heaved up a handful high and set down again. The one at the window seemed... with spread-abread arms to come to E.K. (Edward Kelley), at which sight, he shrieked back somewhat, and then that Creature took up between both his hands the stone and the frame of gold, and mounted up away as he came. E.K. catched at it, but he could not touch it... E.K. was in a great fear and trembling and had tremorem cordis (heart palpitations)... but I was very glad and well pleased.

Kelley was so terrified he left Britain and never saw Dee again. Shortly thereafter Dee was forced out of Britain by the Church. This was a hard time for Dee; his contact with spiritual entities led him to complete ruin. In the public, the popular play by Christopher Marlow, *Dr. Faustus,* was a sharp satire and mockery of the aging wizard.

Later, in 1595, Dee returned to England after things had died down. Queen Elizabeth appointed him to the prestigious role as Warden of Christ's College in Manchester. Elizabeth ordered that Dee was free to continue his magical experiments and funded his research. Dee always kept strict diaries of all his endeavors. All of them exist to this day, except for the ones from this period. It is believed by some that they were intentionally destroyed immediately after Dee's death because Elizabeth was in fact taking part in the rituals at Dee's side.

MISTER CROWLEY: The Hermetic Order of the Golden Dawn was a secret society who continued with the works of John Dee. A leading member and 33rd degree Freemason[19] was Aleister Crowley, later dubbed "the Wickedest Man Alive." He was once expelled from

---

[19] Lawrence Sutin, *Do What Thou Wilt, A Life of Aleister Crowley,* pg 83.

Italy by the dictator Mussolini for an apparent murder which may in fact have been a child sacrifice during a magical ritual. Crowley, who would later refer to himself as "the Beast," built upon Dee's work hoping to realize the epitome of all magical workings, to summon the Watchers.

He kept precise diaries of all his efforts. He celebrated his honeymoon in November 1903, performing rituals in the King's Chamber of the Great Pyramid. A few months later, in February 1904, his wife and he would return for further rituals which would result in her receiving the abilities of a medium. Speaking through his wife Rose Kelly, whom he referred to as his "Scarlet Woman," a name he took from Revelation 17: 3, was a being named Aiwass, pronounced "I was," who declared that a New Age was dawning and that Crowley was to be its prophet. Aiwass commanded him to turn their rented Cairo flat into a temple and to follow a specific ritual. On April 8, 9, and 10 Aiwass dictated the *Book of the Law* to Crowley. The *Book of the Law* spoke of the coming Antichrist as a "living being in form resembling man, and possessing those qualities of man which distinguish him from beasts, namely intellect and the power of speech, but neither begotten in the manner of human generation, nor inhabited by a human soul." Crowley referred to this being as a "Moonchild," a magical child "greater than all the kings of the earth."

On July 28, Crowley's first daughter was born, named Nuit Lilith. Little Nuit died in June 1906. Rose and Crowley would later separate, Rose was declared mentally ill and institutionalized. She would be easily replaced, however, as there would be at least ten more Scarlet Women in Crowley's life, all participants in the rituals.

By 1914 Crowley had Left the Golden Dawn and formed a new secret society, the Ordo Templi Orientis (O.T.O.), where he was absolute overlord. The directions for the IX degree, instructions entitled *On the Homuculus,* were the rites to bring about the Moonchild. The premise was to calculate the correct astrological positioning of the temple and precise timing for the rituals to conceive a nonhuman hybrid child. In 1917 he wrote the fictional novel *Moonchild* which describes, under the veil of fiction, the means to bring about the desired event. From an examination of Crowley's ample records, he never succeeded in attaining the desired union between angel and human. But in 1918 Crowley did succeed when he summoned a physical manifestation of the being known as Lam. A drawing Crowley made of this entity appears exactly as the typical grey alien of modern UFO lore. Crowley's successor as head of the O.T.O, wrote that "Lam is a Great Old One whose archetype is recognizable in accounts of UFO occupants." Another O.T.O. member, Micheal Bertiaux, said Lam[20] was a "subterranean burgeoning of Luciferian Gnosis."

Crowley tells us that Aiwass, who dictated the *Book of the Law* was actually the spirit of Horus, aka: Nimrod, and he has some very disturbing things to say.

> I am the secret serpent coiled about to spring... Get the stele of revealing itself; set it in thy secret temple and that temple is already aright disposed... Sacrifice cattle, little and big: after a child.
> That stele they shall call the Abomination of Desolation... the best blood is of the moon, monthly: then the fresh blood of a child... There cometh a rich man from the West who shall pour his gold upon thee... with my Hawk's head I peck at the eyes of Jesus as he hangs upon the cross.
> Aleister Crowley, *Book of the Law*

Albert Pike says Horus is "the Master of Life" and is present as a symbol in every Masonic Lodge (*Morals and Dogma*, pg 13).

JACK PARSONS: One of Crowley's followers in the O.T.O. was Jack Parsons, a brilliant rocket scientist and co-founder of Jet Propulsion Laboratories (JPL). It would not be an understatement to say that without Parsons, NASA and the current space program would not exist. Crowley was so impressed by Parsons, he made him head of the Agape O.T.O. Californian Lodge in 1942. Parsons took it upon himself to advance upon the work of all his predecessors. He attempted to summon angels to mate with a woman in order to sire a Moonchild. Parsons had an assistant and scribe named L. Ron Hubbard, who later became famous himself for starting the Scientology cult. Parsons carefully documented all his magical workings, and on January 4 through to 15, 1946, they followed Crowley's path with a magical project they called the "Babylon Working." The first phase was to

---

[20] An interesting thing occurred as I was writing this. A typo occurred. I did not capitalize the letter "L." We know that the small letter "L" appears as a capital "I" and the name Lam appeared "I am." The first spirit being Crowley encountered was named Aiwass (I was), then he met Lam, (I am). Who will be next, Iwillbe?

summon the angels using the Enochian calls to help them find a "Scarlet Woman" whose womb they could use. As an added spin they hoped the female would be possessed.

On January 18 Parsons suddenly declared "It is done!" He raced home from the Mojave Desert, where he and Hubbard had been engaged in occult rituals, to mysteriously find a woman named Marjorie Cameron waiting for him at his house. She was a redhead with green eyes, as most of Crowley's women were.

Parsons built a temple with an altar and on March 2, 1946, in a hooded black robe, dagger and chalice, he covered the altar with his own blood. He took Cameron on the altar and later wrote to Crowley that the Babylon working had been successful.

Crowley wrote to Karl Germe, of the Agape O.T.O. Lodge, that "Apparently Parsons or Hubbard or somebody is producing a Moonchild. I get fairly frantic when I contemplate the idiocy of these louts." Parsons does not seem to have succeeded in his quest to bring about the Antichrist, but perhaps he did succeed in unleashing something else. Recall that Crowley had once inadvertently summoned the "grey alien" Lam? Well, during the time of Parson's experiments the first modern UFO sighting by Kenneth Arnold occurred on June 24, 1947, over the Cascade Mountains of Washington State and later on July 4th a UFO crashed near Roswel New Mexico. Did Parsons inadvertently tear open the space time continuum and bring about an invasion of these entities? Is this the end time's return of the Watchers, unleashed by men such as John Dee, Crowley and Parsons?

From this point onward, Parsons' life and career are seen to spiral out of control. He invented and took the oath of Antichrist in 1948, afterwards insisting that he be only referred to as "Antichrist." He even wrote a book entitled *The Book of Antichrist*. Parsons was investigated by the FBI for his odd behavior and soon after fired from JPL which required top security clearance. Adding insult to injury, Hubbard cheated Parsons out of a large sum of money they had invested in a company and ran off with Parson's girl. Parsons died at the age of 37 in a mysterious lab explosion.

ROSWEL'S SATANIC CONNECTION: On the 4th of July 1947, a flying saucer supposedly crashed near Roswell, New Mexico. This is the most famous and talked about UFO encounter in history. Is there any evidence that the Roswell incident is related to Satan and his fallen angels?

When we make maps or measurements of the earth, we utilize a precise system of grids. This network uses imaginary lines known as Longitude and Latitude. There are 360 up and down, vertical lines of Latitude dividing the earth. At present, the *Zero* or Prime Meridian, aka: the International Date Line, passes through Greenwich Village. Greenwich Village has not always been the location of the Prime Meridian. It was originally located running through Paris, France. There has actually been a long standing rivalry between the two, many debating which would be a better location to measure "zero" from on the earth. Henry Lincoln, in his book *The Holy Place,* sides with the Parisian faction. He claims there are many esoteric reasons that the line should be there and that many ancient and sacred pagan sites are located along the line. Surprisingly, the Parisian line was once known as "The Devil's Line," "The Sinister Axis," "The Rose Line," and "the Masonic Axis."

If we look at the world under this system of measurement, we see that the location described in the Book of Enoch where the first fallen angels came to earth, Mount Hermon, in ancient Phoenicia, is situated at exactly 33.33 degrees north and 33.33 degrees east. Mount Hermon is exactly 2012 miles from the equator and 2012 miles from the Parisian Prime Meridian. Can this be just a coincidence?

Occultists will instantly see the numerological significance of these numbers. Thirty-three is a sacred number, thirty-three percent is one third and we know that one third of the angels fell from heaven (Revelation 12: 4). Also, in Elizabeth Van Buren's book *The Secret of the Illuminati,* she reveals that "In Spiritual Numerology, 33 symbolizes the highest spiritual conscious attainable by the human being." 33 is a code for the godhood that followers of Lucifer seek to attain. There are thirty-three vertebrae in the human spine and there are 33 degrees to Scottish Rite Masonry.

There is significance to the name of the land *Phoenicia* as well. It was named after the mythical phoenix, the bird that was consumed by fire but was destined to rise again from the ashes, just as we expect the Antichrist to do.

But what does any of this have to do with Roswell?

The impact crater of the flying saucer, on the Brazell farm near Roswell, is located at precisely 33.33 degrees north Latitude, 2012 miles from the equator. This might be a coincidence. Especially if one was to argue that the remaining line of Longitude here is 104 degrees and does not fit the pattern. But then I could point out that if we take 33.33 degrees and multiply it by the universal constant of Pi (3.1415926571...) the result is 104!

The Roswell incident, where humans first came into publicized contact with aliens was a sign. These aliens are the same entities as the Watchers who came down millennia ago on Mount Hermon. The Watchers alerted their followers in 1947 to the fact that they are back to complete their mission.

The Luciferians always give some sign of their presence, always.

CHARACTERISTICS OF ANGELS: I have reviewed the case reports of several thousand people who claim to have had paranormal encounters and have concluded one thing. All the supernatural powers and abilities displayed by these creatures are also displayed by angels.

The belief in angels is a world wide phenomenon. Every culture speaks of creatures acting as intermediaries between the highest gods and mortals. There are several things we can learn about angels in the Bible. There are different types: Cherubim, Seraphim, Elders, Archangels and Watchers. We can tell that they have a hierarchical system of ranking similar to the military. Angels usually appear in white or in radiant light (John 20: 12, Acts 1: 10, Mark 16: 5). They definitely have an affinity to light, this is interesting because the name Lucifer meant *bearer of light* and it is written that "Satan himself masquerades as an angel of light (2Corinthians 7: 14)."

Throughout scripture we see that angels can become physical beings in our world, Jacob wrestled with a heavenly being (Genesis 32: 24), angels will hunger and require nourishment, as Abraham ate with angels (Genesis 18: 5 and Psalms 78: 25) and they will tire and have need of sleep as two slept at Lot's house in Sodom (Genesis 19: 3). Angels can change their form and appearances at will (Hebrews 13: 2). They can appear, disappear (Judges 6: 21) and remain invisible in our presence (Numbers 22: 31, Daniel 10: 7). Angels can cause people to become paralyzed, incapable of movement and speech (Daniel 10: 8-19). Angels can even cause people to see visions of whatever they choose (Luke 4: 5). They can appear in whatever form they choose to, from E.T. or Bigfoot to the Virgin Mary. Most important to remember is that the angels have certain powers over the minds and spirits of humans. Angels can appear to us in dreams (Genesis 28: 12, and 31: 11, Matthew 1: 20) and remove us from our bodies and let us encounter them while we are in spirit form (2Corinthians 12: 2- 4,

Ezekiel 8: 2, 3, Revelations 4: 2)! It is angels who will take our souls from our bodies at the moment of death (and possibly on other occasions) and lead us to the heavenly dimensions (Luke 16: 22, Matthew 24: 31, Mark 13: 27). All angels have access to the heavenly realms, even the fallen ones (Job 1: 6 and 2: 1). There have been many battles in the unseen dimensions; some feel that political and social events on earth parallel the trials and triumphs of the angels fighting in the heavens (see Daniel 10: 13). Someday the fallen angels will be permanently cast from these realms (Revelations 12: 7- 9).

Angels can appear human and at those times they are essentially just that, human. While in this form they have all the physiological needs that a human would. They hunger, thirst, and may be fertile, but at the same time they are somewhat immortal. They would not have drowned and died in the Flood, otherwise, the special preparations would not have been made for their imprisonment within the earth. Remember, that angels are very powerful, one alone killed 85,000 Syrian men in a single night (2Kings 19: 35, and also see 2Peter 2: 10, 11, Psalm 78: 49 and Jude 1: 9)!

It has been reported that aliens from other far of worlds possess every one of these abilities as well. Some believe that aliens were responsible for all the acts of angels long ago, but primitive peoples merely mistook them for angels, something their *fragile minds* could understand and accept more easily. I propose another, opposite, scenario: perhaps modern people are mistaking old fashioned angels for futuristic aliens.

An important point to remember regarding angels is that Jesus will not be forgiving their sins. Jesus came as a human, for mankind. Humans will be called to judge the angels that have been in our earthly lives, presently unbeknownst to us (1Corinthians 6: 3).

DEMONS IN A NUTSHELL: Fallen angels are different from demons. Satan has angels in his employment (Matthew 25: 41), but he also has demons (aka: unclean spirits) working for him (Matthew 12: 25-28). Fallen angels are not demons. They are two distinct and separate entities (Romans 8: 38, Acts 23: 8). Whenever these two entities are mentioned in scripture, the terms are not used interchangeably, they are very different beings. Angels can materialize into this reality at will and take various forms. Demons are the disembodied spirits, or ghosts, of the ancient giants and therefore remain unseen, instead affecting us with whispers and all out possession when given the chance. They still have the hungers and lusts of this world and want nothing more than a body so they can fulfill these desires. Both fallen angels and demons are very adept liars and tricksters, and both derive great pleasure from our suffering.

Demonic creatures have been noted to only attack those who have somehow opened the door to them, naively invited them in, as it were. Whether summoned through diabolic rituals, incantations or dabbling in witchcraft and the occult (1 Samuel 28: 7), or even continuous sinful behaviors (Matthew 12: 43- 45, John 12: 4- 6, Luke 22: 3), these beings just wait for us to slip up.

Those who experience the paranormal, and especially those who actually make contact with strange beings, are often given certain teachings and messages.

What messages do these paranormal, satanic, beings leave us?

They have deceived many and have completely invaded our pop culture![21] Some who lean toward the New Age world view seem more comfortable believing ancient aliens created humanity than a loving God; aliens who travel unknown light years only to torture and experiment on livestock and humans. These aliens have brought with them a message that reveals exactly who they are and what their intentions are.

RETURN OF THE WATCHERS: We have been trying to solve the riddle of the days of Noah prophecy. We looked at Noah's pre-Flood world in Genesis 6 with the Sons of God and the Nephilim. Since this is all the Bible tells us of Noah's life before the Flood, wouldn't we expect these creatures to return in the end times?

With this in mind let's look at the modern claims of those abducted by aliens. Many have described encounters with tall beings with radiant white skin, beards, hair and robes. Paranormal researchers have named these particular aliens *Nordics* because they resemble the stereotypical light-skinned Norwegian, but these characters are an even closer match to the description of angels given to us by Enoch. These *aliens* also take genetic materials from abducted humans to sire hybrid children! Could this be just a coincidence? They look like Watchers, do what Watchers do... if it quacks like a duck... But the name these beings call themselves is the clincher, as it were. They tell their victims they are...

---

[21] Top UFO researcher Jacques Vallee claimed that this is all a part of an evolving population control system that the aliens have been carefully manipulating over time.

Watchers!

Raymond Fowler has written several books following the ongoing abduction accounts of Betty Andreasson- Luca. She tells us that initially she would be abducted and taken *out of her body* by small grey creatures with large black eyes. After time she was introduced to their superiors, very tall "men in white robes with long white hair." While under hypnosis, she recounted more:

> They're tall people with smooth complexion and maybe a foot taller than me, (wearing) just a long white, long, long thing. It's a white gown, kinda, and it's pure, it's pure white and it fits loose... they instantly changed into a ball of light... it's not light, it's spirit. Those are intelligent. Those orbs are record keepers of intelligence, they can become small as what we know as atoms, or they can become large. They have an intelligence of their own. They're living. Are they a good intelligence? I don't know. They're saying they are record keepers of all intelligence, and that they're all around us, everywhere around us but our eyes cannot see them.
>
> *The Watchers II,* pg 30- 32, 79, 80

Through Betty they claim to be "the caretakers of nature and natural forms: The Watchers. They love the planet earth and have been caring for it and Man since Mankind's beginning. They watch the spirit in all things... they have been taking the form from man... they have collected the seed of Man, male and female (*The Watchers,* pg 202, 203)." When asked why, for what purpose they were doing this, the Watchers explained to Betty that the females of their race have become unable to reproduce as "The (alien) females just don't accept the protoplasm all together. So, they grow and use them (human females) to carry other fetuses. They (alien females) are very weak and cannot be artificially inseminated like humans (*The Watchers,* pg 213)." Recall that Biblically, female angels do not exist.[22] Betty was then taken down into the earth by Watchers who transform into balls of light and encapsulate her. She is shown a mental image of a fiery phoenix dying in blazing fire only to be reborn later. Earlier we saw the phoenix was a

---

[22] "Watcher "males have normal genitals" and "have intercourse with humans in the "normal" manner, bypassing the standard egg and sperm harvesting phase of abductions." David M. Jacobs, Ph. D. *The Threat, Revealing the Alien Agenda,* pg 133.

metaphor for the Antichrist. Betty later meets other beings down there, similar to the Watchers but "old, gnarled, and white scraggly haired." She is told that these beings are called *Elders.*

Betty describes how the Watcher's genetic hybridization experiments create the smaller grey beings "the greys are working for the tall human like beings. And how they can see everything, is through the grey's eyes, and they can command them to do whatever they want… the tall beings in white, with white hair, control the grey ones, to a point, through the eyes and the brain evidently. Those eyes are evidently like cameras for the tall ones to see through, the greys are like walking or living cameras and do the bidding of the tall ones (*The Watchers II,* pg 106, 109)."

So it would appear that certain Watchers use human DNA to create the grey beings that are sent to the earth's surface on occasion. It is the old and gnarled Elders, who fully control, possess, as it were, and see through the grey's eyes (*The Watchers II,* pg 104). Are these *Elders* the fallen angels that were imprisoned and trapped in the centre of the earth since the Flood? Could it be that they are sending out the greys as vehicles for themselves to escape their inner earth prison so they can carry on their dastardly deeds on the earth's surface?

AN ALIEN NAMED PTAAH: Eduard "Billy" Meier (born 1937) has been contacted by extraterrestrials several times and took several photographs of the aliens and their ships. In 1988 a set of books was released entitled *Message from the Pleiades* which documented the messages the aliens have given Meier to spread to us earthlings. The aliens have travelled so far to tell us that not only the earth, but all existence is in great danger! The aliens have recruited Meier to help them save all the alien races in existence from an incredible danger, a danger that originates from earth!

No, it's not our nuclear arsenal; it is one specific earth religion. Earth is the home of one religious path that threatens all living creatures. The aliens have come all this way to stop its spread before other races can learn of it and succumb to it. That one religion which these aliens hate and fear is none other than Christianity!

Meier was told he is the alien's spokesperson on earth, the Prophet of the New Age of Aquarius. Meier was told by a pale blond humanoid named Semjase that "the Christian religion is an unscrupulous and wicked piece of work for stupefying and enslaving." Meier later met the alien leader named Ptaah who told him that the Age of Aquarius, of which he is the prophet, is really the Age of the Antichrist!

Less than 1130 years ago three space traveling races came to Earth and secretly contacted Earth priests, learning religions and thinking themselves falsely led by their own Creation philosophy, thus adopting Christianity and spreading it among their home-worlds, which destroyed the peace they had known for thousands of years by generating conflicts and wars which spread to two other worlds; other space traveling races became aware of this and intervened and forbidding Earth religions, destroying all religious materials; further visits to Earth were forbidden with the decree that if a ship became stranded on Earth it and the crew must eliminate themselves; this regulation was exercised when a large ship was stranded in Russia and had to build an atomic bomb to destroy itself and the 4300 plus life forms aboard.

Is this destructive event an attempt to explain what happened in Tunguska, Russia in 1908? Several square miles of remote forest were destroyed apparently by a meteorite.

Meier has told us many things pertinent to our research. He has told us the alien's believe Christianity is evil, they are sending him out as a prophet of the Antichrist and in Meier's later journal entries he tells us that the aliens often spoke about cloning and hybridization. This all cannot be a coincidence!

In Egypt Ptah was the father of Osiris. Could Meier's Ptaah be the same individual? Meier tells us that Ptaah presides over the earth and his rank is JHWH. JHWH is the Hebrew way of spelling Father God's name! Satan always copies God, and ultimately wants to be God; this Ptaah is calling himself by God's own name! Meier then tells us that Ptaah has one son, who, like Osiris, is "no longer alive."

All too mysterious and co-incidental, I think. So what should Christians conclude about all this? Well, what do the scientific types have to say?

THE EXPERTS WEIGH IN: The great science fiction writer Arthur C. Clark, with all the imagination in the world, simply could not accept the facts regarding UFOs "One theory that can no longer be taken very seriously is that UFO's are interstellar spaceships." The notion that flying saucers are tangible metallic craft made of nuts and bolts just like our present aircraft piloted by alien astronauts from another distant planet is referred to as the *Extraterrestrial Hypothesis.* The most respected scientists to investigate UFOs, aka UFOlogists, have been John Allen Hynek and Jacques Vallee, and they had trouble with the hypothesis as well. It just did not fit the facts. Both worked with the U.S. Government's program looking into the UFO phenomenon: Project Bluebook. In October of 1976 John Allen Hynek fully reversed his original position on the extraterrestrial hypothesis that he had had while with the U.S. Air Force.

> I have come to support less and less the idea that UFO's are 'nuts and bolts' spacecrafts from other worlds. There are just too many things going against this theory. To me, it seems ridiculous that super intelligences would travel great distances to do relatively stupid things like stop cars, collect soil samples, and frighten people. I think we must begin to re-examine the evidence. We must begin to look closer to home.

The majority of UFO encounters occur in the United States. In a memo regarding Project Magnet sent by Wilbert Smith, November 1952, then head of Canada's UFO research program, it was seen that the American government admitted to the existence UFOs and that their research into this subject is their number one most classified secret. Even Presidents have been denied access to their own country's UFO database. Why the extreme secrecy regarding such a strange subject?

What is there to hide?

Perhaps this was partially revealed in a book found in the Library of Congress that was printed for the Air Force Office of Scientific Research. In it we find:

> A large part of available UFO literature is closely linked with mysticism and the metaphysical. It deals with subjects like mental telepathy, automatic writing, and invisible entities, as well as phenomena like poltergeist manifestations and possession... Many UFO reports now being published in the popular press recount alleged incidents that are strikingly similar to demonic possession and psychic phenomena which have been long known to

theologians and parapsychologists.[23]

Dr. Frank Salisbury of Utah State University, a UFO researcher who did consulting work for NASA on three special committees came to a similar conclusion. "Reported UFO activities seem too irrational, too closely related to occult, psychic, and religious phenomena, and generally too full of confusion and controversy to logically represent the activities of visitors from other star systems... for this reason I have decided to withdraw from active UFO research."

A working knowledge of the occult has been found by many UFOlogists to be indispensible to their investigations. Dr. Pierre Guerin has stated that "UFO behavior is more akin to magic than to physics as we know it... the modern UFOnauts and the demons of past days are probably identical."

> We are dealing with highly intelligent beings and in their effort to subvert us, they will use whatever cover they can... we came to think that the phenomenon must be preternatural. Which means something not of our world but interacting with it. And that, of course, is very close to the area of traditional religion. It is our belief that what we are seeing conforms very nicely with orthodox religious teachings on demonic angels.
>
> Nelson Pacheco and Tommy Blann
> *Omni,* October 1994, pg 101

JOHN A. KEEL: John Keel was not so much a scientific based researcher as the others just mentioned, but he became the lead pioneer in comparing the UFO phenomenon to demonic activity with his 1970 book *UFO's: Operation Trojan Horse*. "I abandoned the extraterrestrial hypothesis in 1967 when my own field investigations disclosed an astonishing overlap between psychic phenomena and UFOs... the objects and apparitions do not necessarily originate on another planet and may not even exist as permanent constructions of matter."

Keel's findings come from comparative research of UFOs, hauntings, religious phenomena, demons, faeries, forest and swamp monsters, mystery airships, poltergeists, mediums, New Age channels

---

[23]Lynn E. Catoe, *UFO's and Related Subjects:* USGPO, 1969; prepared under AFOSR Project Order 67-0002 and 68-0003.

and magic to conclude all originate from the same source.

He even says that the non-human or spiritual intelligence behind these phenomena has staged whole events over many thousands of years "in order to propagate and reinforce erroneous belief systems." Keel's work actually stands to verify the claims made in scripture regarding demonic deception:

> The UFO phenomenon is actually a staggering cosmic put-on; a joke perpetrated by invisible entities who have always delighted in frightening, confusing and misleading the human race. The activities of these entities have been carefully recorded through out history. The objects have always chosen to operate in a clandestine manner... the objects chose, most often, to appear in forms which we can readily accept and explain to our own satisfaction. The phenomenon is constantly reaching down to us, creating frames of reference which we can understand and accept. Then whenever we see something unusual in the sky we accept it within that frame of reference and call it a meteor, an airplane, an angel, or a visitor from outer space...
>
> ...the real truth lies in another direction. The contactees from 1897 on have been telling us what they have been told by the ufonauts. The ufonauts are the liars, not the contactees. And they are lying deliberately as part of the bewildering smokescreen which they have established to cover their origin, purpose and motivation.
>
> Victims of demonomania, possession, suffer the very same medical and emotional symptoms as the UFO contactees... the Devil and his demons can, according to the literature, manifest themselves in almost any form and can physically imitate anything from angels to horrifying monsters with glowing eyes. Strange objects and entities materialize and dematerialize in these stories, just as the UFO's and their splendid occupants appear and disappear, walk through walls, and perform supernatural feats...The demons, devils and false angels were recognized as liars and plunderers by early man. These same imposters now appear as long-haired Venusians.
>
> Dabbling with UFO's can be as dangerous as dabbling with black magic. The phenomenon preys upon the neurotic, the gullible and the immature. Paranoid schizophrenia, demonomania, and even suicide can result, and this has resulted in a number of cases. A

mild curiosity about UFO's can turn into a destructive obsession. For this reason, I strongly recommend that parents forbid their children from becoming involved.

> John A. Keel, *Operation Trojan Horse*
> pg 220

The majority of UFO investigators now conclude that they are dealing with the same phenomena to which the Bible calls demonic. A psychiatrist has noticed a similarity between patients abused by satanic cults and those abducted by aliens.

> Alien abductees enter therapy with periods of missing time and unexplained post-traumatic symptoms, just as Satanic ritual abuse survivors do. The abductees reported having hypnotic amnesia barriers deliberately implanted by aliens, while the cult survivors report being similarly programmed by Satanists. Survivors of Satanic ritual abuse also describe ritually enforced pregnancies, medical experimentation in laboratory-like settings, and deliberate removal of the fetuses before term, the difference being that, whereas Satanists use the fetuses for ceremonies, the aliens raise them as children. The myth of the Watcher Angels has returned from behind the historical repression barrier and is active in our culture…the connection between the Watcher Angels and multiple personality disorder occurs in several ways. First, many survivors of Satanic ritual abuse have MPD (Multiple Personality Disorder). More important, both ritually and non-ritually based MPD patients often have Watcher Angels in their personality systems. These are sometimes benign and cognitive in nature, in which case they are called 'Inner Self-Helpers,' while in other patients they may be more closely resemble the Apocalyptic Watchers in character.

> Colin A. Ross M.D, *Satanic Ritual Abuse, Principle of Treatment*

Where do Christians stand on this issue? Well, most stand as far from it as possible, but Hugh Ross discovered that:

> The conclusion that demons are behind the residual UFO phenomenon is a testable one. According to the Bible, demons can attack only those individuals who, through their activities, pursuits,

beliefs, friendships, and possessions, invite the attacks (Leviticus 17: 7; Deuteronomy 32: 15- 43; Judges 9: 22- 57; 1Samuel 15: 1- 16: 23; Psalm 106: 36- 43; Luke 11: 14- 26; Acts 13: 6- 11: 17: 12- 20; 1Corinthians 10: 18- 22; Revelation 9: 20- 21).

Researchers continue to observe a correlation between the degree of invitations in a person's life to demonic attacks (for example, participation in séances, Ouija games, astrology, spiritualism, witchcraft, palm reading, and psychic reading) and the proximity of their UFO encounters… One reason why research scientists and others may be reluctant to say specifically that demons exist behind residual UFOs is because such an answer points too directly to a Christian interpretation of the problem.

> Hugh Ross, *a Closer Look at UFOs,*
> *Lights in the Sky and Little Green Men*

So again we can ask ourselves the question, why is the American Government so bent on keeping this secret? It's known that agents sent to investigate claims of UFO abduction are highly trained in psychological warfare. They've also given four separate and different "official" explanations for what happened at Roswel, New Mexico, in 1947. For what it's worth, it is rumored that President Eisenhower had three secret meetings with the aliens and traded access to citizen's for advanced technology. Many abductees have reported seeing American military personnel present alongside the aliens.

OPENING THE DOOR: Whitley Strieber was a pioneer among UFO abduction researchers. He was one of the first to bring his own well documented case to the public realm. He has had best selling novels and a terrifying motion picture with *Communion.* Strieber admits that he practiced meditative mind training exercises with the Gurdjieff Foundation which is "devoted to the development of consciousness" through "a lot of meditation and effort" to reach a new state of consciousness. Yoga means *union,* we will now see what is being united; this is what the Mystery religion was all about.

I sat cross legged on the floor trying to collect myself… as soon as I relaxed, it was as if I had opened a hatch into another world. They swarmed at me, climbing up my unconscious, grasping at me… it was meeting me on every level, caressing me as well as capturing me. This emergence was a kind of internal birth, but what was being born was no bubbling infant. What came out into my conscious mind was a living, aware force. And I had a relationship with it… what might be hidden in the dark part of my mind? I thought then that I was dancing on the hidden edge of my soul… what lives within?

Deep into a state of meditation… the image had not gone away. On the contrary, it had become far more clear… somehow triggered by hypnosis… I attracted the visitor's attention and they responded. I'd already conjured something awfully disturbing. If I could give up my autonomy to another, I might experience not only fear but also a deep sense of rest. It would be alittle like dying to really give oneself up in that way, and being with her was a little like dying… the sheer helplessness… the fear caused such confusion that one could not be sure how to feel… I could actually feel the presence of that other person within me, which was disturbing.

Strieber describes how hypnosis enhanced his meditative abilities. He was seeking Eastern enlightenment, but what he achieved, in his mindset, was besiegement by *visitor* space aliens.

To all appearances I have had an elaborate personal encounter with intelligent nonhuman beings. But who could they be, and where have they come from? Are unidentified flying objects real? Are there goblins or demons… or visitors? What happened to me was terrifying. It seemed completely real. It was clear normal memory.

Scoffing at people who have been taken by the visitors… is as ugly as laughing at rape victims. We do not know what is happening to these people, but whatever it is, it causes them to react as if they have suffered a great personal trauma… I suffered with this experience. Others suffered and are still suffering… I'm not only scared and upset, frankly I'm curious. It seems to me that it seeks the very depth of the soul.

I became entirely given over to extreme dread. The fear was so powerful that it seemed to make my personality completely evaporate. This was not a theoretical or even a mental experience, but something profoundly physical. "Whitley" ceased to exist. What was left was a body in a state of raw fear so great that it swept about me like a thick, suffocating curtain, turning paralysis into a condition that seemed close to death. I do not think ordinary humanity survived the transition to this little room. I died, and a wild animal appeared in my place. Not everything was gone, though. What remained, although small, never the less was occupied with an essential task of verification. I was looking around as best I could, recording what I saw.

I was in a mental state that separated me from myself so completely that I had no way to filter my emotions or most immediate reactions, nor could my personality initiate anything. I was reduced to raw biologic response. It was as if my forebrain had been separated from the rest of my system, and all that remained was a primitive creature. If I had been afraid before, I now became quite simply crazed with terror.

Steiber's account of yogic union is terrifying. As an experienced writer he communicates the sensations of demonic possession very effectively. The next day he awoke in his bed:

I awoke very much as usual, but grappling with a distinct sense of unease and a very improbable but intense memory of seeing a barn owl staring at me through the window sometime during the night. From that first day my wife noticed a dramatic personality change in me... our nearest neighbors suddenly arrived.... and no sooner had we started talking than I found myself complaining that I thought I had seen the light of a snowmobile in the woods between our houses at about three in the morning. I was horrified at myself. What was I saying? I couldn't remember any such thing, and I knew it even as I spoke... I was not pleased with my own behavior, and found it hard to understand because I had been talking against my will.

My wife reports that my personality deteriorated dramatically over the following weeks. I became hypersensitive, easily confused, and worst of all, short with my son. We have always been a happy family, and there was no change in our life condition or relationship to account for this personality shift... I was aware that something had somehow gone wrong with me... I felt watched... my disposition got worse. I became mercurial, frantic with excitement about some idea one moment, in despair the next. I was suspicious of friends and family, often openly hostile. I came to hate... I thought I had lost my mind... I thought my mind was turning against me

Wave after wave of sorrow passed over me. I looked at the window with hunger. I wanted to jump. I wanted to die... I felt out of control... I felt complex emotions, ranging from the deepest inner unrest to what I can only describe as an urgency to compliance. I wanted to come together with them. The visitors were somehow trying to hide themselves in our folklore... gods of the past... little steel grey gods. Owl-like faces... the owl was also the totem of the Celtic Blodeuwedd, the Triple Goddess of the Moon and... the most common symbolic structure of the visitors, mentioned by many people who have been taken.

(Regarding) their emergence into human consciousness... I wished that I could believe that the experience had never hurt anybody. But I couldn't believe that... they are orchestrating our awareness of them very carefully... I felt watched... I bought my gun. I had the burglar alarm installed. I got the motion sensitive lights... my terror, my paradoxical loyalty to their commands... the old gods, the fairy, and the modern visitors... the huge staring eyes of the old gods... I had no personal freedom at all. I could not speak, could not move as I wished.

Strieber also describes his encounter with the aliens face to face:

Little scampering feet, and intimate intrusions into the soul... there's a hell of a lot of them! Filing into the room! I'm talking about a lot of them... there's like a swarm of them... smells somthin' like cheese in here. Smells kind of nasty, to tell the truth. It's not clean in here... "You know what, I think you are old? Are you old?"

She says, "Yes, I'm old."

"I'm not gonna let you do an operation on me. You have absolutely no right."

"We do have a right."

Strieber had given himself over to these monsters the moment he took the path of the Eastern mystic. This is entirely what the Mysteries were designed to accomplish! Now possessed and abused, the aliens claim to be his benevolent saviors from the stars. Do the experiences that Strieber describes sound like salvation?

The paranormal is entirely related to the Mysteries.

In the end times these types of scenarios will likely be very frequent. Revelation 16: 13 mentions demons with the eyes of frogs. The alien grey on the cover of Strieber's book *Communion* looks rather like this.

INCUBI AND SUCCUBI: No exploration of the demonic would be complete without a look at what transpired in Europe during the Dark Ages. History tells us that claims were rampant that demons were engaging in sexual union with humans.

The Vatican released two books to help its clergy combat the same forces of darkness we have been discussing here: *the Malleus Maleficarum* by Heinrich Kramer and James Sprenger in 1484, and the *Compendium Maleficarum* by Francesco Guazzo in 1608.

At this time the fallen angels were referred to as incubi and succubi. The Catholic Church fully realized that women were being impregnated and men were having their semen stolen. These were facts, but how could this be explained. Those warring against the Watchers thought that the incubi could not generate its own semen. What they presumed occurred rather was that a feminine succubi would take a man's seed, transform its own being into a male incubi and implant that same human semen into a woman.

> It is a very general belief… that Satyrs and Fauns, which are commonly called Incubi, have appeared to women and have sought and obtained coition with them. And that certain devils assiduously attempt and achieve this filthiness is vouched for by so many credible witnesses that it would seem impudent to deny it… many authentic histories, both Catholic and heathen, openly affirm the existence of Incubi… if anyone wishes to further study the histories concerning Incubi and Succubi, let him read Bede's *History of the English.*

The second book was the *Compendium Maleficarum.*

> Almost all the Theologians and learned Philosophers are agreed and it has been the experience of all times and all nations, that witches practice coition with demons, the men with Succubus devils. Plato in the Cratylus, Philo, Josephus, and the Old

Synagogue; St. Cyprian, St. Justin Martyr, Clement of Alexandria, Tertullian, and others have clearly proved that devils can and will fornicate with women… for demons can make for themselves out of air a palpable body like that of flesh, and to these they can impart motion and heat at their will. They can therefore create the appearance of sex which is not naturally present and show themselves to men in a feminine form, and to women in a masculine form, and lie with each accordingly: and they can also produce semen which they have brought from elsewhere, and imitate the ejaculation of it. I add that a child can be born of such copulation with an incubus devil… the devils cannot, as animals do, procreate children by virulence of their own strength and substance… nor are they endowed with any semen… We say then that a child can be born from the copulation of an Incubus with a woman, but that the father of such a child is not the demon but that man whose semen that demon has misused. There are countless examples told by many authors… in Spanish America a demon named Corocoton lies with women and that there are born children with two horns. The Japanese claim that their Shaka is of the same sort… Witches confess that the semen injected by the devil is cold, and that the act brings them no pleasure but rather horror… they rather feel the most acute pain in them… he usually asks the women if she wishes to become pregnant.

> Francesco Maria Guazzo,
> *Compendium Maleficarum,* pg 30, 31

Several of the most renowned and respected of the paranormal researches have come to the same conclusions. These entities are working towards an end goal. David M. Jacobs, in his book *The Threat, Revealing the Alien Agenda,* and Jacques Vallee in *The Invisible College* agree. They are manipulating humanity, implementing a form of population control. They are preparing humanity to accept them. At some point they will make their presence known and land on the White House lawn, as it were.

But how does this fit in with the Biblical end time's scenario?

The Antichrist requires some event that will propel him into the forefront of everyone's minds as a leader and savior. Somehow, I think, he will become the inter-dimensional alien's chosen ambassador. He will somehow make peace with them and save humanity: enabling us all to feel warm and fuzzy. The aliens might even acknowledge him as the great and immortal god Osiris. This would be the ultimate perpetration of the Hegelian Dialectic.

Satan has put a lot into this plan. All the aliens, theft of genetic material, the hybrids; this effort couldn't be for nothing. Prophetically, the end times are the only thing left. It must fit into the Beast's coming to power. The appearance of otherworldly intelligence would without a doubt change the belief systems of billions. But it would all be a deception. The new aliens would still be the same old fallen angels, still trying to separate us from our loving Father in Heaven.

CHAPTER NINE
EVENTS ENGINEERED BY THE LUCIFERIANS

Fallen! Fallen is Babylon the Great!
...all the nations have drunk the wine of her adulteries...
and the merchants of the earth grew rich from her excessive
luxuries.
Revelation 18: 2, 3

THE NEW WORLD ORDER: Upon the American dollar bill,
with all its Masonic symbolism, there is the phrase "Novus Ordo
Seclorum" which in Latin roughly translates as New Order of the Ages,
or New World Order. Prophecy indicates that we will see a one-world
government, what many call a New World Order, in the end times.
Most believe that the Antichrist will establish it, but the Bible indicates
it will already be in place by the time he arrives.

We first hear of this kingdom from Daniel when he interprets the
dream of King Nebuchadnezzar. He describes a statue whose body
parts represent future nations. The head was made of gold and
represented Nebuchadnezzar's Babylon. The chest and arms were made
of silver, the belly and thighs were bronze and the legs were of iron.
Daniel tells us that the feet represent the final kingdom and that the toes
are specifically made of iron and clay. Looking back through history,
scholars believe the silver chest and arms represented the Persian
Empire, the bronze belly and thighs the Greek Empire and the iron legs
the Roman Empire. Because the final kingdom is to be partly iron,
many believe the Roman Empire will somehow make a resurgence in
the future (Daniel 2: 34).

Later Daniel spoke of a ten headed beast and again told us that the
beast is the last kingdom and that, like the feet with ten toes, it will
have ten divisions, each with its own king (Daniel 7: 19- 25, and see
Revelation 13: 1). Daniel then tells us that the Antichrist becomes one
of the kings, he will come up "after them," after the government is
established (Daniel 7: 24)! He will come up "in the latter part of their

reign (Daniel 8: 23)." He will then "subdue" three of the other kings and thereafter take over the entire earth. From this we can conclude that the end time's government, the New World Order, will already be in place by the time the Antichrist comes.

Plato told us that pre-Flood Atlantis had ten kingdoms. There are rumors that ten regions are planned for the New World Order as well.[24] The first zone to be united was Europe; it was consolidated into the European Union on February 7, 1992, with the Maastricht Treaty. Critics say that the Roman Empire was reborn through this document! North America is very nearly united in a similar fashion with many trade agreements and military treaties now standing between the U.S, Canada and Mexico.

On the surface it might appear a good thing to have a single world government, economy and religion. The dream of this is to end all strife and wars based on regional and cultural differences. But what cannot be eliminated with this is man's sinful nature. A globalist government and economy would only serve to broaden the distance between classes: with all the world's natural resources at their disposal the rich will get far richer. And deciding which religion will be the solitary world religion would just lead to incredible turmoil. Do those working to unite the nations understand what they are doing? Do they see beyond the money they stand to make? Maybe they're hoping for a benevolent savior to step in and astound the people?

Who are those pushing the globalist agenda today?

MONEY, MONEY, MONEY: A powerful central bank will be the corner stone of the Antichrist's emerging empire. In Revelation 13 we are told that "everyone, small and great, rich and poor, free and slave" will be forced into a cashless monetary system. I must tell you, when the Bible uses words like *all,* or *everyone,* it means *all* and *everyone!* Every citizen of every country will one day utilize the same financial system, the same central bank. Every soul on earth will be forced to utilize a common means of buying and selling and the Bible says if you are not a part of it… you cannot buy what you and you family need to survive, you starve.

With the debit system we are nearly cashless, and now debit cards

[24] Ten Regions of the NWO: 1. North America, 2. Western Europe, 3. Japan, 4. Australia/South Africa, 5. Eastern Europe/Russia, 6. Latin America, 7. North Africa/Middle East, 8. Central Africa, 9. South/South East Asia, 10. China.

utilize a chip. It is currently possible to inject these chips under the skin. Could such a thing be the Mark of the Beast mentioned in Revelation 13? Or will it simply be a tattooed bar code, similar to the number put on Jews in the concentration camps. Incidentally, the world's first computers were developed by IBM to manage, via a punch card system, those poor souls in the Nazi's camps. How much did IBM profit from their dealings with the Third Reich? How about the Rockefellers who sold them cheap oil, or Prescott Bush, father and grand father of American presidents, he helped fund Hitler? Big business loves to have governments making laws that benefit them. For this reason monetary greed will always draw near to political might. So, in the highest levels of politics we can expect to find greedy souls who will stop at nothing to enrich and empower themselves and their associates. The establishment of global monopolies is the goal of those who would cast their lot in with the devil.

> The love of money is a root of all kinds of evil.
> 1Timothy 6:10

The Rothschilds are a notoriously wealthy and powerful banking family. They would prosper greatly from globalism and have lobbied every level of politics to get a global banking monopoly. The Rockefellers, who acquired much of their wealth through the oil and gas industry, are another super-wealthy family who also desire a global system. These sorts have established and finance politically active bodies to ceaselessly push for a New World Order.

THE COUNCIL ON FOREIGN RELATIONS: Currently the three most prominent organizations dedicated to establishing the New World Order are The Council on Foreign Relations (CFR), the Trilateral Commission (TC) and a group known as the Bilderbergers. Each of these counts as members those we're are all familiar with from the nightly news: politicians, business leaders and the influential.

According to the CFR's own website, of 502 American "government officials in high positions" between 1945 and 1972, over half were CFR members. There are currently 5000 members, and these can be individuals or corporations. Founded in 1921, its more prominent members have been Gerald Ford, Jimmy Carter, George H.W. Bush, Bill and Hilary Clinton, Dick Cheney, Mikhail Gorbachev, David, Nelson and John D. Rockefeller, and Rothschild North America

Inc. Funding has come largely from the Rockefeller family.

> For more than a century ideological extremists at either end of the political spectrum have seized upon well-publicized incidents... to attack the Rockefeller family for the inordinate influence they claim we weld over American political and economic institutions. Some even believe we are part of a secret global cabal working against the best interests of the United States, characterizing my family and me as 'internationalists' and conspiring with others around the world to build a more integrated global political and economic structure; one world, if you will. If that's the charge, I stand guilty and am proud of it.
>
> David Rockefeller, *Memoirs*, pg 405

In 1919, after World War I, with the Treaty of Versailles and the creation of the League of Nations, the CFR just about succeeded in establishing a governing body set above all independent governments. They tried again after World War II by creating the United Nations.

Arizona Governor and 1964 presidential nominee Barry Goldwater blew the whistle on this group with his 1979 book *With No Apologies.* In it he quotes Rear Admiral Chester Ward, a 16 year CFR member who stated "The main purpose of the Council on Foreign Relations is promoting the disarmament of U.S. sovereignty and submergence into an all powerful one-world government... they want the world banking monopoly power to end in the control of global government."

In 2008 the CFR initiated a program called "International Institutions and Global Governance: World Order in the 21st Century," and began creating several institutions to promote "global governance."

THE TRILATERAL COMMISSION: David Rockefeller Sr. convened the first meeting of the Trilateral Commission in 1972 at Pocantico, the family's compound in the Hudson Valley. The TC was founded to extend the reach of the CFR into Europe and primarily Asia. At Kyoto, in 1975, the Commission declared its purpose was to "manage the world economy" and improve "the chances of a smooth and peaceful evolution of a global system."

Like the CFR the membership of the TC is made up of politically powerful individuals, for example the Clinton administration had nearly a dozen TC members.

The Trilateral Commission is intended to be the vehicle for multinational consolidation of the commercial and banking interests by seizing control of the political government of the United States. The Trilateral Commission represents a skilful, coordinated effort to seize control and consolidate the four centers of power; political, monetary, intellectual and ecclesiastical. What the Trilateral Commission intends is to create a worldwide economic power superior to the political governments of the nation states involved.

U.S. Senator Barry Goldwater,
With No Apologies, 1964

THE BILDERBERG GROUP: The third pillar of the New World Order is the Bilderberg Group, of which David Rockefeller attended the inaugural meeting in 1954 and is a life member. This again is a group of those influential in business, media and politics who meet annually to "make a common political line tie between the United States of America and Europe in their... common money interests." There is a tremendous amount of secrecy involving the Bilderbergers and critics maintain that the group exists to feed the careers of ambitious politicians with a similar view for a New World Order.

Daniel Estulin raised an important, yet obvious point, about the Bilderbergers, that applies to all other secret societies of which the elites take part.

Why are world economic forums and G8 meetings discussed in every newspaper, given front page coverage, with thousands of journalists in attendance, while no one covers Bilderberg Group meetings? This blackout exists despite the fact that they are annually attended by Presidents of the International Money fund, the World Bank, the Federal Reserve; by chairmen of 100 of the most powerful corporations in the world such as Daimler Chrysler, Coca Cola, British Petroleum, Chase Manhattan Bank, American Express, Goldman Sachs, and Microsoft; by Vice Presidents of the United States, Directors of the CIA and the FBI, Secretaries General of NATO, American Senators and members of Congress, European Prime Ministers, and leaders of opposition parties; and by top editors and CEOs of the leading newspapers in the world. It is certainly curious that no mainstream media outlet considers a gathering of such figures, whose wealth far exceeds the combined wealth of all United States citizens, to be newsworthy, when a trip by any one of them on their own makes headline news on TV.

Daniel Estulin, *The True Story of the Bilderberg Group,* pg 14

The first chairman of the Bilderbergers was Prince Bernhard, a Nazi SS Officer. Also at this first meeting were other Nazi's, such as Dr. Hermann Josef Abs, the Banker in charge of the Nazi's funds. Rather suspicious and unsavory individuals to be seen with in those post war years. How could the Rockefellers be leading members of these three secretive organizations, who function only to incrementally destroy every nation's sovereignty, without the people's slightest knowledge? David Rockefeller gave us the answer.

We are grateful to The Washington Post, The New York Times, Time Magazine and other great publications whose directors have attended our meetings and respected our promises of discretion for almost forty years. It would have been impossible to develop our plan for the world if we had been subject to the bright lights of publicity during those years. But, the work is now much more sophisticated and prepared to march toward a world government. The supranational sovereignty of an intellectual elite and world bankers is surely preferable to the national autodetermination practiced in past centuries.

David Rockefeller, June 1991 Address to the Trilateral Commission

Seeking to rule the entire world, making all people his idiot worker drones, David Rockefeller showed his fascist authoritarian side in an August 10, 1973, *New York Times* article when he stated "Whatever the price of the Chinese Revolution, it has obviously succeeded... the social experiment in China under chairman Mao's leadership is one of the most important and successful in human history." The cost was eighty-million people dead! Many politicians and leaders from around the globe have noticed the ruthless power wielded by the Rockefellers and have tried to utter warnings.

The drive of the Rockefellers and their allies is to create a one-world government combining supercapitalism and Communism under the same tent, all under their control... Do I mean conspiracy? Yes I do. I am convinced that there is such a plot, international in scope, generations old in the planning, and incredibly evil in intent.

> Congressman Larry McDonald, 1976, just before his 747 was *accidentally* shot down.

The real menace of our republic is the invisible government which like a giant octopus sprawls its slimy length over city, state and nation. Like the octopus of real life it operates under cover of a self created screen... At the head of this octopus are the Rockefeller Standard Oil interests and a small group of powerful banking houses generally referred to as international bankers. The little coterie of powerful international bankers virtually run the United States government for their own selfish purposes. They practically control both parties.

> John F. Hylan, Mayor of New York, 1922

Jesus said it is easier for a camel to fit through the eye of a needle than for a rich man to get into heaven (Matthew 19: 24). The Bible says that in the end times it will be these wealthy merchants that will be our rulers (Revelation 18: 23).

SILENT WEAPONS FOR QUIET WARS: On July 7, 1986, an employee of Boeing Aircraft Co. purchased a broken down IBM photocopy machine to use for spare parts. Much to his surprise, someone had left inside it a short, highly detailed manual on how to take over the world!

Conspiracy researcher William Cooper had reason to believe the document originated from the Bilderberg Group. Cooper was never able to reveal his sources for this presumption, as he was suspiciously shot to death on his own property by an off duty police officer. The document was entitled *Silent Weapons for Quiet Wars, an Introductory Planning Manual.* Some have claimed that the document is an elaborate forgery. But this is unlikely because the document reveals a revolutionary teaching on economic theory bordering on genius, that one would be foolish not to stand up and take credit for. The document itself claims to have been funded by the Rockefeller Foundation and states the economic theory it contains was invented by Mayer Rothschild, one of the wealthiest men ever to live. None the less, the plans for global-economic conquest include steps which can be seen to have been implemented since the document's discovery.

In order to achieve a totally predictable economy, the lower class elements of the society must be brought under total control, ie: must be housebroken, trained, and assigned a yoke and long term social duties from an early age, before they have an opportunity to question the propriety of the matter. In order to achieve such conformity, the lower class family unit must be disintegrated by a process of increasing preoccupation of the parents and the establishment of government operated day care centres for the occupationally orphaned children.

The quality of education to the lower class must be the poorest sort, so the moat of ignorance isolating the inferior class from the superior class is and remains incomprehensible to the inferior class. With such a handicap, even bright lower class individuals have little if any hope of extricating themselves from their assigned lot in life. This form of slavery is essential to maintaining some measure of social order, peace, and tranquility for the upper ruling class.

Experience has proven that the simplest method of securing a silent weapon and gaining control of the public is to keep the public undisciplined and ignorant of basic systems and principles on the one hand, while keeping them confused, disorganized, and distracted with matters of no real importance on the other hand.

This is achieved by: (1) disengaging their minds, sabotaging their mental activities, by providing a low quality program of public education in mathematics, logic, systems design, and economics, and by discouraging technical creativity. (2) Engaging their emotions, increasing their self indulgence and their indulgence in emotional and physical activities, by (a) unrelenting emotional affrontations and attacks, mental and emotional rape, by way of a constant barrage of sex, violence, and wars in the media, especially the T.V. and the newspapers. (b) Giving them what they desire, in excess, 'junk food for thought,' and depriving them of what they really need. (3) Rewriting history and law and subjecting the public to the deviant creation…

The general rule is that there is profit in confusion; the more confusion, the more profit. Therefore, the best approach is to create problems, and then offer the solutions.

DIVERSION SUMMARY
MEDIA: keep the adult public attention diverted away from the real social issues, and captivated by matters of no real importance.
SCHOOLS: Keep the young public ignorant of real mathematics, real economics, real law, real history.
ENTERTAINMENT: Keep the public entertainment below a sixth grade level.
WORK: Keep the public busy, busy, busy, with no time to think; back on the farm with the other animals.

THE PROTOCOLS OF ZION: *Silent Weapons for a Quiet War* was not the first manifesto to surface describing the means to take over the world. During the Russian Revolution, in 1905, a similar document appeared. The new Soviet Government, upon taking power, commanded that all copies be destroyed and that anybody with one was to be put to death, but one copy escaped and found its way to the British Museum in 1906.

The steps described in the document do show how a secret group may not only be attempting to take over the world, but now, more than a hundred years later, it appears they are well on their way to accomplishing this!

This document is presently known as *The Protocols of the Learned Elders of Zion*. But this might not be a document made by Jews as it appears. Someone may have attempted to make the plan appear to be a Jewish one by inserting a few bits of Jewish phraseology and thoughts, but a careful analysis shows that the individual perpetrating the "Jewification" of the plan had little knowledge of the Hebrew culture. They did succeed in rousing anti-Semitic fury in Europe however, thirty years later Adolf Hitler would use the *Protocols* as evidence that the Jews were dangerous and should be wiped from the earth. Interestingly, Freemasonry is mentioned in this document far more than Judaism. It claims that Freemasonry will be the screen they will hide behind (Protocol 4: 2). "We shall create and multiply Freemasonic lodges in all the countries of the world, absorb into them all who may become or who are prominent in public activity, for these lodges shall find our principle intelligence office and means of influence (Protocol 15: 4)."

When we examine the *Protocols,* being the steps to world domination, we can actually see that many steps of the plan have been successfully implemented. If the process is allowed to continue, these steps will clearly lead us to the end time's scenario seen in the Bible. The writers of the *Protocols* desire to be acknowledged "supreme lords of the world" and their leader as "King of all the World (Protocol 12: 5)." This should remind us of Genesis 3, where Lucifer told his followers they could be gods. Accordingly, in Protocol 3: 1 it says that this organization has been represented by the image of a serpent. The view in the *Protocols* is that they have superior minds and therefore deserve to rule, "by the law of nature right lies in force… our right lies in force" Hence the old adage, "might is right." Similar to the teachings of Plato, they think that mankind left to his own ends will destroy itself with the weak liberal and democratic governments now in place, which they strive to further twist and weaken.

To quote the first of the *Protocols,* "I find a new right… to become the sovereign lord of those who have left us the rights of their power by laying them down voluntarily to their liberalism. Our power will remain invisible until the moment when it has gained such strength that no cunning can any longer deny it. Out of the unshakable evil we are now compelled to commit, will emerge the good of an unshakable rule… before us is a plan which has been laid down strategically, the labor of many centuries (Protocol 1: 14- 17)."

They plan to implement the harshest dictatorship ever conceived upon the planet. To achieve this and have the people accept them they plan to have "violence be the principle, and lies the rule for the government… to maintain terror which produces blind submission (Protocol 1: 23, 24)." Wars are essential, but they must not result in any real gains for the victors. They have, and will continue to create wars between the various peoples they supply arms to (Protocol 3: 3). Political leaders will be specially selected for their weakness and gullibility and then surrounded by corrupt advisors. Judges, senators, bankers, economists, industrialists and capitalists will be taken under control via blackmail or bought outright. Because of governmental laws, worldwide monopolies will be established over industry and trade (Protocol 5: 7).

The media and press will create discontent among the people. The Protocols reveal that the educated person is the only thing that they fear. Protocol 12: 3 tells us that they fear information reaching the hands of the common people. To protect themselves they will take control over the media and press. Books and publications will be closely monitored for dissent. "Not a single announcement will reach the public without our control." To control a person they must control what influences them, "we will swallow up and confiscate to our own use the last scintilla of independence of thought (Protocol 16: 8)." People will be distracted from the assault upon their liberties by various forms of captivating entertainment, greed and heavy work loads.

In the schools it will be taught that there are divisions among the people and that equality is impossible. This will create envy and hatred among the people. Also, it is stated that "We have fooled, bemused and corrupted the youth by rearing them on principles and theories which are known by us to be false (Protocol 9: 10)." "We have persuaded them to accept the dictates of science. It is with this object in view that we are constantly, by means of our press, arousing a blind confidence in these theories (Protocol 2: 2)." "Think carefully of the successes we arranged for Darwinism (Protocol 2: 3)." It was all planned long ago, to destroy the concept of God "and put in its place arithmetical calculations and material needs (Protocol 4: 3)."

Educational curriculums will be altered in favor of promoting their objectives and history lessons will be greatly distorted to make their acts seem good and those of the Christian Church seem terrible. They say that minds must be diverted to materialism, swallowed up in pursuit of gain so that the people do not focus on the real foe. Ultimately they also wish to see the traditional family unit destroyed, because the home is where the majority of ethical and moral teaching should take place (Protocol 10: 5).

In accordance with the Illuminati's long term goal, the Church will be discredited "and thereby ruin their mission on earth… day by day its influence on people is falling lower… now only years divide us from the moment of the complete wrecking of that Christian Religion (Protocol 17: 2)." Their religion will be the only religion allowed, but they say that only their elite will fully understand its secrets, ie: a Mystery Religion (Protocol 14: 1, 4).

Terrorist attacks will be staged as a pretext for the implementation of super surveillance (Protocol 18: 1). People will be praised and rewarded for turning in their neighbors and families. It will be everyone's duty to keep others under observation (Protocol 17: 7).

Liberties will be taken away, but only temporarily they will say, for the good of the people during the time of war and crisis. To protect the people, a one world super-government will be created with new laws and a new police force. All will be forced to submit to the state. Torture and execution will be allowed, people will starve and be secretly inoculated with plagues and disease to keep them fearful and dependant upon the state (Protocol 10: 19). Simultaneously, inflation will become rampant (Protocol 6: 7). All the money in the world will be concentrated in their hands. The middle class will be destroyed through high taxes (Protocol 20: 5, 6). The Protocols tell us that any transfer of wealth, goods, or services will be taxed. People and Nations will become addicted to credit and loans eventually making them slaves. With banks demanding their money back and by withdrawing their money from the system, they will cause a devastating economic collapse. A global economic crisis will be created and industry will come to a halt. Raging mobs will form. "Men will fight even against God himself (Protocol 3: 20)." "Our power is in the chronic shortages of food and physical weakness of the worker, because by all that this implies he is made slave to our will (Protocol 3: 7)."

Then out of the chaos their savior will take the throne, "in order that he who rules may be seated firmly in the hearts and minds of his subjects it is necessary to instruct them of his actions and beneficent initiatives (Protocol 16: 4, 6)." "Then will it be possible for us to say to the peoples of the world: give thanks and bow the knee before him who bears the seal of the predestination of man, to which god has led his star that none other than him might free us from all evil (Protocol 23: 5)." "And they will acknowledge our ruler with a devotion bordering on deification... we are obliged without hesitation to sacrifice individuals... when the king sets upon his sacred head the crown he will become patriarch of the world (Protocol 15: 20, 21)."

We can regularly see evidence on our nightly news which shows that this is all incrementally coming to fruition.

They only wait for the right moment. David Rockefeller said "We are on the verge of a global transformation. All we need is the right major crisis and nations will accept the New World Order."

A Washington D.C. based think tank called the Project for a New American Century had a mandate "to promote American global leadership" via "military strength." They planned to lead American interests to dominate the emerging New World Order, to use the military to excess and totally neglect diplomacy. They end off Section V, entitled *Creating Tomorrow's Dominant Force,* with the statement "Further, the process of transformation, even if it brings revolutionary change, is likely to be a long one, absent some catastrophic and catalyzing event, like a new Pearl Harbor." Donald Rumsfeld, Secretary of Defense, was a contributor and Dick Cheney, Vice President, signed to the Statement of Principles.

By all means they were waiting for an opportunity, but if the right crisis doesn't come along on time, do you think it is possible for the richest people in the world to orchestrate one?

SEPTEMBER 11: Let us examine what occurred on September 11, 2001, when the United States suffered an unprecedented terrorist attack which propelled the world into a war between many Islamic nations and the West.

Could the attacks have been engineered? Could September 11, where nearly three thousand people died, have been a purposefully planned and staged event? What has come from these attacks, how has our world changed since then?

Conspiracy theorists have had a lot to say about the World Trade Center towers but let us focus for a moment solely on the attack on the Pentagon, the center of American military might. Is there any evidence that the attack here is not what is was portrayed to be?

The American government tells us that NORAD and the FAA, who both monitor air traffic over the United States and Canada, were supposedly unable to track the planes once hijacked. The truth is that those in air traffic control towers requested and even begged for the standard military intercept of wayward planes in that area. At nearby Andrews Air Force Base there are two squadrons of fighters whose job it is to defend the airspace over Washington, D.C. These crews are standing by twenty-four hours a day, ready to defend the President and the Nation's Capital. Between September 2000 and June 2001, the Pentagon had ordered to launch fighter interceptors sixty-seven times to escort wayward aircraft from the area.

What happened on the morning of September 11, 2001?

For some reason, the fighters were directly ordered by White House officials to "Stand Down," not to launch for almost one and a half hours. Never before in NORAD's fifty year history has such a "Stand

Down" order been given.

The Pentagon itself is a five sided building that covers 29 acres and only rises to 80 feet in height. It is the most well protected building on the planet with five batteries of anti-missile rocket launchers on the roof that are programmed to shoot down anything entering the area. Hitting a jumbo jet would be the easiest conceivable target for these computerized killers. The only way an aircraft can come near the building is if it sends a coded signal saying "friendly." Now what has gone unaddressed is the fact that these missiles never fired on American Airlines Flight 77, did they fail or did the terrorists infiltrate America's tightest security and steal the codes? If that is the case, what about the launch codes for America's arsenal of nuclear weapons? Either scenario is a huge black-spot for American safety and security.

Another interesting element is the terrorist who supposedly flew the passenger jet into the Pentagon, Hani Hanjour, was kicked out of the flight school he attended because he was such a terrible student that the instructors feared flying with him. Despite this, Washington officials insist that Hanjour was able to put the jumbo jet through impossible maneuvers. He put the plane into a 330-degree turn while descending 2200 feet, while simultaneously advancing the throttles to maximum power, all while keeping the plane out of a dive and come in horizontal at tree top level. He somehow then managed to drop the plane down only after passing the light poles just meters from the Pentagon itself. A highly skilled combat pilot in a fighter jet would have tremendous difficulty performing this feat. Because it would be an impossibility for a hundred-ton plane to move this way, engineers tell us that its wings would have been torn off, many aviation authorities believe it was actually some sort of cruise missile that was performing the maneuvers recorded on radar.

The most interesting curiosities are found dealing with the wreckage of Flight 77. In the photos taken immediately after the crash there is no wreckage from an airplane seen outside of the Pentagon. What is curious about this is that the wing span of a 757-passenger plane is 125 feet across, the height at the tail is about 44 feet, yet the hole in the building was only 15 to 20 feet in diameter. This ultimately means that the wings of Flight 77 never would've entered the Pentagon and would have to be outside on the lawn where photos show there was no wreckage whatsoever.

Fire crews and rescue personnel denied seeing any jet plane

wreckage within the Pentagon. Since then government sources have insisted that the plane disintegrated and was vaporized by the fires caused by the impact.[25] The heat necessary to melt the plane's steel frame would have to be in excess of 2770 degrees Fahrenheit. To completely vaporize steel, the fires would have to be considerably hotter yet. The problem here is that jet fuel burns at only 1700 degrees Fahrenheit. A conflicting statement was then issued by the government, that the deceased passengers of flight 77 were all identified by their fingerprints![26]

How could a steel framed jet be made to pass entirely through an 18-foot hole and then burn to vaporization until not a scrap of it was left while not harming the flesh of those on board?

One must next ask "what is the American Government trying to hide?" Did Donald Rumsfeld experience a "Freudian slip" when he was interviewed by *Parade* (WWW.Defenselink.mil)? He clearly stated that "...the missile used to damage this building..."

With the Pentagon being the most secure structure on the planet there are video cameras everywhere. Yet the only video footage released by the government of the attack has had the frames removed that would have shown the aircraft itself. Even the gas station down the road had its security cameras and tapes confiscated minutes after the attack.

The eyewitnesses now fall into two categories. Those few who claim they saw a jumbo jet are all higher up in the American military. The mass of other, nonmilitary, witnesses all claim to have seen a much smaller aircraft, some witnesses described hearing a high-pitched roar, similar to a fighter jet or a missile. These witnesses adamantly deny seeing a jumbo jet. Mike Walter told CNN that what he saw "was like a cruise missile with wings."

And what an odd coincidence that the section of the Pentagon hit was closed for renovations and the vast majority of the 125 souls that perished there were civilians working on the renovations.

The absurdities, *coincidences* and questions here are endless, but we must note that of the FBI's list of the nineteen terrorists who committed

---

[25] *NFPA Journal,* November 1, 2001.

[26] *Washington Post* November 21, 2001.

suicide by flying jets into targets, that six of them have turned out to be still very much alive. The FBI went into great detail in the media telling us the actions of these crazed men in the days before the attacks and what their roles and responsibilities were during the events. For example they told us that Waleed al-Shehri stabbed each of the flight attendants on American Airlines Flight 11 with a box cutter knife. In the London based Arabic newspaper *Al-Quds al-Arabi,* however, Waleed al-Shehri has stated that he was not on board that flight, on which everyone perished, that he never stabbed anyone, that he is not a terrorist and that he is not dead!

The American Government still insists, however, that he is a dead highjacker, that five other living men are dead and that a seventh man who died years before the attacks was alive enough to also hijack an airplane.

Isn't it also odd that warnings were given to important persons around the world not to be on board flights passing anywhere near the North Eastern United States on September 11? Several have come forward saying they too received similar warnings.

Another huge coincidence is the fact that on September 11 military *War Games* were being practiced. The scenario designed by CIA officer John Fulton was that there was a terrorist attack on the United States. The mode of attack was that planes were crashing into buildings! The fake attacks were taking place in New York, Washington, D.C. and Pennsylvania! Air traffic controllers were totally disoriented by the "games" but also by as many as two dozen fake "blips" put on the FAA's radar screens and monitors by the military.

Here is a huge irony. *Newsweek* magazine for October 1, 2001, tells us that in the weeks prior to 9-11, President George W. Bush signed a secret national security order entitled W199-EYE. This document told FBI agents and other intelligence and defense officers that if they tried to stop al-Qaeda they would be arrested under national security implications. Shortly after Bush put W199-EYE into effect, FBI deputy director John O'Neill resigned in disgust. O'Neill would die on the first day of his new job, on September 11, when he started as the new head of security for the World Trade Center.

On November 10, 2001, before the General Assembly of the United Nations, Bush gave his first post attack speech. He stated "Let us never tolerate outrageous conspiracy theories concerning the attacks of September 11th."

Why? What to do the conspiracy theorists have to say?

What was known as WTC 7 of the World Trade Center Plaza was supposedly severely damaged from the attacks on the twin towers, buildings 1 and 2. The leaseholder on the World Trade Center properties was Larry Silverstein; he won the right to the ninety-nine year lease only six weeks before 9-11. Silverstein said in a 2002 PBS documentary, *America Rebuilds: a Year at Ground Zero,* that it was decided WTC 7 would be "pulled," a construction term for demolished.

> I remember getting a call from the fire department commander, telling me that they were not sure they were gonna be able to contain the fire, and I said, 'We've had such terrible loss of life, maybe the smartest thing to do is pull it.' And they made that decision to pull and then we watched the building collapse.
> Larry Silverstein

That certainly sounds reasonable, but what is not is the fact the building was brought down the evening of September 11th. It takes months to plan that kind of demolition, and they're trying to tell us that some crew with explosives accessed the absolutely chaotic crime scene and did the job in just a few hours? Those capable of this kind of structure demolition are far and few between, and none have come forward to take credit for WTC 7.

What was in building 7?

Building 7 was a 47 story skyscraper housing the NYC Office of Emergency Management's Emergency Operation's Center, which is a bunker designed to withstand nearly any kind of attack. It also had offices for the CIA and Department of Defense. This would be an ideal location for anyone wanting to orchestrate this kind of attack.

Clearly there are too many coincidences and too many questions here. As mentioned earlier the attacks on the World Trade Centre buildings are not without a tremendous list of valid concerns as well. For example, why was the evidence, the steel from the fallen towers, removed and melted down, much to the ire of firefighters and those investigating the crime? What we must conclude from all of this is that the Government's story just does not add up. Period.

If this was an event organized by the world elite, why would they do it? For what purpose would such chaos be instigated?

Indeed, what have the attacks brought us?

LIFE AFTER 9-11: Let's say a governing body has something they want to implement, but they fear the people will react against it. Now let's say that governing body was corrupt and greedy and cared little for the people. That government might use the Hegelian Dialectic, a means of population control.

The system can be remembered as: Problem-Reaction-Solution. Keep in mind, the government has their "solution" ready before any manipulation occurs; this is whatever horrible thing they want to impose upon the people. So, first they engineer a problem, they purposefully arrange a crisis of some sort. Next, the people react to the crisis, demanding a resolution. Then come the government with their solution, what they already had in mind, they just could not implement it without the planned "problem." But with the people literally begging for their solution, really any solution, the government gets what they wanted and the public none the wiser, has lost something.

Immediately after 9-11 we saw the outrage of the Western world. Americans were calling for something to be done, to avenge the attacks and ensure that this could not happen again. If the clandestine Hegelian system were in place here the attacks were the crisis, and the people definitely reacted. We should expect to see a solution offered, possibly measures taken that the New World Order types and Luciferians have all along desired but were unable to implement until they had the people begging for them.

Indeed, what solutions were offered?

The USA Patriot Act was rammed through congress a mere eight days after 9- 11, showing the world that the massive document was waiting in the wings ready to go long before the attacks took place. Attorney General Ashcroft told Congress that further attacks were immanent and that if the Act was not passed the blood of innocents would be on their hands. This occurred in an unprecedented, middle of the night session. Very few copies of the utterly massive document, which would have taken many years to design, were available for the Congressmen to even glance at, let alone read, study and debate, the way an Act should be treated before passing. President Bush signed the Patriot Act into law on October 26, 2001.

Critics now say this was a trap and that the Act not only weakened civil liberties but has suspended the Constitution taking away all the rights of the people.

As if to foreshadow the birth of such a document, America's

Founding Father Ben Franklin once wrote that "Any society that would give up a little liberty to gain a little security will deserve neither and lose both." The first provision of America's Constitution, which Franklin helped pen, is the right to freedom of speech and religion, the second is the right to keep firearms to protect the people from… their own government; should it fall into tyranny and reject the first provision!

The stated purpose of the Patriot Act is to "deter and punish American terrorists in the United States and around the world, to enhance law enforcement investigatory tools, and for other purposes." This is a law aimed entirely against American citizens! This law does nothing to protect the country from attackers on the other side of the world. The Act then defines "domestic terrorism" as: any misdemeanor. This essentially makes anyone, at any time the authorities say so, a terrorist. Also under section 802 we see that the definition of "terrorist" expands to those who would dare to coerce a civilian population or influence the government. This makes a terrorist out of anyone who disagrees with the state's policies and any activist who would protest against the state attempting to educate people to their opinion.
Few Americans even recognize that this fully nullifies the American Constitution. The right to freedom of speech is now absolutely gone, if you bring this fact up publically you will be called a terrorist!

Who is terrorizing who?

A big part of the Patriot Act is surveillance. Law enforcement agencies may now search or monitor any form of your communications or data, all without search warrants, your knowledge or consent. The Information Awareness Office (IAO), whose official symbol is the All Seeing Eye perched above a pyramid overseeing the planet earth, was established in January 2002 as the mass surveillance system to monitor the flow of information in America. Every individual has a file into which goes data regarding their debit or credit card purchases, which web sites they've visited, what library books they've taken out, movies rented, phone numbers dialed, everything in the cyber world is monitored and recorded in huge data bases.

Initiated in 2008, another data base, known as Main Core, contains information on over eight million American civilians deemed to be terrorist threats! Those individuals seen as threats, likely those reading about Luciferians and conspiracies, are bumped up and observed even more closely. Intelligence gathering is not always this sophisticated.

Tyrants have always relied heavily on neighbors turning in neighbors and children their parents.

With the Patriot Act now in place, they can search any location, your home or workplace; remove your belongings or plant objects all without your knowledge or consent. Ultimately you may be subject to indefinite detention should any suspicion arise. You would not be allowed to contact your family to alert them of your abduction or contact a lawyer.

Another part of the Patriot Act is the militarization of police. Traditionally the police have been there to "Protect and Serve." Meanwhile, the military are there to kill, destroy and blow stuff up, to utterly defeat an enemy. Now with the establishment of the Department of Homeland Security, the citizens of America have been deemed the enemy. In many centers Police now carry assault rifles, wear black balaclavas, storm trooper outfits and armor which obviously creates an element of intimidation in the people they once protected and served. After the American Civil War (1867- 1877) the Posse Comitatus Act was put into place to prevent the Federal Government from ever using the Military against the citizenry. Soon after invoking the Patriot Act, President Bush killed Posse Comitatus when he signed the Military Commissions Act of 2006. The military can police the people and any citizen can be secretly arrested, stripped of their citizenship, flown out of the country to regions where torture is condoned and available, and even secretly executed. The victim would never be allowed to formally speak on his own behalf. His family would only know that one day he just disappeared.

Another Act related to Posse Comitatus, designed to protect the American people from their own government was the Insurrection Act of 1807. Bush put an end to this with the Defense Authorization Bill in 2007. The Defense Authorization Act made it possible, so that any time the President deems it necessary, regional governors and legislatures could be stripped of their powers and all power transferred to the Federal Government. Since May 9, 2007, with President Bush's National Security and Homeland Security Presidential Directive (NSPD 51), all Federal powers could be placed on the American President whenever he would deem it necessary, thus laying the legal requirements enabling an American dictatorship. These nullify the Legislative, Judicial, and Executive branches of government, the very measures the Founding Fathers had put in place to prevent such a scenario.

On October 1, 2002, NorthCom was created. The 3rd Infantry Division's 1st Brigade Combat Team is now a domestic army that can be "called upon to help with civil unrest and crowd control" and can "subdue unruly or dangerous individuals" in the U.S. and Canada. As of 2011 NorthCom would have 20,000 troops, plus Canadian reservists. Two documents have already been prepared for the implementation of martial law, with REX-84 and Operation Garden Plot. Tyranny is already on the books.

WAR: After 9-11, war was declared first in Afghanistan and the Taliban regime was ousted. The direct result of this has been a dramatic increase in the world wide opium supply. Afghanistan has traditionally been the world's key opium exporter, but under the Taliban government the crop was banned, now with that regime quashed the amount of illegal narcotics on the streets of North America has skyrocketed and the prices have plummeted. After Afghanistan, the Americans set their sites to invade Iraq and topple Saddam Hussein despite the fact that there was no evidence he was involved with 9-11 whatsoever. They CIA said he had "Weapons of Mass Destruction," but he didn't. U.S. citizens realized it too late, the war was already on.

Arms dealers and the Military Industrial Complex were profiteering like never before. American Vice President Dick Cheney, once CEO of Halliburton, saw his stock options increase by 3281% in 2004 alone. Halliburton KBR received more than $21 billion in American contracts in Iraq. Secretary of Defense Dick Cheney has simultaneously collected a salary from both the American citizens, whose finest young men and women he sends off to war, and monies from Halliburton, which he positioned to "provide logistical support for U.S. forces around the world."

There are many profiteers, but the visible losers in the post 9-11 world are the common people.

SKULL AND BONES: In modern day America, at Yale University, there is a secret society that prides itself on their Druidic Mysteries called the Order of the Skull and Bones, aka: the Order of Death. Their lodge is called the Tomb and annually, since 1832, only fifteen senior students are selected and asked to join.

The Skull and Bones was founded by William H. Russells, whose family had grown very wealthy from the opium trade. Russells had spent time in Bavaria and apparently became affiliated with Adam

Weishaupt's Illuminati. He was charged with setting up an American chapter. By 1856 their headquarters had been built and The Russell Trust Association was established as a holding company to handle their finances. Next to the Thirty-third degree of Scottish Rite Masonry, the Skull and Bones fraternity is the most obvious stepping stone into the Illuminati. Members believe the number 322 has a secret and magical meaning. The Order was founded in 1832 as the 2nd chapter of the Illuminati: 32- 2.

In politics a disproportionate amount of Bonesmen become top movers and shakers, the cream rising to the top. Often, when one becomes a Bonesman, it becomes a hereditary thing, with member's sons later also being selected. Notable Bones families have been Bush, Goodyear, Ford, Dodge, Heintz, Pillsbury, Kellogg, Rockefeller, Taft, Weyerhaeuser and Cheney. The CIA also has a long history of recruiting agents from the fraternity. Now, the fact with the CIA is this, the agency was caught completely unaware when the Berlin Wall went up, and when it came down, the two most important events in the Cold War. They also grossly over-estimated Russia's nuclear attack capabilities. The CIA also said there were weapons of mass destruction in Iraq and that Saddam Hussein had a hand in the 9-11 attacks, both later proven false. So what have America's spies been doing with their time all these years? Has the agency been serving the Illuminati or the American people? The wealthiest people have time and again been caught funding secret CIA "black" operations that Congress had refused to finance. These operations of course often provided nice payoffs for those involved.

For at least three generations the Bush family has been members of the strange Skull and Bones fraternity. George H.W. Bush is still avidly involved with the Order and before he was President of the United States he was head of the CIA. He can also be tied to the Bay of Pigs fiasco, the ousting of President Nixon and JFK's assassination. His son would later also become a Bonesman and American President as well. George W. Bush wrote in his autobiography that "In my senior year I joined the Skull and Bones, a secret society, so secret that I can't say anything more."

Bush repeated this remark when he was interviewed on the NBC television show *Meet the Press*. The host, Tim Russert, while interviewing George W. Bush addressed the little known fact that both Bush and John Kerry, who were at that time both running in the 2000

Presidential election race, were Bonesmen.

> Host: "You were both in Skull and Bones the secret society."
> Bush: "It's so secret we can't talk about it."
> Host: "What does that mean for America?"
> There is a long pause as Bush nervously adjusts himself in his seat.
> Host: "The conspiracy theorists are going to go wild."
> Bush: "I'm sure they will... (Laughing nervously)."
> Host: "Number three-two-two?"
> Bush: changing the subject "First of all he's not the nominee..."

John Kerry was also later interviewed on *Meet the Press* and asked similar questions:

> Host: "You both were members of Skull and Bones, a secret society at Yale, what does that tell us?"
> Kerry: "Uhhh, not much because it's a secret."
> Host: "Is there a secret handshake? Is there a secret code?"
> Kerry: "I wish there was something secret that I could manifest."
> Host: "Three twenty-two, a secret number?"
> Kerry: "There's all kinds of secrets, but there's one thing that is not a secret, I disagree with this president's direction..."

Kerry nervously changes the subject. Unfortunately the host of *Meet the Press* never addressed another fact, that both Bush and Kerry were not only fellow Bonesmen from the same senior year, but also first cousins.

In the September 25, 2002, issue of *USA Today,* Alexandra Robbins wrote that Bush was a particularly active member and that when he came into office he brought many fellow Bonesmen such as Robert McCallum and Edward McNally with him placing them in key White House positions.

When we see a group of men claiming to be of the Order of Death and spend time happily chanting "The devil equals death" we know they are not a group based upon Christian morals. To be initiated into the Order, to be a Bonesman, the aspirant, which they term a "neophyte," has to kiss a human skull and pass the tests of courage. On one past occasion this consisted of stealing, from a museum, the actual silver wear used by Adolf Hitler and at another time allegedly stealing the skull of Indian war hero Geronimo. After this test they are placed in a coffin and forced to divulge all their secrets, especially sexual. As they rise from the coffin, they are said to be Druids and to be "born again." George W. Bush was asked while campaigning for the presidency if he was a Christian. His answer was rather cryptic, as he was admittedly desperately seeking "the Evangelical vote," he replied "If you mean that if I am "born again," then you can say that I am."

BOHEMIAN GROVE: A good portion of Skull and Bones members became involved in the CIA, the American spy network. In 1973 a retired CIA agent named Victor Marchetti tried to publish a book called *The CIA and the Cult of Intelligence.* The CIA at first blocked its publication, but after wide protests a heavily censored version was allowed to be printed. He discovered some very frightening things while working with the agency. He stated that:

> There exists in our world today a powerful and dangerous secret cult… Its patrons and protectors are the highest officials of the federal government. Its membership extending far beyond government circles, reaches into the power-centers of industry, commerce, finance and labor. Its friends are many in the areas of important public influence, the academic world and communications media. The Cult of Intelligence is a secret fraternity of the American political aristocracy. The purpose of this cult is to… foster a world order in which America would reign supreme.

Is there any evidence of such a cult's existence?

Just 70 miles north of San Francisco, every July, world leaders come to a "country club" amid a beautiful redwood forest, which members consider sacred, to take the cares of the world off their shoulders, this club is called Bohemian Grove. The club was founded in 1872 and despite the fact that more than 2300 of the most powerful men in the world meet there annually we never hear much of it.

In July of 1991 Dirk Mathison, San Francisco bureau chief for *People* Magazine, snuck into the Grove. He saw "Druidic rituals" and even former Attorney General Elliott Richardson give a speech called "Defining the New World Order." He saw the heads of many nations, leaders in business, as well as media moguls, his very employers… who recognized him and promptly had Grove security escort him from the premises! These same executives from Time Warner, who published *People* Magazine, blocked and prevented Mathison from running his article on the pagan rites and political manipulations occurring in Bohemian Grove.

This was not the first time someone had infiltrated the Grove. Philip Weiss of *Spy Magazine* snuck in during the summer of 1989 and also saw odd "Druidic tree worship and bizarre rites." He heard that the men were officially summoned over loud speakers with the hail "Brother Bohemians: The Sun is once again in the clutches of the Lion, and the encircling season bids us to the forest, there to celebrate the awful Mysteries!" Wow! Evidence that those who attend this "country club," world leaders such as the Presidents Bush, are there for the Mystery Religion! Weiss also mentioned that there is copious consumption of alcohol and a great deal of homosexual promiscuity. He wrote that Grove regulars had even informed him that "AIDS has put a damper on the Grove's... pickup scene."

Of the Grove's pagan rituals is the paramount "Cremation of Care" ceremony which is held before a forty-foot tall, moss-covered statue of stone and steel at the south end of the lake. The idol is horned and is rather owl shaped.[27] Bohemians refer to it as Moloch! Weiss tells us that he was informed by Grove members that the "ceremony derives from Druid rites and American (Masonic) Lodge rites."

Moloch is the Ammonite's name for Nimrod! These men are not only following the Mystery Religion, they are worshipping Nimrod outright!

Every year there is a dramatic performance for the members to watch and learn from. The performance of 1989 had a budget of more than $75,000, an orchestra, hundreds of back stage personnel, dozens of on-stage extras and was masterfully produced, but it was only to be seen once by the elite gathered there that day.

I obtained, off E-Bay, the script from the July 30, 1976,

---

[27] The owl is the official logo of Bohemian Grove. In Talmudic lore the owl is the consort of the goddess Lilith. Lilith is described as the first created female, part serpent and responsible for revealing the mysteries of the Garden of Eden to Adam. One legend claims she then desired to return to the Cherubim in heaven but instead found herself cast out. Angels loyal to God then threatened to drown her. Undoubtedly, she bears quite a resemblance to Lucifer.

performance of *Noah.* The script sets the scene for the first act, amid "various orgiastic activities… devils dance and cavort among the people as they encourage and inspire their wickedness. We hear a chant offstage: Baal, Baal, Baal, We offer sacrifice to thee, This sacrifice! Praise be to Baal, Glory be to Baal, Baal, Baal, Baal." Actors also portray the heroes, Lucifer and Moloch, in the performance.

German Chancellor Helmut Schmidt wrote in his autobiography, *Men and Powers,* that he regularly attends these rituals in German Groves, but prefers those at the Bohemian Grove most of all.

> Allegations by former Republican Senator John DeCamp of murder and snuff films shot in Bohemian Grove (are) in his book, *The Franklin Cover-Up.* Former Republican Nebraska State Senator John DeCamp writes that Paul Bonacci was an eyewitness to the rape and ritualistic murder of a young boy in the Bohemian Grove in the summer of 1984… More details are available in *Bohemian Grove: Cult of Conspiracy,* by Mike Hansen. They are far beyond the most gruesome and grotesque things one could imagine, and are not included here because simply reading the details will make many readers physically ill. It will leave images in the mind that most readers would wish they had never seen.
>
> Mark Dice, *The Resistance Manifesto,*
> pgs 218, 273, 274

On July 15, 2000, two men again snuck past the ultra high security made up of the most elite Special Forces Operatives. This time with hidden cameras to show the world what exactly was going on there. Their video taped footage was shown in the United Kingdom as part of a four part TV special entitled *The Secret Rulers of the World.* These two men, Alex Jones and Mike Hansen, were witness to an occult ritual involving the leaders of the free-world. The video showed the elite before the enormous idol of Moloch chanting in ceremonial robes. The video also shows what Jones and Hansen hoped was a mock child sacrifice, amid roaring flames at Moloch's feet. The Bible tells us that this was Moloch's traditional ritual (Leviticus 18: 21).

What few people picked up on, awed with the frightening imagery alone, was a man wearing a Sonoma County Sheriff's Department uniform, presuming these two reporters were supposed to be there, asked them "Were you here in 1913? Are you one of the Old Ones?"

Jones and Hanson bluffed their way past this individual and got away with their video proof that the pagan Mysteries were alive among the elite of America. But what of the comment regarding the "Old Ones," what was this all about? These were men born in the early 1970's. There is no way that Jones and Hansen were old enough to have lived in 1913. In Francis X. King's book *Witchcraft and Demonology,* while discussing the famed occultist and writer H.P. Lovecraft, he has this to say about the "Old Ones:"

> Firstly, that humanity is ignorant of the real nature of the universe, there are other dimensions of space which are full of beings of terrifying power and malignancy. Secondly, that earth was once ruled by some of these beings, the Great Old Ones, who somehow or other lost control of it but are perpetually endeavoring to regain their lost dominion. And, finally, that all over the world exist individuals and groups who have chosen to ally themselves with the Great Old Ones... the Great Old Ones are Lucifer and his angels; their human allies are witches and black magicians.
>
> Francis X. King, *Witchcraft and Demonology,* pg 151

DEAD PRESIDENTS: Some great men have stood against the Luciferian threat. For example Abraham Lincoln tried to stop the Rothschild banking family from loaning their currency to the American people. Lincoln realized the interest rate they charged for loaning the paper money, inflation, would enslave a nation. If the Rothschilds wanted their money back they could take it. It was theirs, but they were loaning it for a fee. If they took it all back they would leave the people with no money to pay that fee, how would the people repay the interest? Lincoln called the bankers the "Money-Power:"

> The money-power preys upon the nation in times of peace and conspires against it in times of adversity. It is more despotic than monarchy, more insolent than autocracy, more selfish than bureaucracy. I see in the near future a crisis approaching that unnerves me, and causes me to tremble for the safety of our country. Corporations have been enthroned, an era of corruption will follow, and the money-power of the country will endeavor to prolong its reign by working upon the prejudices of the people,

until the wealth is aggregated in a few hands, and the republic is destroyed.

Lincoln was shot dead shortly after issuing America's own paper money called Greenbacks.

In 1835 Andrew Jackson also spoke out against the bankers. "You are a den of vipers. I intend to rout you out and by the eternal God I will rout you out. If the people understood the rank injustice of our money and banking system, there would be a revolution by morning." Jackson was shot, as he lay bleeding he told Vice President, Martin Van Buren "The bank, Mr. Van Buren, is trying to kill me."

James Garfield was the 20th President of the United States. He said that whoever controls the supply of America's paper money would control the business and activities of all the people. After only four months in office, on July 2, 1881, he was shot dead in a railway station.

In 1863 Mayer Amschel Rothschild said "Give me control of a nation's money and I care not who makes the laws."

Today the Federal Reserve is responsible for printing America's money, do not let the name fool you, they are not federal in any way. They are a private entity ultimately owned by the same central bankers. "Some people think the Federal Reserve Banks are the U.S. government's institutions. They are not... they are private credit monopolies which prey upon the people of the United States for the benefit of themselves and their foreign swindlers."[28]

Once a man came to lead the American Government; he saw the conspiracy there and went to war against it. He was an intellectual reared within one of the most elite families. He knew full well the corruption he faced when he became president. Instead of joining in as the Luciferians had hoped this man fought against them.

The enemy could not get control over him; because of his family's wealth he could not be bought or bribed. He went to war on organized crime, those responsible for prostitution, drugs, intimidation and violence. He went after big-business. He vowed to take away the Texas oilmen's lucrative oil-depletion allowance. International bankers, such as the Rothschilds, trembled when this heroic president signed Executive Order 11110, which would shut down the Federal Reserve

---

[28] Congressional Record 12595-12603, Louis T McFadden, Chairman of the Committee on Banking and Currency, Jun 10, 1932.

System and have the Treasury Department begin printing its own money. He tried to end the Cold War by signing the Nuclear Test Ban treaty with Russia. He planned to withdraw American troops from Vietnam by the end of 1965. He fired the corrupt top spies and intelligence agents that had become a government of their own, a shadow government, he even signed an order to abolish the entire CIA. The Vice-president was also to be terminated from office.

This man was President John F. Kennedy.

He spoke out against the secret societies he saw acting behind the scenes pushing for the New World Order. He stated "The very word secrecy is repugnant in a free and open society. And we are as a people, inherently and historically, opposed to secret societies, to secret oaths, and to secret proceedings."

In a speech at Columbia University, November 12, 1963, he expanded on this, "The office of the President has been used to foment a plot to destroy America's freedom and before I leave office, I must inform the citizen of this plight."

He was assassinated just ten days later.

Conclusive research, like that by Jim Marrs, in *Crossfire, the Plot that Killed Kennedy,* indicates that Kennedy's murder was organized by those within every branch of the Luciferian chain: Big-business, Big-oil, Big-banking, Big military-industrial complex, Big-organized crime, Big CIA and intelligence community.[29]

Despite the fact that JFK's assassination was very public, to send a message to others that may follow his lead, there was another Kennedy waiting in the wings and ready to become President and finish what his brother had started. JFK's brother Bobby Kennedy was similarly murdered, along with the man who was alleged to soon be revealed as his presidential running mate, Dr. Martin Luther King.

Those who hang out at Bohemian Grove, worshipping Moloch have been implicated in many dastardly things. They are admittedly trying to manipulate and steer the people of the world and they eliminate anyone who gets in their way, even Presidents and world leaders. As followers of Nimrod it cannot be a coincidence that the direction they're leading us is the Biblical end times.

---

[29] Alex Jones produced a documentary, *JFK II,* which showed that Texas oilman and CIA head, George H.W. Bush, may have had a larger roll in the assassination than anyone previously thought.

CHAPTER TEN
NIMROD RESSURRECTED: THE ANTICHRIST RETURNS

The spirit of the Antichrist, which you have heard is coming...
is now already in the world.
1John 4: 3

THE AMERICAN DOLLAR BILL: Luciferians need only look to
the American dollar bill for a reminder of their savior's identity as well
as their mission. Believe it or not, the Freemasons laid out their full
intentions, their great "undertaking," here; the most notorious and
widely distributed piece of paper on earth.

The Latin words around the pyramid in the Great Seal: ANNUIT
COEPTIS, NOVUS ORDO SECLORUM, comes from an ancient work
by the Roman poet Virgil (70- 19 BC), *the Aeneid.* This phrase is from
a prayer to Jupiter asking his favor in an "undertaking."

Remember, quite simply, an *undertaker* is someone who buries and
exhumes dead bodies.

The lower line, NOVUS ORDO SECULORUM, refers to the New
World Order. The symbolism on the bill implies that somehow the
Great Pyramid of Egypt would be involved in this. Furthermore, things
will come to fruition when the All Seeing Eye of Osiris becomes the
capstone that finishes the work.

What was Osiris undertaking?

Osiris is another name for Nimrod, and we know that he was intent
upon two things. Nimrod wanted to unite all the people and then
involve them in a rebellion against God.

THE RESTORATION OF BABEL: Nimrod's base of operations
was Babylon. The Biblical name Babel is in fact a pun. To Bible
readers we see the term related to "babbling," like gobble-de-gook
mixed up speech. To the Sumerians, those who built the tower, in their
language it meant "gateway to god."

In 1563 the artist Pieter Bruegel completed a painting called "the
Tower of Babel," it has become the most famous rendering of

Nimrod's unholy Tower. In the early 1990s, during the formation of the European Union, apparently the first kingdom of the New World Order, a promotional poster and symbol were adopted. They are easily seen to be the Tower of Babel from Bruegel's painting. It had the caption "Europe: Many Tongues, One Voice" and the image was of the Tower under construction. There were several inverted pentagrams above it and Egyptian pyramids seen in the background. Soon after, the European Union's parliament building was constructed in Stasboug, it is also easily recognizable as Bruegel's Tower of Babel. Why make such an effort to emulate a construct that long ago offended God?

If Nimrod were alive today and saw this, he would certainly feel at home.

OSIRIS: Egyptians prophesied about Osiris long ago that he would live again and lead the people. "Raise yourself, O Osiris, first-born son of Geb, at whom the Two Enneads tremble... Your hand is taken by the Souls of On, your hand is grasped by Ra, your head is raised by the Two Enneads, and they have set you, O Osiris, at the head of the Conclave of the Souls of On. Live, live and raise yourself (Pyramid Texts, Utterance 532)!" It has been recorded in the Theban Recension in the *Book of the Dead,* chapter 64, that Osiris said: "I am Yesterday and I am Today; and I have the power to be born a second time!" This is incredibly similar to the Biblical verse regarding the Beast who once was, now is not, and yet will come (Revelation 17: 8)!

> Osiris appears... "Here comes **the Dweller in the Abyss**," says Atum. "We have come," say they, say the gods to you, O Osiris... The sky has conceived him, the dawn has borne him... You support the earth with your left side, possessing dominion; you live, you live, because the gods have ordered that you shall live.
>
> Pyramid Texts, Utterance 577

> The sky reels, the earth quakes, Horus comes, Thoth appears, they raise Osiris from upon his side and make him stand up... Orion, long of leg and lengthy of stride, who presides over Upper Egypt. Raise yourself, O Osiris... The sky is given to you, the earth is given to you, and the towns are given to you and he who speaks about it is Geb.
>
> Pyramid Texts, Utterance 477

> Raise yourself, my father... Traverse the sky, make your abode in the Field of Offerings among the gods... Sit upon your iron throne, take your mace and your scepter, that you may **lead those who are in the Abyss,** give orders to the gods, and set a spirit in its spirit-state... O my father, raise yourself, go in your spirit-state.
> Pyramid Texts, Utterance 512

All these statements say Osiris will rise from the dead. But how could a long dead, hacked up mummified Egyptian god be reborn?

> The coming of the lawless one will be in accordance with the work of Satan displayed in all kinds of counterfeit miracles, signs and wonders, and in every sort of evil that deceives those who are perishing.
> 2Thessalonians 2: 9, 10

The coming of the Antichrist will be "in accordance" with the work of Satan. "In accordance with" means *in agreement* or *in conjunction with,* this means that certain humans will be working in conjunction with Satan to produce the "lawless one." It will be one of the most spectacular events ever. Everyone will be aware of it.

GENETIC ENGINEERING: In 1953 DNA was discovered to have a double-helical structure, like two snakes winding around each other. Biological reproduction occurs when the male's sperm and the female's egg each contribute one chromosomal strand, or snake, to combine into a new individual. One half of the very complex DNA comes from the mom, one from the dad. DNA is incredibly small, but full of an incredible amount of data. Each molecule represents the entire blue print of that individual. Their entire body, all their physical traits and many elements of their character are programmed into the smallest of molecules.

With just one intact set of DNA blueprints, say from a single cell, many wondered, could the DNA of a creature be isolated and reproduced to create an identical individual? How about from a dead creature? Could the DNA blue print be retrieved from a dead creature to bring it back to life? This was the premise of Steven Spielberg's film *Jurassic Park,* to clone dinosaur DNA and get a theme park full of giant prehistoric lizards. It was actually considered for the Wooly Mammoths discovered in the Siberian and Alaskan permafrost.

Unfortunately, the freezing processes irreparably damaged the prehistoric creature's cells. Those scientists could only hope something preserved in a hotter and dryer environment might be clonable.

Then the Science Journal *Nature* reported a breakthrough on April 18, 1985, with the article *Molecular Cloning of Ancient Egyptian Mummy DNA*. Svante Paabo of the Department of Cell Research at the University of Uppsala Sweden had found that the mummification processes of the ancient Egyptians were sufficient to preserve DNA over several millennia so that it "could be molecularly cloned in a plasmid vector." No one really paid much attention to this, they knew it was possible, but more work was necessary to actually clone and resurrect anything, let alone a dead mummy. But then Dolly came along.

Dolly the cloned sheep was presented before the media in July 1996. She was a living breathing clone. The process had worked! But to clone a human being still required a giant leap.

The Human Genome Project was that *leap*. The mapping of the entire human DNA molecule was completed in 2003. With the map of the molecule the possibilities became endless. Manipulation became possible, human traits and characteristics could all be modified before conception. Sexes could be predetermined. Your child's eye or hair color, height or athleticism could all be picked ahead of time. Say a gene for cancer was apparent, it could be removed. Any desire became a possibility. The potential for abuses also became endless.

Since President Obama took office more money has been set aside for genetic research than ever imagined. Thanks to him, this is now the hottest field in research science. Do you think we can trust them not to find ways to abuse DNA technology?

The Daily Mail reported on July 22, 2011 that "150 human animal hybrids were grown in UK labs: Embryos have been produced secretively for the past three years." The paper names the three locations where it occurred and calls the human animal hybrids "chimeras." Images were shown of half human and half rabbit creatures, a combination of human and cow, and a half human and half mouse creature.

We are to be watching for the events of Noah's day in our own. Could this be a part of it?

NIMROD RETURNS: Recall that Nimrod's body was cut to pieces and parts sent to all the lands he terrorized. Egyptians explained that is why there were so many locations for Osiris' tomb, such as the Osirion at Abydos and even the tomb of Gilgamesh found by archeologist Jorg Fassbinder in Iraq on April 13, 2003.

But none of these compare to what lies bellow Giza. The ancient Greek traveler and historian Herodotus tells us in his *Histories* that the primary Tomb of Osiris was at Giza, home of the Great Pyramids.

> Adorned with pillars… the sepulcher of the king …the burial place of one whom I think it not right to mention… large stone obelisks in the enclosure, and there is a lake… On this lake it is that the Egyptians represent by night his sufferings whose name I refrain from mentioning and this representation they call their Mysteries. I know well the whole course of the proceedings in these ceremonies, but they shall not pass my lips.
>
> Herodotus, *Histories* 2: 168- 171

Albert Pike also quotes from Herodotus and discusses the Tomb of his god. "Here we reach the most mysterious part of the ancient initiations, and that most interesting to the Mason who laments the death of his Grand Master Khir-Om (Hiram). Over it Herodotus throws the august veil of mystery and silence… he speaks of a tomb… this God was Osiris, put to death by Typhon, and who descended to the Shades (*Morals and Dogma,* pg 405)." Obviously the Mason puts the utmost importance on the tomb of their god. Manly P. Hall speaks of a similar underground island adorned with pillars in his book *The Secret Destiny* of *America* (pg 52- 55).

Explorers and archeologists have been banned from the lower levels of the Great Pyramid and the tunnel riddled Giza complex for several decades now, but the first archeologists had free access to the area. From their records we can tell they found an unopened tomb with four squared pillars on a small subterranean island which was surrounded by a few feet of water, precisely how Herodotus described the legendary resting place of Osiris.[30]

Working under the profiteer and scoundrel Howard Vyse the Italian Captain Giovanni Battista Caviglia (1770- 1845) found a sand and rubble filled shaft-way in 1816, leading 114 feet straight down. A map

---

[30] The Osirion at Abydos also matches this description but is out in the sun… as above, so bellow.

was made and this location the vertical passage was labeled "Shaft #1."

Next we come across the thorough documentation of Selim Hassan. While exploring Shaft #1, and after cleaning out a large amount of the rubble, Hassan saw it matched Herodotus' ancient description of Osiris' tomb! *The Daily Telegraph* of England carried the amazing story of this discovery on March 10, 1935. It was documented that Hassan found an opening near the Sphinx. He entered the underground causeway now known to lead to the middle pyramid. Midway there was a shaft that descended straight down ninety-five feet. In 1944 Hassan documented that the four pillars were completely intact and covered with strange ancient writing.

In 1997 Borris Said again found the Tomb, but Zahi Hawass, the boisterous and arrogant Egyptian Minister of State Antiquities, a very controversial character to put it mildly, took credit for the discovery. He has taken credit for most Egyptian archeological discoveries since he came to power. Hawass has even had a brief reality TV program where he can be seen yelling fanatically at his archeology students. Unfortunately this madman has dictated exactly who could and could not get archeological permits in his country. For years he has absolutely banned anyone and everyone, except for himself, from Giza's locked lower subterranean levels.

Despite documented explorers previously entering the hidden tomb, Hawass went to the media and claimed he had discovered the Tomb of Osiris! His account can be seen in an article called *The Sandpit of Royalty.*

> I have found a shaft, going 29 meters vertically down into the ground, exactly half way between the Chrefren Pyramid and the Sphinx. At the bottom which was filled with water, we have found a burial chamber with four pillars. In the middle is a large granite sarcophagus, which I expect to be the grave of Osiris, the god... I have been digging in Egypt's sand for more than 30 years, and up to date this is the most exciting discovery I have made... we found the shaft in November and began pumping up the water recently. So several years will pass before we have finished investigating the find.
>
> Dorte Quist, *Extra Bladet*
> (Newspaper), Copenhagen,
> January 31, 1999.

Not years but days later on FOX television, March 2, 1999, Hawass had his own TV special entitled *Opening the Lost Tombs, Live from Egypt*. Here Hawass shows the Tomb for the whole world to see. The water filled Sarcophagus was more than nine feet long and lying open, its lid upon heavy wooded beams, a chain and hoist hanging from the ceiling. Also to note, the four inscribed stone pillars were completely smashed!

Hawass concluded after finding the tomb empty that it was merely a symbolic representation of Osiris' grave. He never mentioned the vandalism of the stone pillars. But as the absolute overlord of Giza, he should've had some knowledge of this.

THE VANDALISM: Egyptologist Robert Temple was granted the extremely rare opportunity to explore the tomb, and revealed his discoveries in the book *Egyptian Dawn*. He was able to prove that the Tomb of Osiris was added later, long after the Pyramids were constructed and long after the level above, level two, was carved out.

Temple tells us that the vandalism of the four pillars had to have happened between 1944 and 1956. He offers one very brief guess at who did it. Keep in mind this is coming from a scholar, a scientifically minded person, not someone chasing after shadows or conspiracy theories.

> The hacking away of the four stone columns is so utterly vicious and must have required such prolonged and exhausting effort over a substantial period of time that it seems to me that it could only have had a fanatical religious motivation of some kind. Certainly it was far beyond the capability of any casual vandals, and must have been consciously planned… the destruction could conceivably have been carried out for some sinister occult purpose by a secret society, Freemasons or the Rosicrucians.
>
> Robert Temple, *Egyptian Dawn*,
> pg 64, 65

Temple admits this would be unlikely because these groups "would be more inclined to take a favorable interest in such a site than damage it." What if, however, the Freemasons had something to hide here?

THE SYMBOLIC TOMB: It is quite likely Hawass was correct in assuming that the tomb was a symbolic one. No mummy could be expected to survive in a coffer that was constantly filled with water.

The room was crudely cut, roughly hewn, not with the usual perfection we'd expect of a Giza site. The tomb was small and without the usual religious paraphernalia and inscriptions to take the dead through the underworld. The tomb only had enough room for a few priests and an initiate. It is known that pharaohs had particular initiation ceremonies upon taking the crown, ceremonies where they might become possessed by the spirit of Osiris. This was probably the place where the ritual re-enactment of the death of Osiris was performed. Recall Nimrod/Osiris was put in a box by Shem, it was sealed shut and he was drowned. The pharaoh may have had some secret means of breathing, say from a tube, as he lay meditating in the water with the heavy stone lid closed over him. When the lid was raised he too would have been symbolically raised from the dead.

THE DACITE COFFER: Let's back up a level now. On level two, the older middle level above Osiris' symbolic tomb, we see something very strange. All the attention was on the symbolic tomb so everyone missed a very pertinent clue. On level two there sit two extremely large, enormous, 9 feet long, 40 ton coffers.

Using new scientific dating techniques Robert Temple tells us these coffers were placed there around 2250 BC. Arch Bishop Usher, who made a time line of the Biblical personalities and events, tells us that Nimrod died at about this time.

One of these large coffers has been found to be carved out of a piece of dacite.

In all of Egypt this is the only artifact made from dacite. It is an extremely rare mineral "found in lava flows as small intrusions." This coffer is probably the largest known piece of dacite on earth! Ever!

But what's the big deal about dacite, besides the obvious question: where did the ancient Egyptians get it?

Dacite is radioactive.[31]

Anything stored in a dacite coffer such as this would be preserved forever free from fungal rot and bugs, the arch enemies of mummies everywhere. Whatever was kept in this giant coffer was preserved in a fashion similar to irradiated supermarket food.

If we examine the Mystery lore of the Sumerian god Dumuzi, the same deity as the Babylonian Tammuz, we see reference to this particular method of preservation. In the story of *Inanna's Descent to*

---

[31] Robert Temple took a Geiger counter to it, *Egyptian Dawn* pg 60.

the Lower World we are told that after Dumuzi's death, his wife Inanna takes his corpse to Bad-Tibira (Cush/Thoth) to embalm it. She says "It should be preserved, so that one day, on the Final Day, Dumuzi will return from the dead." There is wailing as he is embalmed and Inanna orders the mummy placed on a stone slab of lapis lazuli rather than buried. The mineral lapis lazuli is not dacite; dacite is far too rare, lapis lazuli was the substitute chosen in ancient Sumeria and Egypt. Almost all the dead were buried with a scarab beetle made of this semi precious blue mineral.

We won't even ask how the ancients understood what it means to be "irradiated." They were guided by Watchers. Only one thing was to be preserved like this. Only one thing was so precious to necessitate this extreme.

1947: THE YEAR THE CLOCK STARTED TICKING: What was happening on the Giza Plateau during the 1944- 1956 period when Robert Temple says the vandalism of the four pillars occurred?

World War II had just ended. Politically the British were in charge, led by Winston Churchill a Freemason[32] and Druid. His close ally during the war was Harry S. Truman, the thirty-third American President and thirty-third degree Freemason. Truman was the president who dared use the nuclear bomb. Freemasonry was popular in Cairo, as Lodges were formed for the many servicemen, such as the Bulwer Lodge and Lord Kitchener Lodge.

In 1947 everything changed. The United Nations General Assembly approved the creation of the Jewish State on November 29, right next to Egypt. As the British were leaving the country the first act of free Egypt was to go to war against Israel! At the same time a rampant plague of cholera had broken out, killing at least 20,000 people.

Somewhere here, amidst the chaos of 1947, the mummified remains of Osiris were exhumed from the dacite coffer. There was so much turmoil in the region no one would have noticed the endeavor. It could have been a British military force who supplied the manpower and perhaps led by elite members of secret societies, such as Masons like Churchill.

1947 was the year the prophetic clock started ticking again. This was without a doubt when the birth pains of the end times began

---

[32] Churchill became a Freemason in 1901 according to the records of Studholme Lodge no. 1591 in London.

(Matthew 24: 8, Mark 13: 8). Firstly, Israel returned to the Holy Land. Also the ancient knowledge of both God and Lucifer were found on ancient parchments; the Dead Sea Scrolls were found accompanied by the Book of Enoch, and the Nag Hammadi Library was translated and released, the source of modern Gnosticism. There was the prophetically significant UFO crash near Roswel New Mexico. The CIA was formed by Skull and Bones alumni. The Cold War began. The agents of world government, the WTO and IMF were formed. George Orwell wrote *Nineteen Eighty Four.* The American MKUltra mind control program was formed, Aleister Crowley died and many other important incidents occurred all pointing towards the end times.

And ever since, the Secret Societies have likely had possession of Nimrod's remains.

HOW THE FREEMASONS REVIVE THE BEAST: Albert Pike referred to Osiris as "the Savior" that rises from death (*Morals and Dogma,* pg 589) and as "the Redeemer (*Morals and Dogma,* pg 640)." Manly P. Hall wrote:

> The Dying God shall rise again! The secret room in the House of the Hidden Places shall be rediscovered. The Pyramid again shall stand as the ideal emblem of solidarity, inspiration, aspiration, resurrection, and regeneration.
>
> Manly P. Hall, *The Secret Teaching of All Ages,* pg 120

Hall said more in *The Lost Keys of Freemasonry* (aka: *the Secret of Hiram Abif*).

> The Grand Master dying in the midst of his labors... he is not dead; he is asleep. Who will awaken him? His labors are not done... He must remain asleep... until they raise their Master from the dead... This eternal quest is yours until ye have found your Builder, until the cup giveth up its secret, until the grave giveth up its ghosts. No more shall I speak until ye have found and raised my beloved Son, and have listened to the words of my Messenger and with Him as your guide have finished the Temple which I shall inhabit.

Hall seems to be channeling Satan here, commanding his followers to find his son and raise him from the dead. But how can the Masons, as the preeminent surviving Mystery cult, awaken their Grand Master?

The third Masonic degree, that of Master Mason has a ritual which has been called their most important because of what is hidden in the symbolism involved. In the ritual the candidate plays the role of Hiram Abif in a dramatic reenactment of his life. Abif is killed, lies dead, and is restored to life. This has been widely acknowledged by senior Masons, such as Albert Pike and Mackey, as a reenactment of Osiris' life. Here we must pay attention to the language regarding the revival of Osiris.

Captain William Morgan was martyred by Freemasons in 1826 for revealing this secret ritual in his book *Morgan's Freemasonry Exposed and Explained.* From his writings we will paraphrase parts of the initiation ritual for the degree of Master Mason.

> The Third, or Master Mason's Degree: The traditional account of the death, several burials, and resurrection of Hiram Abiff, the widow's son.
>
> *Q.* "Why do you leave the West, and travel to the East?"
> *Ans.* "In search of more light."
>
> "Teach the Candidate how to approach the East... you are about to receive all the light that can be conferred on you in a Master's Lodge."
>
> They report that they had found the grave of their Grand Master, Hiram Abiff... "Try to raise the body by the Master's grip, or lion's paw." ...he proceeds to raise the Candidate, alias the representative of the dead body of Hiram Abiff... "Whisper the word Mah-hah-bone." The Master's grip is given by taking hold of each other's right hand as though you were going to shake hands, and sticking the nails of each of your fingers into the joint of the other's wrist where it unites with the hand. In this position the candidate is raised... the Master whispers the word Mah-hah-bone in his ear and causes the Candidate to repeat it, telling him at the same time that he must never give it in any manner other than that which he receives it. He is told that Mah-hah-bone signifies marrow in the bone.
>
> William Morgan, *Morgan's Masonry,*
> pgs 54- 64

The Lion's Grip secret handshake is significant because in ancient Egypt the lion was symbolic of eternal life. The Masons have claimed: "In ancient Egypt as we learn from the stone carvings on the ruins of temples a lion raised Osiris from a dead level to a living perpendicular by a grip of his paw (Carl H. Claudy, *Introduction to Freemasonry*, pg 135)." Apparently, somewhere in Egypt, there is an image of a lion raising Osiris from the dead. A replica is seen in *Morals and Dogma*, the only illustration in Pike's book.

We now know the secret handshake of the Master Mason, and it certainly won't raise a dead mummy back to life, but what of this Mah-hah-bone business? Masonry has many secret passwords. The ultimate password is believed to have been lost, or forgotten. Masons tell us that Mah-hah-bone is the substitute secret word until the original sacred "Lost Word" is rediscovered. Morgan tells us that Mah-hah-bone is a word pertaining to bone marrow, what does bone marrow have to do with resurrecting Osiris?

No matter the creature, when it has lain dead for centuries, the bone marrow is the best place to look for intact DNA. This is where the Antichrist's DNA will be found. Did the ancients understand the significance of this, keeping the secret hidden in the Master's word and the bone clawing handshake of the Masons? It cannot be believed that the ancient Egyptians understood DNA and such, but their gods certainly would have.

The Greek philosopher Plato, whose efforts the Masons claim to be reviving (Albert Pike, *Morals and Dogma*, pg 221) said some interesting things about bone-marrow. In his book *Timaeus* Plato tells us that in his day the belief was that the soul was tied to the body by the marrow. Very interesting considering our topic is cloning and regeneration, but Plato went even further and said bone marrow is where the unique "universal seed" of every living "kind" dwells. *Seed* and *kind*, these are the words we reviewed in Genesis when we were considering if the topics of DNA and genetics were at all covered in the Bible! Was Plato trying to get the same point across to us? These ancient writers were certainly not familiar with our current and modern terminology, but were they still trying to convey the same message?

It seems likely.

The Freemasons admittedly follow Plato's reasoning. They have this super important word: Mah-hah-bone, which has been handed down for thousands of years. They say it pertains to bone marrow. But when we add Plato's input, that it really has to do with *seed* and *kind,* we can conclude that the Freemason's word Mah-hah-bone pertains directly to DNA! Plato tells us to look to a creature's bone marrow to find their *seed,* certainly he knew the genitals were the seed producing organ for sexual reproduction, but the *universal* seed, the means to genetically copy an individual, would be found in the marrow. In fact, Plato taught that *marrow* and *seed* were two words for the same thing, and not only that he wrote that the *seed* emitted by the male's genitals comes from the marrow of the spine.[33] So all those pagan phallic symbols in the Mystery religions not only pertain to mere sexual reproduction, they pertain to genetic reproduction which includes processes akin to our modern cloning! The Mysteries have many secrets buried in layers upon layers of symbolism.

THE LOST WORD: This book has been the first ever to reveal the real secrets of Freemasonry. For all the Masons that are reading this, sitting on the edges of their seats excitedly discovering the meanings behind their vows, actions and symbols, there is one mystery left so far unrevealed, the mythic Lost Word.

The Masons have several mysterious words like *Mah-hah-bone.* Another phrase is one of the names for their deity, T.G.A.O.T.U. The acronym spelt out is: The Great Architect of the Universe. But the Lost Word is different, the word itself is has never been revealed, nor the meaning.

How can anyone ever hope to discover the secret meaning of a word if we don't even know what the word is?

Many explanations have been offered, but none make any sense when considering the clues offered. Freemasonry has claimed that the secret of the Lost Word is just that, entirely lost. The martyr William Morgan gave the only hint Masons know regarding the Lost Word when he revealed the script of the ritual drama for the third degree. We will again paraphrase this teaching of the Master Mason degree. The context is that Solomon has just discovered that Hiram Abif has been murdered by "three ruffians" who demanded to know the secret Master's Word. Hiram Abif refused to tell the word and he was killed and his corpse hidden. Solomon is now sending out agents to search for the body…

---

[33] Plato, Timaeus 91: B.

...and charges them if they find the body to examine carefully on and about it for the Master's word, or a key to it... they report that they had found the grave of their grand master, Hiram Abiff, and on moving the earth until they come to the body, they involuntarily found their hands raised in this position to guard their nostrils against the offensive effluvia which arose from the grave, and that they had searched carefully on and about the body for the Master's word, but had not discovered anything but a faint resemblance of the letter G on his left breast... that is not the Master's word, nor a key to it. I fear the Master's word is forever lost! ...is there no help for the widow's son?

They all then assemble around the candidate, the Master having declared that the first word spoken after the body was raised, should be adopted as a substitute for the Master's word, for the government of Master-Mason's Lodges in all future generations.

William Morgan, *Morgan's Masonry*

Mah-hah-bone is now the appointed substitute for the Master's word until the original is discovered. What clues are revealed in this passage as to what the original secret, or "Lost," word of Freemasonry is?

There are three clues: One, they found the body and smelled such a stink they had to hold their noses.

Two: the mysterious letter G.

And thirdly we are told that the first word uttered immediately after exhuming the rotted corpse had to do with the secret Master's word.

In Freemasonry they refer to their god as: TGAOTU, the Great Architect of the Universe. There is a G here, as in "Great Architect," which is the common name of the Mason's god. The riddle of the letter G on Hiram's left breast appears to be solved with this and it gives us a further clue as to the Lost Word: the Lost Word is the secret name of the Mason's god!

Now, the next clue is interesting. They raised their hands because the corpse stunk, buried fifteen days according to the legend. What was the first word they uttered?

In all honesty they must have said "PEE-YEW!" as they raised their hands to their noses.

Well, the Lost Word is not PEE YEW, but it is very close.

PEE-YEW sounds like P-tah, which is the name of an Egyptian god. An Egyptian god with some startling attributes.

Ptah is the oldest god of ancient Egypt (Masonry and the Mysteries were born in Egypt).

Ptah was the Egyptian god of craftsmen (Masonry has often been referred to as *the Craft*).

More specifically, Ptah was the god of stone based crafts, and the inventor of stone work and masonry!

Ptah was also the Egyptian god of resurrection.

Ptah has as symbols the serpent and the Djed pillar.

Ptah is related to the era immediately after the Flood when the land was still soaked and saturated with water, he helped reclaim the land.

Ptah is the father of the sun god Osiris.

Herodotus tells us that Ptah was the father of Apis, who we know to be the bull the Hebrews worshipped while Moses was on the mountain receiving the Ten Commandments. Apis is another version of Osiris/Nimrod.

Many scholars have seen the similarities and made comparisons between Ptah and the Sumerian serpent god ENKI.

The Memphis Triad tells us that Ptah is "the universal architect god and the patron of masons."

The Book of the Dead tells us that Thoth wrote down the teachings of Ptah and referred to him as "the Great Architect." We can clearly conclude that Ptah is the 'G,' the Great Architect, the god, of the Freemasons. And Ptah, as the father of the sun god Osiris, is Satan.

Therefore, the Lost Word of Freemasonry, the Master's Word, is Ptah, which is the ancient Egyptian name for Satan.

We should always remember fitting way in which the Freemason's chose to remember the Lost Word, the name of their god, by the sound one makes when uncovering something stinky and rotten.

Ptah's sacred symbol was not only the serpent, but more specifically the entwined serpents of the caduceus symbol, which we've mentioned many times, resemble the helical DNA molecule. Judy Kay King has put forward what she calls *the Isis Thesis,* in her book of the same title, she runs with the notion that the caduceus represents DNA. She shows that 870 other Egyptian symbols seem to map the complete sequence for cloning DNA! In her second book, a work of fiction, *The Road from Orion,* she describes how the hidden technology could indeed be used to clone a dead pharaoh!

Zecharia Sitchin is another researcher who has had some pretty far out ideas. He was one of the first to translate the old Sumerian clay tablets, with an odd bias that the ancients were in contact with extra-terrestrial space-men! He believed that Noah's Ark was a submarine, that Babylon was a space port city and that the Tower of Babel was a rocket ship that could take its occupants to Nibiru. His ideas seemed rather flakey, but he hit a homerun with his work showing the ancients had advanced sciences in the field of DNA.

In Sitchin's work, *the Cosmic Code,* he mentions ancient Egyptian documents which describe the processes of genetic engineering, *Tales of the Magicians* (Cairo Papyrus 30646) and the *Westcar Papyrus.* Both of these also claim that the Book of Thoth was the original source of this knowledge: what Cush had copied off of the Great Pyramid and what Manly P. Hall insists is still kept by elite Luciferian families!

CONCLUSION: From buying a stack of Masonic books and comparing their teachings to the Word of God I learned more than I ever thought possible about the end times. Understanding how events from the past are supposed to happen again, as in the days of Noah prophecy, is easier now. From the mythological records of many ancient cultures we were able to get a glimpse of their beliefs and maybe a history lesson as well. What these ancients were eyewitnesses to may be seen again in the end times.

We learned many of the different names various cultures had for Nimrod. There was very little about him in the Bible, but there was enough that we could follow his trail.

We learned that Nimrod was a hybrid Nephilim, son of Lucifer. He was a tyrant obsessed with uniting the world in rebellion against God. He was truly evil, hunting down souls to deceive them and turn them away from their own loving Father.

Fortunately, Shem, the son of Noah, decided to do something about this. He went to Nimrod and tricked the master of deception. Nimrod died, but he would not stay that way for long. The beast's wife retrieved the body and tried to somehow restore him to life. Shem discovered this and cut up the body and destroyed the "seed" generating parts hoping to prevent any resurrection or genetic manipulation, which the fallen angels were apparently known for before the Flood. Shem was of course eyewitness to these kind of evil acts.

The Egyptian legends tell us that Isis and Thoth were unrelenting, they used the knowledge of the Watchers left on the Great Pyramid to acquire, not the seed of Osiris, but his genetic "essence," his DNA.

They cloned Osiris and used Isis's womb to grow the embryo. The child Horus was born in secret, hidden from Shem. Later the demon ghost of the Nephilim Osiris possessed his own cloned body.

Horus would eventually die and Egyptian legends claim that his spirit then came to possess each succeeding Pharaoh afterwards, facilitated via certain rituals.

The Mystery Religion came into being as a means to preserve this story, the ancient science and the rituals involved. Freemasonry is now the living head of the Mysteries. Those involved in the conspiracy are preparing for their god's return. Their members include elite leaders of the world, studied experts, trained in population control and mass manipulation. They attend pagan rituals at places like Bohemian Grove where they pray to Moloch, the Ammonite version of Nimrod. They believe he will rise from the grave to again lead the world, Christians should be aware of this because the Holy Bible agrees! It would seem the Luciferians are presently orchestrating changes in several of the world's governments to prepare a one world government, a New World Order, which the Beast will arise to take control of. They are also preparing the world's citizens via carefully managed movements in our pop culture and entertainment.

The remains of his body will be found, if they haven't been already. Osiris will be cloned again. Horus will be reborn and again inhabited by Osiris' spirit. We have seen that the mummified remains may already be in the hands of secret societies that finance experiments related to DNA technology.

Revelation 9: 11 tells us that a comet will hit the earth and free the demon spirits from the Abyss. The Sumerians named that space borne object Encke, a name similar to Enki who originally sired Nimrod. If Enki is Lucifer, it fits that the Comet Encke's return will release *his seed* from the pit.

Nimrod's demon spirit will possess his clone midway through the seven year tribulation. Anyone following God will suffer as Nimrod will focus his attention on them. Then Christ our Lord will come and crush the Beast's head!

Jesus will come down on the Mount of Olives. The entire earth will shudder in the presence of the Creator. When our Lord comes every soul will be overcome by his presence; left still and silent in the awesome perfection radiating from him. Sinners will see the error of their ways and recognize the love God always intended for us all to receive. It will be the most glorious moment humanity will ever witness! Enoch prophesied that "the Lord is coming with thousands upon thousands of His holy ones" by his side (Jude 14). I believe that means every follower of Jesus Christ will come down with him. I intend to be there! I pray you will be too.

We have learned what to watch for, some of the signs the enemy displays. I pray we can educate our neighbors, warn our friends and families of the enemy's deceptive tactics and, most of all, tell everyone that they are loved by the one who created them.

HOW MUCH LONGER? ARE WE THERE YET? This is the biggest question for most Christians when it comes to this subject. Some preachers are ravenous in claiming the end is near, others ignore the topic all together. Jesus said that even he did not know when it would happen, that only the Father knows (Mark 13: 32). But we were told to be on guard, to watch carefully for certain signs and from these we can get a rough estimate of where we are in the scheme of things, we can know the season in which we live.

During the last two thousand years since the prophecies were given it has only been in recent decades that cloning was at all fathomable. So with this in mind we may be near the end times. We are also told in the Bible that a great rebellion against the Church will come before the Tribulation. There certainly seems to be a lot of rebellion in Western society and no one can argue that Church attendance has plummeted over the last generation. With these things in mind we may be close, but recall that the Tribulation does not actually start until the fatally wounded beast gets into politics and calls for a truce between Israel and her enemies (Daniel 9: 27). This truce will be the final sign! Wars between Israel and her enemies have been a near constant since her rebirth in 1948; tensions in the Mid-East seem to be constantly escalating. These things could go on for sometime. But the Antichrist's peace treaty seems to follow a devastating and catastrophic war, something that will not be mistaken for the current skirmishes there now.

And when the resurrected Nimrod does appear on the scene he will be impossible to miss. The Masons claimed he was eighteen feet tall! There will be no mistaking somebody even half that tall when they enter the international political realm.

Until then, what we should be watching for is the formation of a world government made up of ten states. Daniel spoke of a statue with ten toes and later a ten headed beast and told us that these represent the ten divisions of the last kingdom. He said that the Antichrist will become one of the ten kings, he will come up "after them," after the government is established (Daniel 7: 24)! He will come up "in the latter part of their reign (Daniel 8: 23)." He will then "subdue" three of the other kings and thereafter take over the entire earth. From this we can conclude that the end time's government, the New World Order, will already be in place by the time the Antichrist comes.[34] How long would it take to set up such an organization? It certainly couldn't be done overnight, it took years to unite the countries involved in the European Union, and they were friends! Unless some unprecedented event happens to speed up the process, like an *alien invasion,* I think evidence shows we are at least several decades from the end times. But watch out for events which could be a catalyst, speed things along, and manipulate the peoples of the world toward this end. Be alert for propaganda, watch for acts of population manipulation and control that will steer us this way. Remember that Jesus emphasized: do not be deceived (Matthew 24: 4, Mark 13: 5, Luke 21: 8). We are commanded to watch for these things (Matthew 24: 42) and to alert and educate our neighbors (Matthew 24: 10- 20).

Such a world government is the desire of those politicians with a globalist agenda. Politicians owned by the rich elite who fund, influence and guide them. Watch the behavior of rich families like the Rockefellers and Rothschilds. Look at those elite who attend pagan ritual meetings like those at Bohemian Grove. It is difficult because these folks own the media but Wiki-Leaks released the names of all 3000 individuals who attended the 2012 meeting. Do not be afraid to enter the political realm and chastise those who would take our God given rights from us. Be careful what you allow to influence you. Pop culture is not so innocent. There are people who are working day and night, trying to manipulate you and our society so we will accept what they want. Do not sit idly by. Get off your couch. Tear yourself away from entertainment that insults your intelligence! Every moment we can delay the Beast's arrival is a moment that somebody will find a relationship with Our Father in Heaven! We must pray constantly, and

---

[34] Similar to how the Emperor and tyrant Napoleon did not rise up until after the rebellion of the French Revolution occurred and an antichristian government was already firmly in place.

be on guard that we remain innocent as doves, but wise to the ways of the serpents. Our Creator loves us more than we can comprehend! He does not want us to fixate on the enemy's darkness. He does not want our lives to be filled with paranoia, depression or fear, but he does want us to understand the dangers that are out there so they can be avoided. Jesus has given his followers the authority to trample on snakes, to crush the heads of serpents (Luke 10: 18)! He has given us victory over the darkness, but we cannot thwart it if we do not know something of it and we cannot combat it unless we act!

Spread the Word.

APPENDIX:
A BRIEF HISTORY OF THE NEPHILIM

The Antichrist will be the son of Satan, who was once an angel named Lucifer. Human/angel hybrids are referred to in the Bible as Nephilim. As I researched the Nephilim I was astonished to find there weren't just a few of them, there was once an entire race! They literally had an empire that spanned the globe! Hear me out before you condemn me as a fool; there is a lot of evidence that backs this claim up. We'll look first to the irrefutable Biblical Scriptures, then historical documentation of their existence.

GIANTS IN GENESIS: In Genesis 6 we found the first mention of the Nephilim, we've been over that enough though. Let's move onto the story of Abraham who lived several years after the Flood. Here we will see that he encountered some people with strange sounding names, let's see what these names mean, maybe they can tell us something about these people.

In Genesis 14 we hear that Abraham's nephew, Lot, took up residence in a town called Sodom. Sodom was eventually taken by the nation of Shinar and its allies the Rephaites, the Zuzites and the Emites (Genesis 14: 5). Shinar is the Hebrew name for Sumeria, later known as Babylon, which was Nimrod's homeland, but who were these other peoples?

In Hebrew the name *Rephaites* literally means the "strong ones" and the name *Zuzims* means the "powerful ones."

> The Emites used to live there, a people strong and numerous, and as tall as the Anakites, they too were considered Rephaites, but the Moabites called them Emites... the Rephaites who the Ammonites called Zamzummites. They were a people strong and numerous as Anakites.
> Deuteronomy 2: 10, 11, 20

Okay, great, who are the Anakites then? Numbers 13: 33 tells us that "the descendants of Anak come from the Nephilim."

Wow! Did you follow that?

If the Anakites are Nephilim, then the Rephaites, Zuzites and Emites are all giants as well!

Clearly, Abram was at war with the Nephilim.

Abram was forced to form a small army and fight the Nephilim to see Lot returned. Incidentally, the king of the neighboring city of Gomorrah was Birsha (Genesis 14: 2), whose name means "Large man," he may also be a giant and Arioch, another king, involved in the skirmish (Genesis 14: 1), has a name meaning "tall among the giants."

MOSES AND THE GIANTS: Before the Flood Satan had seen to it that the world was filled with hybrids. It seems his plan was to breed humanity out of the equation. There could be no Savior to defeat him if man's genetic seed was entirely corrupted. Later he used the same strategy again, but this time he was going to spoil the Promised Land, hoping to corrupt the Hebrew's genetics and therefore prevent the birth of the Messiah.

After Moses and the Israelites escaped from Egypt and approached the Promised Land they decided that scouts should be sent ahead to "spy out the land." When the scouts returned their reports were mixed. Indeed the land was found to be "flowing with milk and honey" but they had seen a big problem.

> The people who live there are powerful… we even saw the descendants of Anak there… all the people we saw there are of great size. We saw the Nephilim there, the descendants of Anak come from the Nephilim. We seemed like grasshoppers in our own eyes, and we looked the same to them.
> Numbers 13: 28, 32, 33

> There were till then left the race of giants, who had bodies so large, and countenances so entirely different from other men, that they were surprising to the sight, and terrible to the hearing. The bones of these men are still shown to this day, unlike to any creditable relations of other men.
> Josephus, *Antiquities of the Jews*, 5. 2. 3

The Promised Land was populated with giants. Some were of the same tribes that Abraham had fought earlier. Furthermore, Numbers 13: 22 states this was "where Ahiman, Sheshai, and Talmai, the descendants of Anak lived…" these are even more tribal names seen in Scripture belonging to Nephilim.

For these were none other than the seed of the angels fallen…

sprung from their union with the daughters of men, and being half angels, half men, these giants were only half mortal… they were of such enormous size that the spies, listening one day while the giants discussed them, heard them say, pointing to the Israelites: "There are grasshoppers by the trees that have the semblance of men."

Ginzberg, *Legends of the Jews,*
Bk. III, pgs 269, 270

The report of giants in the Promised Land led the Hebrew people to rebel against the Lord's leadership. They feared entering the land even though God said he would be with them and miraculously protect them! "If only we had died in Egypt! Or in this desert! Why is the Lord bringing us to this land only to let us fall by the sword? Our wives will be taken as plunder. Wouldn't it be better for us to go back to Egypt? We should choose a leader and go back to Egypt (Numbers 14: 2-4)."

The Hebrews forgot all about God and declared "The people are strong and tall Anakites! Who can stand up against the Anakites (Deuteronomy 9: 2)?" God's frustration with the Jewish people led to a severe punishment. They would not be allowed to enter the Promised Land for forty more years, until that generation of fighting men had grown old and passed on. So, for the next forty years they wandered the desert in circles.

MOSES' WARS WITH THE GIANTS: While in the desert God set up situations to help his people acquire some battle experience and develop some strategies against these monsters. A lost book of the Bible is *the Book of the Wars of the Lord* (Numbers 21: 14), if it still existed we would no doubt find in it many details of Moses' battles with the Nephilim. We do know that they faced the army of:

Og, king of Bashan who was of the remnant of the Rephaites. His bed was more than thirteen feet long and six feet wide. It is still in Rabbah of the Ammonites… the whole region of Argob in Bashan used to be known as the land of the Rephaites.
Deuteronomy 3: 11, 13

The land was full of these satanic beings and God once again had a plan to get rid of them, but this time he wasn't going to use a flood. He would lead the Israeli army.

HOW TO FIGHT GIANTS: In the Rabbinical literature, based on ancient Hebrew oral traditions, we can find more of Og. He supposedly had a brother named Sihon, king of the Amorites (Numbers 21: 21). Apparently, Sihon took out his army of giants to fight the nomadic Hebrews thinking they could easily be massacred, but the Israelites instead put them to the sword and took over their land (Numbers 21: 24). The ancient Rabbis recorded that Sihon matched Og in stature and bravery. These brothers are spoken of in Psalm 136 where they are counted among the greatest antagonists Israel would face after Pharaoh himself.

The oral traditions of the Rabbis tell us that every one of the Amorite people were in fact giants, we're also told of the parentage of these two giant kings; their grandfather was an angel named Shamhazai (Niddah 61a)!

> Sihon, the king of the Amorites... and likewise Og, the king of Bashan, were sons of Ahiah, whose father Shemhazai was one of the fallen angels. In accordance with his celestial origin Sihon was a giant whom none could withstand, for he was of enormous stature... (until) God put Sihon's and Og's guardian angels in chains... after the angels of Sihon and his people had fallen, Moses had nothing more to fear.
>
> Ginsberg, *Legends of the Jews,*
> Book III, pg 340

Did you notice that Og's army could only be defeated after their protectors, the Watchers, were dealt with by God?

Wars were being fought in multiple dimensions; humans were fighting humans while holy angels were fighting fallen Watchers. This is why it was so important for the Hebrews to coordinate their attacks with God via prayer. There might be a lesson in here for all of us.

Deuteronomy 3: 4 tells us that the Hebrews eventually took all sixty cities in Og's kingdom. These victories must have encouraged the Israelites greatly.

After Moses' death, Joshua led the Hebrew people. God's command still stood, to take the Promised Land and wipe out all the inhabitants before them, all the people were to be put to the sword until they completely destroyed them, not sparing anyone (Deuteronomy 7: 1- 5). Until now many have not known the whole story and have asked "Why would God make such a militant and violent command?" We must understand, not only were those pagans in the Promised Land following the Luciferian religion, many would have had the blood of the Watchers in their veins. They had to be wiped out as they were with Noah's Flood.

JOSHUA'S WARS WITH THE GIANTS: Joshua led the Hebrew's army north from the Sinai desert into the Promised Land. He wrote that:

> This hill country that the Lord promised... the Anakites were there and their cities were large and fortified, but, the Lord helping me, I will drive them out just as he said... Hebron used to be called Kiriath Arba after Arba, who was the greatest man among the Anakites.
>
> Joshua 14 12- 15

> ...Kiriath Abar, that is Hebron. Arba was the forefather of Anak. From Hebron Caleb drove out the three Anakites; Sheshai, Ahiman and Talmai, descendants of Anak.
>
> Joshua 15: 13, 14

Remember, the descendants of Anak were Nephilim giants. From scripture we can see the direction of the war to drive them from the Promised Land. The fortified city of Jericho was the first Joshua and the Hebrew army had to face.

JERICHO: According to the *Jewish Encyclopaedia* (Vol. 5, page 659) Jericho was once widely known as the "City of the Giants." If we look at Joshua 6: 2, God says "See, I have delivered Jericho into your hands, along with its king and it's fighting men." In the original Hebrew, for the phrase *fighting men* the word *Gibborim* is used, this is one of the Hebrew words for *giant.* We can then conclude that the inhabitants of Jericho were Nephilim giants!

Since Jericho was a home to giants we would expect its fortifications, masonry and walls to have been exceptional and that is exactly what archeologists found when they discovered the city in the 1930s. The German-Austrian team, headed by John Garstang, found the remains of the once great city in the Tell es-Sultan mound. They also reported that "traces of intense fire are plain to see, including reddened masses of brick, cracked stones, charred timbers and ashes. Houses alongside the wall are found burned to the ground… the walls fell outwards so completely that the attackers would be able to clamber up and over their ruins into the city." This is an amazing find, because historically, besieged cities always have their walls forced inward as the invading army pushed ahead. Examining Jericho's walls makes one think that the walls were pushed out from within.

Sir Charles Marston, another archeologist to examine the Jericho site stated that the "study of the geological strata, in addition to archeological work on the walls themselves, now has revealed undoubted evidence that the wall was raised by an earthquake." Indeed God's power would appear as an earthquake, which enabled Joshua's forces to storm the city.

Interestingly, legends persist that a few giants escaped the destruction. The *Jewish Encyclopaedia* tells us that "Those who survived were led by a certain Ifrikish ibn Kais to Africa, and having killed the king of that country, settled there. The Berbers are their descendants (Vol. 5 page 659)." Ancient historians actually verify this by telling us of a monument left in the Numidian town of Tigisis. A Phoenician inscription was engraved into the pillar which Procopius translated as "We are those who fled from the face of Joshua the robber, the son of Nun." Suidas translated this as "We are the Canaanites, whom Joshua the robber drove out."

CITIES OF THE GIANTS: We know that the Hebrew armies were coming from the southern desert regions, pushing north, and that they would have to face the giants in "all the hill country of Israel (Joshua 11: 21)." Today there is evidence that giants did inhabit these cities.

The Baqa valley is three miles long and stretches from Bethlehem to the valley of Hinnom. Before it was called Baqa, the Hebrews referred to it as the Valley of the Rephaim, the Valley of Giants. Here odd remains can be found in several ancient cities that seem to indicate they once housed giant people. These were the fortified cities that the Hebrews had to take, cities such as Ashod (Joshua 11: 22). The ancient Egyptian *Execration Texts* refer to Ashod as "the City of Giants." The *Execration Texts* date to the Twelfth Dynasty, about 1900 BC and clearly state that the Egyptian's had huge Anakim in their territory. The texts are presently in the Berlin Museum and name many of the Anakim tribal leaders.

There are further representations of the sons of Anak in Egypt. The

Temple of Abu Simbel, the royal tombs of Biban-el-Molukat in Karnak and the tomb of Oimenepthah I all display images of giant blond men with white skin. The hieroglyphics in Oimenepthah I's tomb tell us of a particular giant called Tanmahu or Talmia. Amazingly, the Bible tells us that one of the children of Anak was indeed named Talmia (Numbers 13: 22). The same verse tells us of Talmia's brother Ahiman, who the ancient Jewish traditions say was the most feared of all the Nephilim. Apparently he would often taunt passers by, by demanding "Whose brother will fight with me?" It was customary at the time for entire armies to select their best men to fight one on one rather than all of those assembled risk their lives, precisely what we see in the story of David and Goliath.

Near Gaza, the town of Beit Jibrim still stands today. Its name means House of the Gibborim: House of the Giants. Here can be found a complex underground city, part natural cave, part laborious construct. Pick marks are visible on the walls of the sixty separate chambers whose ceilings reach enormous heights.

Along the Syrian Coast is the city of Ras Sharma, once known as Ugarit, where, in 1928, ancient volumes were found describing life in that ancient city. Besides religion, history and the local economy, the texts also frequently mention the Rephaim giants.

The city of Amon was spoken of by the Prophet Amos and he described its inhabitants as "Tall as the cedars and strong as the oaks (Amos 2: 9)."

The chief city of the Anakim giants was Kiriath Arba, later renamed by the Hebrews Hebron. The Bible tells us that Arba was "the mightiest of giants (Joshua 14: 15, 21: 11)."

Archeologists report that the remains of the city of Gezer "bear out the unusually tall stature of individuals in ancient Palestine (*The Wycliffe Bible Encyclopaedia*, Vol. 1, page 709)." According to archeological expert R.H. Hall, in his book *The Ancient History of the Near East*, "Recent excavations of the Palestine Exploration Fund at Gezer and various other researches have shown that... the Anakim or Rephaim, the 'Giants' of tradition, built the megalithic monuments, the dolmens and menhirs, of Moab and eastern Palestine. To them may be due the earliest stone walls of the Canaanite cities." Archeologist Cyril Graham states that the stone work of this time was inexplicably "Perfect... stone doors are still hanging on their hinges... all betoken the workmanship of a race endowed with powers far exceeding those of ordinary men… and give credibility to the supposition that we have in them the dwellings of a giant race… (we were) forced to the conclusion that its original inhabitants, the people who had constructed those cities, were not only a mighty nation, but individuals of greater strength than ourselves." Professor J.L. Porter agrees in his book *The Giant Cities of Bashan* where he also discusses the giant's incredible abilities and skills as stone masons.

Structures meant to last have always been built of stone. The Bible tells us that all these cities which the Hebrews faced were surrounded by imposing defensive walls, they "were large and fortified (Joshua 14: 12)," "the cities are large, with walls up to the sky (Deuteronomy 1: 28)." These ancient giants were not only strong enough to heave, manipulate and lift the massive stones found making up these walls, but they were accomplished stone masons, perhaps the greatest of masons. The dolmens and menhirs they constructed were the ritual locations, the high places mentioned in Leviticus 26: 30, which were apparently required to summon the Watchers, their own fathers. Fields of these stone objects are still to be seen across the northern Jordan.

STOPPING THE HEBREW'S ADVANCE: Despite all their defensive stone works, as word spread of the powerful invading Hebrew armies the giants must have grown fearful. We cannot forget it was through God that the Hebrew armies had their strength. Isaiah 17: 9 (LXX) tells us that the Amorites and Hittites never even fought the Hebrews; instead they fled their fortified cities. After hearing that their neighbors, fellow giants, were being massacred in city after city, they opted to go further north and hide.

The Hebrew armies went as far north as the city of Jerusalem. But Joshua did not take actual control over the city. Joshua's attack was stopped when he was deceived and erred greatly by allowing a treaty of peace to be made with the Gibeonites (Joshua 9: 15). Unfortunately this set a trend that became worse as time passed. The Hebrew forces allowed more and more treaties to be made (Judges 1: 27- 35). This was in direct contradiction to what God had commanded earlier (Deuteronomy 7: 2). God voiced his displeasure but the damage was done (Judges 2: 1- 3). The Israelites began to take part in their pagan neighbor's religion, bowing to the gods of the peoples around them.

So, with this, Joshua's seven year campaign against the Nephilim ended. He had conquered thirty-one Canaanite kings and taken their cities (Joshua 12: 7- 24). Unfortunately, however, Nephilim remained in Israeli territory, in Gaza, Gath, and Ashod (Joshua 11: 22). As long as any survived, obviously so did the Luciferian religion.

TALL KING SAUL: Saul was the first king of the Israelites, reigning from about 1050- 1040 BC. The Hebrew people rejected having God be their leader, and later rejected the Judges which God had appointed to govern on his behalf. Instead, in their desire to be like other nations with glorious giant kings, the Hebrews, with almost mob-like mentality chose Saul, who was naturally of above average height and size, as their king (1Samuel 9: 2).

Once again God would use the Hebrew army, now led by Saul, to destroy the Nephilim. The city of Gath was one of those places where Joshua had allowed the giants to exist. Saul led the Hebrews to war against the Philistines of Gath and their Champion, Goliath.

GOLIATH: MOST FAMOUS OF THE NEPHILIM: Both the armies of the Hebrews and the Philistines lined up at opposite ends of the battlefield. For days Saul and his army were fearful of the giant who stood and taunted them, regularly challenging the bravest to come fight him one on one. Saul, who did not have the greatest relationship with God, soon found it was David, a only lowly shepherd-boy and musician, who came forward to face the giant. Without armor or sword, relying only on faith in God, David went out to fight the giant:

> A champion named Goliath, who was from Gath, came out of the Philistine camp, he was over nine feet tall… (David) chose five smooth stones from the stream… the Philistine cursed David by his gods… David said… "You come against me with sword and spear and javelin, but I come against you in the name of the Lord Almighty… it is not by sword or spear that the Lord saves; for the battle is the Lords, and he will give all of you into our hands."
> The Philistine moved closer to attack him… Reaching into his bag and taking out a stone, (David) slung it and struck the Philistine on the forehead. The stone sank into his forehead, and he fell facedown on the ground… David ran and stood over him. He took hold of the Philistine's sword… and cut off his head… David put the Philistine's weapons in his own tent.
> 1Samuel 17: 4, 40, 43, 45, 47, 54

Saul soon became resentful of David's success. Because the people loved David, Saul sought to destroy the young slayer of giants. Saul turned his back on God and abandoned the fight against the Hebrew's enemies in the Promised Land. David and a band of his friends were forced to flee as the jealous Hebrew king did everything he could to kill the Sheppard boy.

The prophet Samuel tells us that because Saul meddled in pagan magic by consulting "the Witch of Endor" in his search for David, he was destroyed by God (1Samuel 28: 7-19). David eventually became the great king the Israelites wanted, reigning from about 1040 to 970 BC. Scripture tells us that God considered David to be "a man after God's own heart (1Samuel 13: 14)."

DAVID'S WARS WITH THE GIANTS: Now David went to war against the pagan nations and their Nephilim armies. When David first went to fight Goliath we were told he took five smooth stones from the stream with him, the four extra were not incase he might miss Goliath's mark, there were four other giants to slay! It is written that:

> David went down with his men to fight against the Philistines, and he became exhausted. And **Ishbi-Benob,** one of the descendants of Rapha, whose bronze spear head weighed 7½ pounds, said he would kill David. But Abishai son of Zeruiah came to David's rescue.
> In another battle, **Saph,** one of the descendants of Rapha...
> **Lahmi the brother of Goliath,** who had a spear with a shaft like a weaver's rod...
> There was **a huge man with six fingers** on each hand and six fingers on each foot, twenty four in all. He also was descended from Rapha...
> **These four** were descendants of Rapha in Gath, and they fell at the hands of David and his men.
> 2Samuel 21:15-22

> (David) slew two lionlike men of Moab... also he slew an Egyptian, a man of great stature, five cubits high; and in the Egyptian's hand was a spear like a weaver's beam.
> 1Chronicles 11: 22, 23 (KJV)

Earlier it was noticed that when the Hebrew armies were at war with the giants, holy angels were simultaneously fighting against the fallen Watcher angels in the spiritual realm. We see this occur again during

David's time. Jewish legend tells us that "in the battle that took place in the Valley of Giants, God had commanded David not to attack the host of the Philistines until he heard "The sound of marching in the tops of the mulberry trees." God desired to pass judgment upon the tutelary angels of the heathen, before surrendering the heathen themselves to the pious, and the motion of the tops of the trees was to indicate that the battle could proceed (Ginzberg, *Legends of the Jews,* Book IV, pg. 92, 93)." The Lord went out in front to strike the Watchers, thus making way for the Hebrew armies to advance (2Samuel 5: 24).

DAVID'S DOWNFALL: On one occasion, word came to David that his general, Joab, was victorious over the armies of Rabbah. David came up from Jerusalem, and took the crown from the head of their king. Its weight was found to be 75 pounds of gold and it was set with precious stones (1Chronicles 20: 2). Clearly only a giant could handle such headwear.

Afterwards, David returned to Jerusalem, where he had been taking it easy and the Hebrew armies continued their fight against the Philistines. Clearly the forces of the giants were being systematically crushed and routed. Then suddenly… this is the last mention of the wars with the giants. How does it end? Did David and his mighty men kill every last one of the Nephilim? Were they wiped out as God had commanded?

No.

It would seem that Satan slyly manipulated events in order to come to the aid of his monstrous forces. David, living a pleasant life in Jerusalem, had fallen into lust, adultery and murder. Since he was no longer following the Lord he could no longer provide solid leadership for the Hebrews. Then, because of David's personal weakness "Satan rose up against Israel (1Chronicles 21: 1)." He manipulated the Hebrews by working on their leader's pride. David was basking in the glory of his military victories, he marveled at his mighty men (2Samuel 23). He recounted all their exploits and then he ordered Joab to halt any combat in order to count all the members of his army and then count all the population that David felt he was master over (1Chronicles 21: 1-6). These actions made God very angry (1Chronicles 21: 7), so angry that he sent an angel to attack the Hebrew people (1Chronicle 14, 15)!

Satan halted God's assault on his followers by exploiting David's human weaknesses. He was able to buy his followers time to flee to the north. The Nephilim giants were not completely destroyed. They survived and as we'll see, took up life in Northwestern Europe.

LEGENDS OF THE GIANTS IN THE NORTH: Stephen Quayle, in his book *Genesis 6 Giants,* explains how "the Anakim, or giants that... were pushed out of Canaan by the Israelites, going northward and eventually travelling westward over Europe and, with the passage of several millennia, finally settled in the Celtic nations."

In 1703, a French priest named Paul Pezron, from Brittany, wrote in his *Antiquite de la Nation, et de Langue des Celtes* that he had managed to trace these Celtic giants' migrations. He stated "We may be confident, and that upon very good grounds, that this colony of the Cimbrians, or rather Nomadan Sacae, was very ancient, since it preceded the time of Inachus, who reigned in Greece about two-thousand years before the Nativity of our Savior. Further, I have met with some ancient fragments, which may be produced elsewhere, wherein the Cimmerians acknowledge themselves, they were originally descended from those Scythians, called Sacae; that they formerly dwelt in Asia."

Pezron taught that many of these giants were descendants of Gomer, the son of Japheth, son of Noah (Genesis 10: 2). Gomer was likely the founder of the ancient city of Gomorrah. Josephus confirmed this when he documented that Gomer's descendants make up the Celtic peoples (*Antiquities of the Jews,* 1: 6: 1).

Amazingly, the names of the giant chieftains of the Gomarian Sacae have survived, two princes, Acmon and Doeas, sons of Maneus, were the leaders of the giants when David's army forced them north. Acmon had a son named Uranus, and he a son named Saturn, and he a son named Jupiter. Pezron's research showed that these individuals all had various deformities and were worshipped by their followers. Records show that they built cities all through Central and Northern Europe.

ALEXANDER THE GREAT: It was the ancient historian Ptolemy Soter's assigned task to follow Alexander the Great as he formed the Greek Empire. Early on he recorded that Alexander's father, Philip, had formed an alliance with the tribe known as Celts "who dwelt by the Ionian Gulf." These men were ferocious fighters and feared throughout the region. Alexander knew he could not defeat them, so his first act in forming his empire was to make peace with them.

Soter described these men as haughty men of great stature, and... as giants! Once the pact was concluded the Celtic ambassadors began drinking with the Greek King. Alexander asked these mighty men what, if anything, they feared? They replied "We fear no man; there is but one thing we fear, namely that the sky should fall on us; but we regard nothing so much as the friendship of a man such as thou… if we observe not this engagement, may the earth gape and swallow us up, may the sea burst out and overwhelm us." The giant's believed that a cataclysmic flood had once come upon the earth. They recalled tales of the sky falling, the earth shaking and opening up to swallow their ancestors. This is obviously a reference to Noah's Flood.

THE NEPHILIM IN ROME: After the fall of the Greek Empire, the Roman Empire emerged. They too encountered giants from Northern Europe. The historian Polybius tells us that during the summer of 387 BC, the Romans saw an army of 30,000 Senone giants come down through northern Italy. Apparently they were a tribe from the Adriatic coast where northern populations were expanding and more fruitful lands were needed. It is known that their king was Livy Ambicatus and that their chieftain Brennus led the army through the Apennine Mountains and down into Italy.

When these giants came down from the north, they first met Rome's immediate neighbors, the Etruscans. The Etruscans rapidly mustered an army to defend themselves against the invaders. They met the giants on the Plain of Po and were promptly crushed. The Etruscans were old enemies of Rome, but relented and sent an envoy pleading for their assistance. Rome sent out three noble sons of Fabian Ambustus to mediate the dispute. The giants stated that this was the first time they had heard of the Romans, but assumed they must be a courageous people, because it was to them that the Etruscans had turned in their hour of need. The giants however stated that their right to that land now "lay in their arms; to the brave belong all things." At this, a small skirmish erupted between the leadership of the Etruscans and the chieftains of the giant Celts. One of the mediators, Quintus Fabius, then found himself involved in the brawl. He also found he had taken a side when he helped kill one of the giants.

The Celts saw this as an act of war that had to be avenged.

The Roman historian, Livy, described the scene: as the army of giants began their march, they terrified "the whole region with their wild singing and horrible and diverse yelling," and having put fear into all around with their frenzy, they cried "To Rome!"

THE BATTLE OF ALLIA: Rome's legionnaires barely had time to prepare, they marched out to intercept the giants and only a mere eleven miles from Capitoline Hill, at the river Allia, they faced off on July 18. Diodorus tells us that the Celts were "tall in stature, with rippling muscles, and white of skin, and their hair is blond (Diodorus, 5. 28. 31)." The swords of the giants were as long as a Roman javelin. Archeologists, such as Henri Hubert, have found some as long as eight feet. Needless to say the Romans were terrified, they had never seen anything like them, but all had heard the folk tales of giants and knew of their wrath.

At first the mightiest and proudest of the Celtic warriors would step forward from their lines and challenge anyone to one-on-one combat. Remember, this is what occurred with David and Goliath; as was customary for the giants. No Roman accepted the offer. Further intimidating their opponents many giants stripped off their clothes, to go to battle naked, all shrieking wildly in a frenzied altered state, called a Berserker Frenzy.

The resulting battle was a slaughter. The Celts turned the flank of the Roman army and annihilated it in one tremendous charge. The survivors fled while the giants butchered the bodies of their victims. Herodotus and Strabo both tell us that the Celts cut off the heads of their victims and kept them for trophies and used the skulls in ceremonies. A Celt would always drink the blood of their victim. They kept scalps and further desecrated their victim's bodies. This behavior went on for three or four more days, thus giving the city of Rome an opportunity to evacuate.

When the Celtic barbarians arrived, they ransacked and burned most of the city. Only a small band of Roman youths were still held out there, led by Marcus Manilus. They were positioned at the top of one of the city's steepest hills so that the giants could not easily come against them. So instead the Celts lay siege to the band. After many months, both sides were suffering from plague, dysentery and starvation. The giants delivered an offer and promised to leave Rome if they were paid one bushel of gold. The Romans were barely able to come up with the amount requested, and when the Celts actually measured the weight, their scales showed the amount lacking. This was remembered shamefully and as the worst humiliation Rome ever suffered.

Over the next century the Romans rebuilt their city but small Celtic raiding parties were a constant problem. The Celts always bragged of their own great size, and referred to the Romans as "the little men."

But, one hundred and fifty years later the Romans would avenge themselves.

THE BATTLE OF TELAMON: In the spring of 225 BC, another, even larger, army of 70,000 Celts again came down through the Apennine Mountains. When the invaders arrived at Clustidium, one hundred miles north of Rome, the Romans began to make preparations. Two armies were dispatched, one under Lucius Aemilius, the other under Gaius Atilius and met at Telamon in Etruria. This time the two Roman armies would converge on the naked invaders from both the east and the west, catching them in crossfire of arrows and spears. Polybius tells us that the giants "in their impotent rage, rushed wildly at the enemy and sacrificed their lives." Many, with several arrows protruding from their mortally wounded bodies, still continued to roar and fight.

In the end the Romans killed forty-thousand Celts and captured ten-thousand more. The Roman people were greatly encouraged with this victory but the Romans had not seen the end of the threat posed by the giants. Their sanctuary still lie to the north, from there the giants staged many smaller incursions and raids into Roman territories during the next century.

THE BATTLE OF NOREIA: About one hundred years later, around 113 BC, the Romans found exactly what had been pushing the Celtic giants down from the north. They saw a different tribe of even more terrifying giants. They were obviously looking for a land to conquer and establish as their own as they had their women and children following in leather covered wagons. These men were far worse than the previous monstrosities the Roman Legions had fought. Caesar wrote of these German giants that they were even taller, blonder and far meaner (*Commentary,* 6. 19), that they were more enormous in physique, were more valiant and had extraordinary military training (*Commentary,* 1. 39). He also remarked that the giants whom they had already encountered were all fearful of the German giants, whose name *Germanii,* means genuine, or original. Amazingly, some of the earlier Celtic invaders even requested Roman aid in defending themselves against the Germans!

Roman historians all agreed, these Germans were something to be feared. Plutarch wrote of the German giants as being "invincible of strength and courage: in battle they attack with the force and speed of five and no one can withstand them." Columella stated that "Nature has made Germany remarkable for armies of very tall men." Hegesippus declared the Germans "are superior to other nations in the largeness of their bodies and their contempt for death." Vegetius lamented "What could our undersized men have done against the tall Germans?"

The German giants systematically crushed four entire Roman armies on the battlefield. When they defeated Papirius Carbo's last army at the Battle of Noreia all of Northern Italy was open to an invasion. Then suddenly the Germans simply disappeared! They had headed west for some unknown reason, leaving Rome ample time to regroup. As the giants roamed through Spain they came across many smaller local militias to smite. They also found time to form an alliance with other Celtic tribes, the Cimbri, Teutoness and Ambrones, who had come down earlier.

THE BATTLE OF PROVENCE: In 109 BC the alliance of Celtic giants appeared in Provence. A Roman army led by consul Silanus was sent out to face them, but was almost immediately crushed. With this the Romans knew they had to prepare and quickly restore their national defenses against an even mightier united hoard. The Roman Senate called for Gaius Marius to come home from Africa. This twenty-five-year-old general then spent every possible hour reshaping his army and preparing to defend Rome against the giants. Plutarch tells us the training process for these men was more than severe.

THE BATTLE OF RHONE RIVER: By 105 BC the giant's armies had advanced as far as Orange. Two Roman armies were sent out just to check their advance, one led by Caepio, the other by Manlius. The giants attacked and crushed both armies, leaving only ten men and the two generals to escape.

By 102 BC the giants were at the gates of Rome to push the people from their lands and into the Mediterranean Sea. But Marius' new army, which he had personally trained up over the last three years, was ready. He moved them to the lower Rhone River and encamped opposite the giants. There, Marius forced all his troops to go "in turn to the wall and ordered them to look around and thus get use to the appearance of their enemies and their hideous savage yelling (Plutarch, *Lives of the Noble Grecians and Romans,* page 502- 503)." After some days of this continuing exercise, the Roman troops were literally begging Marius to let them avenge the giant's shouted insults. But Marius was not ready.

On three occasions the giants attacked the Roman encampment, but

Marius only allowed his men to defend the line. The giants eventually grew tired of this and decided to move on. Marius' men then secretly pursued and stalked the giants, waiting for the right moment to attack.

THE BATTLE OF AQUAE SEXTIAE: At Aquae Sextiae the Romans drew out one camp of giants to attack what they thought was a small Roman force, but from the heights above the river bank, the trap was sprung. The giants suffered a severe loss.

All night long the survivor's horrific cries of lamentation for their fallen comrades haunted the victorious Romans. By morning the giant's calls for revenge filled the air.

For two days the giants tried to engage the Romans, when suddenly Marius led his cavalry away, in the direction of Rome. The giants thought they had given flight and attacked the hill which the remaining Romans were positioned upon. The Roman infantry forces bravely held their position. Then the Roman cavalry reappeared, they had ridden out and turned back in order to encircle the giants. Once surrounded, the giants were eventually beaten.

The Romans learned that even with armor the giants had a weakness: their height. Marius found they could utilize this against them by striking strike low, below their shields. The giants could be injured and brought down, not with clumsy swinging and slashes from the Roman's cumbersome long swords, but with thrusts and jabs from newly fabricated short swords.

Even with the new strategies the "little men" of Rome took severe losses at Aquae Sextiae, but in the end the giants suffered worse, only three thousand escaped. One of the giant chieftains actually fled the combat in fear. His own men would later hunt him down and deliver him to the Romans in chains. The historian Florus tells us this chieftain, Teutobokh, "was a warrior of colossal height." That even above all the trophies the triumphant Marius brought back to Rome, hanging from the tips of upraised nine foot spears, Teutobokh could still be seen towering above them. The giant spent his remaining days awing his captors by performing feats of strength and dexterity, such as leaping over more than six horses stood side by side.

Word of the defeat and Teutobokh's humiliation eventually reached the giant's king Boiorix in Germany. Enraged, he threw together the ultimate force of 180,000 men. After an exhausting journey, with hardly a rest for his men or horses, Boiorix road boldly into Marius' encampment and challenged him to a decisive battle. In three days they agreed to pit their forces against one another on the plain of Vercellae.

THE BATTLE OF VERCELLAE: The giants appeared with their typical ferocious shrieks, calls and threats. They came with headgear that made them appear to be even taller and part bestial. They came chained together. They had attached iron chains to their belts so that if any one man fell, the lines could still be held solid and the Romans would be unable to penetrate their ranks.

As the giants worked themselves into their typical frenzy, Marius and his men circled to the east where the bright August sun and the wind would be at their backs. They then caused a huge dust cloud to be raised, thus blinding the giants, and they attacked. The giants raised their shields to protect their vision from the dust and the sun; the Romans again attacked low, under their enemy's shields.

When King Boiorix fell, struck dead, in the midst of the battle, it was seen by many and destroyed the morale of the Celts. They lost the initiative, fear set in and some began to flee. They cut their iron chains and ran to their wives and families in the distance. As they neared their goal, the Romans saw a most horrifying sight. The German women stood fast and slew all who retreated. They then killed their own children by smashing them onto the rocks. The women then finished off the battle, decisively in the Roman's favor, by strangling one-another.

JULIUS CAESAR AND THE BRITISH GIANTS: Marius' nephew, Julius Caesar, capitalized upon his uncle's victories and, during what are now referred to as the Gaelic Wars (58- 51 BC), took the Roman armies north driving whatever giants were left back into their own land. Bohemia was regarded as the giant's sacred land where they celebrated their Mystery religion in groves of oak trees. By the historian Plutarch's ambitious estimates, Caesar crushed eight hundred Celtic towns, killing more than 1.2 million.

The ancient British historian, Geoffrey of Monmouth, a Welsh monk, documented his nation's origins. The legends say a man named Brutus was the first to colonize Britain, and that he had to displace an indigenous tribe of giants to do so. Brutus was said to be a survivor of the legendary Trojan wars, where gods fought along side their chosen mortals, and could trace his family's history back to Japheth, son of Noah. Brutus reigned over New Troy, which later became known as London, from 1104 to 1081 BC. During this time some of the giants became accepted as allies. According to Strabo, in 55 BC, Caesar went as far north as Great Britain determined to wipe out the Celtic giant's threat.

Here Caesar discovered the famous Druids who were the priesthood of the Celts. Roman historians thoroughly documented their religious practices. Athenaeus made comments regarding their sexual rituals and abuses. Diodorus speaks of rituals where by victims were sacrificed and blood was consumed, but it was Julius Caesar himself who recorded that "The Gauls believe that the power of the immortal gods can be appeased only if one human life is exchanged for another and they have sacrifices of this kind regularly established in the community. Some of them have enormous images made of wickerwork, the limbs of which they fill with living men; these are set on fire and the men perish, enveloped in the flames (Julius Caesar, *Commentary*, 6. 16)."

As Caesar came to Britain, Strabo documented that they found men there "taller than the Celti, and not so yellow haired." The population of giants there was extremely large, so large that the Romans had to leave and organize a return the following year with more forces.

That following year Caesar encountered fierce resistance, but after three major battles the giant's alliance began to crumble as separate factions sought treaties of peace with the Romans. Julius Caesar's eight year, scorched earth campaign against the Nephilim ended when he was assassinated on the Ides of March, 44 BC.

In 43 AD, Britain became a Roman province. Under the Edict of Caracalla, most Celts came to be Roman citizens. Caesar Augustus (27 BC- 14 AD) had two giants, each more than ten feet tall, lead his armies into battle. Pliny wrote, that after the death of these men, their bodies "were preserved in the tomb in Sallust's Gardens; their names were Pusio and Secundilla." There were even occasions when the Roman Empire would be led by giant men: Jovian, who reigned for seven months beginning in August 363 AD, Maximinus (173- 238 AD) and Maximilian (1493- 1519 AD).

The effect the giants had on the emerging Roman Empire was paramount. Rome was forced to extend her territories north to create a buffer zone. A huge amount of land had to be taken to ensure the giants could not crouch at the city's gates awaiting an opportunity to pounce. As the Celts were driven further north, so spread the Roman Empire. Another major effect the giants had on Rome was on her armies. The wars with the giants strengthened Rome's military might. After defeating giants, the soldiers found combat with mere mortals very easy. In the records of the legionnaires they often bragged of their prowess against giant supermen.

300 years after the time of Christ the giants were still in existence. When Ammianus Marcellinus visited Gaul, he noted that the people were "Of the great stature, fairness and arrogant bearing of the Gallic warrior." The women he describes as "very tall, blue-eyed and singularly beautiful." His analysis turned to awe when he stated it would be bad enough to get into a dispute with a Gallic man, but it was far worse if his wife with her "huge snowy arms," which could strike like catapults, came to his assistance.

Before the emergence of the Roman Empire the giants held a huge territory. The extent of it has been sorely underestimated. I was very surprised to learn that their remains have been found in burial mounds around the world, not just in Northern Europe but in the Americas!

GIANTS IN THE NEW WORLD: After Columbus discovered America many expeditions followed. The famous explorer Magellan, who sailed around the Southern-most parts of Argentina and Chile in 1520, reported an encounter with a race of giants. Magellan referred to these giants as *Patagons,* or Bigfoot, because of their big feet. This area later became known as Patagonia. Pigafetta, a member of Magellan's crew, documented a "man so tall that our heads scarcely came up to his waist, his voice was like that of a bull." They managed to capture two of these giants to take back to Europe but they died en route.

Later in 1578, the ship's chaplain aboard Sir Francis Drake's ship recorded in his journal that they had come across Magellan's Patagonian race of giants inhabiting the Southern tip of South America. While docked in the Port of San Julian some of Drake's crew got into a fight with some of these "men of large stature" and two crew members died. These men were estimated to be more than seven and a half feet tall.

In the 1590s, Anthonie Knivet, who sailed with Sir Thomas Cavendish, also reported seeing giants in the same region. The dead body of one measured more than twelve feet in length.

In 1598 ten foot tall natives were seen and documented by Sebald de Weert.

In 1776 the crew of the ship commanded by Commodore John Byron, the Dolphin, after circumnavigating the globe and upon return to London, leaked that they had also encountered the tribe of nine-foot giants of Patagonia. Their story appeared in print in the *Gentleman's*

Magazine and other newspapers such as the *London Chronicle*.

Most remember Charles Darwin for his theory of Evolution but few know that he documented sighting the South American giants in his book *The Voyage of the Beagle,* "altogether they are certainly the tallest race that we ever saw."

In 1880, the Rocca expedition to South America boasted that they had wiped out the tribe of giants, which had referred to themselves as Tehuelches. Since then no one has ever reported seeing any trace of the Patagonian giants again. When the Spanish explorer and conquistador Captain Cortez came to the Americas in 1519 he learned of the native's reverence for the giants. Cortez' chronicler, Bernal Diaz del Castillo, wrote "They said that their ancestors had told them that in times past there had lived among them man and women of giant size with huge bones… and because they were a very bad people of evil manners they fought with them and killed them and those which remained had died off. So that we could see how high and tall these people were, they brought us the leg bone of one which was very thick and the height of a man of ordinary stature and that was the bone from hip to knee. We were all amazed at seeing those bones and felt sure that there must have been giants in this country. Our Captain Cortez said to us that it might be well to send the bone to Castille so that his Majesty might see it, so we sent it with the first of our agents who went there."

AMERICAN NEPHILIM: The Egyptians and Romans, those who faced the giants, often noted that their hair was either blond or red. Would it be surprising to find the same trait among American giants? This has been seen with the mummified remains in South America and those found in burial mounds in the United States. The remains of literally thousands of giants were uncovered when farm land was being broke. It was once common knowledge that a race of giants once lived there.

At the turn of the twentieth century there was a national awareness of the mound builders and their extensive earth works that far exceeded contemporary consciousness on the subject. Since the majority of the country was agrarian lifestyle, awareness of the mounds was reinforced by daily contact with the actual sites themselves. Current estimates put the number of known American mounds at well over one hundred thousand. They ranged in shape from the great pyramids of Illinois to the fantastic pictorial mounds of Wisconsin. It seemed to be common knowledge that giants were found buried in many of these mounds and that these giants were not related to the present-day American Indians living in the region.

> Richard J. Dewhurst, *the Ancient Giants Who Ruled America, the Missing Skeletons and the Great Smithsonian Cover-Up*, pg.136

As the colonists came across the Appalachian Mountains into the Ohio Valley in the 1700s they wrote of mounds, large ruined buildings, sacred circles and standing stones left by a mysterious people. Since their remains were found in these mounds, they became known as the *mound people*. There were over ten thousand mounds in the Ohio Valley alone. Some structures in the Mississippi Valley stretch as far as twenty-five miles. As colonists came west through North America many sites were demolished as land was needed for agriculture. To build the cities of Nashville, Pittsburgh, Cincinnati and St. Louis thousands of ancient structures were destroyed. It was estimated in 1948 that ninety per-cent of these structures had disappeared.

Mounds were often constructed in terraces and had flattened tops with temples, just like the Ziggurats of ancient Babylon. Towards the lower Mississippi, the mounds all took the form of pyramids. Roger G Kennedy wrote in *Hidden Cities* that these monuments are as old as the structures of ancient Egypt, Stonehenge and Teotihuacan. There is a pyramid at Cahokia, Illinois, on the east bank of the Mississippi, that dwarfs the Great Pyramid of Egypt, at over 100 feet high and covering over 16 acres. But few consider the American structures equal to the monuments of Egypt because they are made from ridiculously hard packed dirt rather than stone. The impressions of the wicker-like baskets that were used to pack the dirt can still be seen. Of the largest mounds, estimates tell us that more than ten million basket loads of earth were needed, or 60,000 tons of earth. They often had inner structural reinforcement made of log beams and were aligned to the solstices and equinoxes.

Archeologists tell us that at some distant point in time the construction of these mounds suddenly stopped and the mysterious builders disappeared. The mound builder's populations would have been enormous, unlike anything seen by the early American settlers.

What happened to them?

The indigenous peoples said that the mounds were left by "the Old Ones" who had lived there prior to their own settlement. The Natives of North America were equally curious about these sites, at times imitating the mound and sacred circle construction or attempting to expand upon them, but always passing on the legends that these people were unknown and from a time before their own. The Cherokees' tell us that the mounds were there before they moved into the area and that they too constructed temples atop the mounds for their own use.

The Anasazi Natives of the United States lived among the remains of this past civilization and even referred to themselves as "The Old Ones." But they could not take credit for the construction of these sacred and mystical sites, they too spoke of a mysterious culture prior to their own which constructed these monstrous works. Curiously, no Native Americans ever lived in the area of West Virginia; the legends said an evil presence lived among the mounds.

In 1894 Cyrus Thomas wrote in *The Twelfth Annual Report of the Bureau of Ethnology*, that humans, as tall as nine feet, were found in the mounds he excavated. At times the giant's bodies were incased in stone. Could these petrified remains be of pre-Flood Nephilim? He also wrote that the remains he found frequently had blond hair. In Northern Europe there are identical mounds, called Tumulus. In Olaf Rudbeck's 1679 book *Atlantica,* he describes how he dug into many burial mounds on the plains of Uppsala. "I have diligently examined all the burial mounds, where skulls and whole skeletons have been found... the largest ones have been five to six aln (ten to twelve feet), although there were not many of them, but I found countless skeletons four aln long (eight feet) or thereabouts."

George Washington, before becoming the first American President, worked on surveying expeditions in 1757 and 1770, and knew the mounds were the largest man made structures he would ever see. In 1788, Washington wrote "Those works which are found upon the Ohio... show traces of the country's having been once inhabited by a race of people more ingenious, at least, if not more civilized than those who present dwell there" (George Washington, *Writings*, vol. 29).

Thomas Jefferson studied the mounds for twenty-five years, documenting his own excavations. In his later years he constructed his dream home, among a circuit of octagon shaped mounds. The home, he named Poplar Forest, was also itself shaped like an octagon, with octagon shaped rooms and an octagon shaped table. He even went so far as to reconstruct temples at the tops of specific mounds!

As president, Jefferson sent out many explorers, such as Lewis and Clark, to study and map the great ancient structures of America. On October 25, 1804, Lewis and Clark documented that they found a "Mountain of evil spirits" on the present Vermillion River. They saw the temples on top and erroneously decided that they must be forts. To this day these are still known as the Utz Site and the Old Fort.

The most famous American mound is Serpent Mound. Lying on the Ohio River near Marietta, it definitely appears to be a snake with an egg or sphere in its mouth, and stretches out over a quarter mile. It was designed so that on certain days the sun would illuminate the gravel in its coiled section making its true appearance more obvious.

INSIDE THE MOUNDS: Upon excavation, the mounds usually contained artifacts and skeletons, in many cases giant skeletons. They were buried sitting up and often each mound had more than one set of remains. The skeletons were usually complete as they were found in well constructed log tombs covered by literally tons of dirt. Obviously the giants took great pains to care for their dead.

Most mounds were entered by farmers as they broke cropland, only a few were excavated by trained archeologists, but ample scientific documentation does exist. In the August 14, 1880 issue of *Scientific American*, pg. 106, there is an article on the opening of a mound in Bush Creek Township, Ohio. There was found a clay coffin with a woman inside who measured eight feet in length. Also in her coffin was that of a child, three feet in length. In a similar grave there was found the skeletons of a man and a woman, the man was nine feet, and the woman was eight feet in length. In another grave was another pair, male and female, the man was nine-foot four, and the woman was again eight feet in length. Also in the mound was an engraved stone tablet, which was taken to Cincinnati. There a Dr. Everhart and a Mr. Bowers concluded that the giants were of a race of sun worshippers.

American settlers in the upper Ohio region were told legends by the natives of cannibal giants. Then the pioneers began to dig up the remains, from Lake Erie to the Ohio River, of skeletons of giants with double rows of teeth! In 1833, at Lopock Rancho, California a twelve foot tall human was unearthed. It had these double rows of teeth. Another ancient skeleton was found later with the same dental peculiarity on Santa Rosa Island, off the coast of California.

In Europe and Australia these prehistoric giants are known as *meganthropus*, a giant *ape* that stood between seven and twelve feet tall. Meganthropus was apparently a very intelligent giant ape to made use of tools, such as a thirty-seven pound copper axe, which one was found clutching. This was one smart monkey, not only able to use a tool, but able to smelt and refine metals and all. In Java and China the remains of these giants are known as *gianthropithicus blacki*, named after the discoverer. These would have stood around twelve feet tall, and weighed about 1200 pounds. As mentioned earlier, many of these skulls had a strange anomaly. They had two rows of teeth compared to ours. But there was more, the giants frequently had six fingers and toes! This is identical to the Biblical accounts of the Nephilim (2Samuel 21: 20, 1Chronicles 20: 6). These traits suggest there were differences in the giant's genetics.

SETTLING AMERICA: In the old western TV shows, with gun fights between cowboys and Indians, we often saw the stereotypical Indian raise his right hand and say "How" when meeting someone. In reality this was not just a means of saying "Hello, how are you doing today?" This was in fact was the means the Native Americans had of discerning friend from foe. The significance of the raised hand was to show genetic ancestry. Good people had five fingers, enemy's had six.

Few know that the famous cowboy William F. "Buffalo Bill" Cody wrote this. In his book he documented:

> While we were in the sand-hills, scouting the Niobrara country, the Pawnee Indians brought into camp, one night, some very large bones, one of which a surgeon of the expedition pronounced to be the thigh-bone of a human being. The Indians claimed that the bones they had found were those of a person belonging to a race of people who a long time ago lived in this country. That there was a race of men on the earth whose size was about three times that of an ordinary man, and they were so swift and powerful that they could run along-side a buffalo, and taking the animal in one arm could tear off a leg and eat the meat as they walked. These giants denied the existence of a Great Spirit, and when they heard the thunder or saw the lightening they laughed at it and said that they were greater than either. This so displeased the Great Spirit that he caused a great rain-storm to come, and the water kept rising higher and higher so that it drove those proud and conceited giants from

the low grounds to the hills, and thence to the mountains, but at last even the mountain tops were submerged, and then those mammoth men were all drowned… they claim that this story is a matter of Indian history, which has been handed down among them from time immemorial. As we had no wagons with us at the time this large and heavy bone was found, we were obliged to leave it.

William F. Cody, the Life of Buffalo Bill, pg. 266

The giants and their mounds are mostly forgotten today, but they played a huge role in our history. For example, the Mormon religion, which believes that Jesus came to preach to advanced North American peoples after his departure from Israel, was started by Joseph Smith who spent his early years digging into the mounds with his father searching for gold artifacts. No doubt the mounds inspired his belief of an advanced pre-Columbian race in the Americas.

THE SMITHSONIAN: In America, the strange artifacts discovered in the mounds were mostly shipped to the Smithsonian. Countless local newspapers report that Smithsonian representatives came to retrieve the skeletons. Then what happened? The Smithsonian is the great national museum, why do we not see anything relating to the giants on display there? The better question is why do they deny the giants ever existed? Some suspect a conspiracy is afoot.

When someone who sent artifacts to the Smithsonian would inquire about them, perhaps in hopes of seeing their discoveries on display, the Smithsonian always gave the same response, they lost them. This same story is told in many small town newspapers across the States: giant bones found, sent to the Smithsonian and shortly thereafter *lost*.

Today the Smithsonian deny loosing the evidence of giants, they deny ever receiving it… *because giants don't exist.* There is a rumor on the internet that the Smithsonian once loaded all the artifacts relating to the giants onto a barge and dumped them into the Atlantic Ocean. It seems the giants just don't fit into the Theory of Evolution; creatures evolve from smaller to larger. But we all realize the Bible disagrees with the Theory of Evolution.

BIBLIOGRAPHY

Agrippa, Henry Cornelius. *Three Books of Occult Philosophy.* Woodbury,MN: Llewellyn Publications, 2006.

Baker, Russ. *Family of Secrets, the Bush Dynasty.* New York, NY. BloomsburyPress, 2009.

Barnstone, Willis, editor. *The Other Bible.* San Francisco: Harper San Francisco, 1984.

Bauval, Robert. *The Orion Mystery.* Toronto: Doubleday Canada Ltd, 1994.

Blavatsky, Helena. *Isis Unveiled.* Los Angeles: The Theosophy Company, 1931

Blavatsky, Helena. *The Secret Doctrine.* Pasadena: Theosophical University Press, 1999.

Brenton, Lancelot. *The Septuagint with Apocrypha: Greek and English.* London: Hendrickson Publishers, 2003.

Broderick, Robert editor. *The Catholic Encyclopdia.* New York: Thomas Nelson Inc. Publishers, 1976.

Bulwer-Lytton. *The Coming Race.* Magoria Books, 2007.

Carlyon, Richard. *A Guide to the Gods.* New York: Quill, 1981.

Carter, John. *Sex and Rockets, the Occult World of Jack Parsons.* Venice, CA: Feral House, 1999

Charles, R.H. *Pseudepigrapha.* Berkeley, CA: The Apocryphile Press, 2004.

Charles, R.H. *The Book of the Secrets of Enoch.* London: The University of Oxford, 1999.

Collier, Peter and Horowitz, David. *The Rockefellers and American Dynasty.* New York: New American Library, 1977.

Cooper, John M. (Editor). *Plato Complete Works.* Indianapolis: Hackett Publishing, 1997.

Cooper, William. *Behold a Pale Horse.* Sedona, AZ. Light Technology Publishing, 1991.

Cotterell, Arthur. (General Editor), *World Mythology.* Bath, U.K: Paragon Publishing, 2005.

Crowley, Aleister. *The Book of Thoth.* New York: Lancer Books.

Crowley, Aleister. *Moonchild.* York Beach, Maine: Samuel Weiser, Inc, 1999.

Crowley, Aleister. *Magick in Theory and Practice.* New York: Castle Books.

Crowley, Aleister. *The Book of the Law.* Boston: Weiser Books, 1976.

England, Robert B. *Noah, the Seventy-First Grove Play of the Bohemian Club.* Printed by Lawton and Alfred Kennedy, 1976

Estulin, Daniel. *The True Story of the Bilderberg Group.* Waterville, OR: TrineDay, 2007.

Fowler, Raymond E. *The Watchers.* Toronto: Bantam 1990.

Fowler, Raymond E. *The Watchers II.* Newberg, OR: Wild Flower Press, 1995.

Freke, Timothy and Candy, Peter. *The Hermetica.* London: Piatkus, 1997.

Gardner, Philip and Osborn, Gary. *The Shining Ones, the Worlds Most Powerful Secret Society Revealed.* London: Watkins Publishing, 2006.

Ginzberg, Louis. *The Legends of the Jews* (vols 1- 7). Philadelphia: The Jewish Publication Society of America, 1968.

Guazzo, Francesco Maria. *Compendium Maleficarum the Montague Summers Edition.* New York: Dover Publications Inc, 1988.

Hall, Manly P. *The Secret Destiny of America.* Los Angeles: The Philosophical Research Society Inc, 1991.

Hall, Manly P. *The Secret Teachings of All Ages.* New York: Tarcher/Penguin Books, 2003.

Hall, Manly P. *The Lost Keys of Freemasonry.* New York: Tarcher/Penguin, 2006.

Heidel, Alexander. *The Babylonian Genesis.* Chicago: Phoenix Books, the University of Chicago Press, 1965.

Herodotus. *Histories.* Hertfordshire: Wordsworth Classics of World Literature, 1996.

Hislop, Alexander. *The Two Babylons.* New York: A&B Publishers Group.

Hunt, Dave. *A Woman Rides the Beast.* Eugene, Oregon: Harvest House Publishers, 1994.

Jeffrey, Grant R. *Messiah: War in the Middle East.* Toronto: Frontier Research Publications, 1991.

Jennings, Hargrave. *Ophiolatreia.* Kessinger Publishing.

Keel, John A. *Our Haunted Planet.* Greenwich CN: Fawcett Publications, 1971.

Keel, John A. *Why UFOs.* New York: Manor Books, 1976.

King, Francis X. *Witchcraft and Demonology.* Twickenham, England: Hamlyn Publishing, 1987.

Kramer, Heinrich and Sprenger, James. *The Malleus Maleficarum.* New York: Dover Publications Inc, 1971

Krishna, Gopi. *Kundalini, the Evolutionary Energy in Man.* Boulder, Colorado:1970.

Laycock, Donald C. *The Complete Enochian Dictionary.* York Beach, Maine: Samuel Weiser, Inc, 1994.

Levi, Eliphas (translated by Aleister Crowley). *The Key of the Mysteries.* Boston: Weiser Books, 2002.

Mackey, Albert G. *An Encyclopaedia of Freemasonry.* New York: The Masonic History Company, 1924.

Mackey, Albert G. *The History of Freemasonry* Volumes 1 - 7, New York and London: the Masonic History Company, 1906.

Mathers, S.L. MacGregor. *The Kabbalah Unveiled.* Chicago: The De Laurence Company, Inc, 1938.

Martin, Malachi. *Windswept House.* New York: Doubleday, 1996.

Mead, G.R.S. *The Corpus Hermeticum.* Kessinger.

Melanson, Terry. *Perfectibilists, the 18th Century Bavarian Illuminati.* Walterville, OR. TrineDay Publishing, 2009.

Morgan, William. *Morgan's Freemasonry Exposed and Explained.* Pomeroy, WA: Health Research.

Norman, Eric. *This Hollow Earth.* New York: Lancer Books, 1972.

Orwell, George. *Nineteen Eighty-Four.* Harmondsworth, England: Penguin Books, 1981.

Pike, Albert. *Morals and Dogma.* Richmond, VA: L.H. Jenkins Inc, 1947.

Randle, Kevin D. *A History of UFO Crashes.* New York: Avon Books, 1995.

Relitz, Chris. *Antichrist Osiris, the History of the Luciferian Conspiracy,* Lulu Books, 2012.

Regardie, Israel. *The Golden Dawn.* St. Paul MN: Llewellyn Publications, 2005.

Robinson, James M. *The Nag Hammadi Library.* San Francisco: Harper San Francisco, 1990.

Ross, Colin A. M.D. *Satanic Ritual Abuse: Principles of Treatment.* Toronto: University of Toronto Press, 1995.

Ross, Colin A. M.D. *The C.I.A. Doctors.* Richardson, TX: Manitou Communications Inc, 2006.

Saint-Yves D'Alveydre, Marquis Alexandre. *The Kingdom of Agarttha, A Journey into the Hollow Earth.* Rochester, Vermont. Inner Traditions, 2008.

Schoch, Robert M. *Pyramid Quest.* New York: Tarcher/Penguin Books, 2005.

Shaver, Richard and Childress, David Hatcher. *Lost Continents and the Hollow Earth.* Kempton, IL: Adventures Unlimited Press, 1999.

Sitchin, Zecharia. *The Cosmic Code,* New York: Avon Books, 1998.

Spence, Lewis. *The Mysteries of Egypt.* New York: Rudolf Steiner Publications, 1972.

Strong, James. *The New Strong's Complete Dictionary of Bible Words.* Nashville: Thomas Nelson Publishers, 1996.

Sutin, Lawrence. *Do What Thou Wilt, A Life of Aleister Crowley.* New York: St. Martin's Griffin. 2000.

Sutton, William. *The Illuminati 666.* New York: Teach Services Inc, 1995.

Temple, Robert. *Egyptian Dawn.* London: Random House, 2011.

Tenney, Merrill C. *The Zondervan Pictorial Bible Dictionary.* Grand Rapids, MI: Zondervan Publishing House, 1967.

Waddell, L. Austine. *Makers of Civilization in Race and History.* Kessinger Publishing.

West, John Anthony. *Serpent in the Sky.* New York: Julian Press, 1987.

Whiston, William translator. *Josephus The Complete Works.* Nashville: Thomas Nelson Publishers, 1998

Wilmshurst, W.L. *The Meaning of Masonry.* New York: Bell Publishing Company, 1980.

Wise, Abegg, Cook. *The Dead Sea Scrolls.* San Francisco: HarperSanFrancisco, 1996.

Lightning Source UK Ltd.
Milton Keynes UK
UKHW010631190819
348215UK00001B/17/P